Development of new ideas, processes, and products—and the ability to bring them to market through entrepreneurship—is fundamental to the growth and development process and to a vibrant economy. But innovation is an elusive topic, particularly in rural communities. In this volume, leading scholars of rural economic growth and development have come together to discuss various dimensions of innovation, and more importantly, how rural communities can foster a more innovative environment. This is an excellent read for both scholars of rural economics as well as practitioners.

— **Steven C. Deller**, *Professor and Community Development Specialist, Center for Community and Economic Development, Department of Agricultural and Applied Economics*

An excellent collection of works exploring the important role innovation and entrepreneurship play in community-based rural economic development across the United States. A must read for anyone working in the field of rural economic development.

— **James C. McConnon**, *Jr., Extension Specialist and Professor Emeritus of Economics, University of Maine*

The premise of the book is that innovation is far more than patent counts. For rural areas across OECD countries that face demographic decline and new forms of competition, innovation by firms, governments and organizations will be key to their future viability. The chapters provide a highly eclectic set of ideas and approaches to rural innovation that help identify ways to increase productivity and revitalize struggling communities.

— **David Freshwater**, *Professor Emeritus, Agricultural Economics, University of Kentucky*

Most of the discussion about growth and innovation tends to focus on urban advantages, yet the reality is that some rural areas are thriving—or doing better than expected. This collection of articles explores the drivers of rural innovation and ways in which rural communities can support this innovation and bolster their economic outcomes. It is a valuable resource for both researchers and practitioners focused on rural economies.

— **Heather Stephens**, *Ph.D., Associate Professor, Resource Economics and Management, West Virginia University*

This book provides an holistic, ecosystems-based approach to community-economic development. This work helps us understand how communities—especially rural communities—can create the conditions for innovation and vitality, which is timely and important.

— **Thaddeus Guldbrandsen**, *Ph.D., High-Impact Departments, LLC, Formerly Vice Provost for Research and Director of the Center for Rural Affairs, Plymouth State University*

BUILDING RURAL COMMUNITY RESILIENCE THROUGH INNOVATION AND ENTREPRENEURSHIP

Drawing from empirical analyses, case studies, and a synthesis of best practices, this book explores how innovation manifests itself in rural places and how it contributes to entrepreneurial development and resilience. Innovation in rural places may come about as a result of new forms of collaboration; policies that leverage rural assets and address critical service or product gaps, novel strategies for accessing financial capital; infusion of arts into aspects of community life; and cultivation of networks that bridge entrepreneurs, organizations, and institutions.

The chapters illustrate how a number of innovation-related characteristics relate to economic vibrancy in rural places such as a strong connection to the arts, adaptive and sustainable use of natural resources, value-chain integrated food systems, robust bridging social capital networks, creative leveraging of technology, and presence of innovation-focused entrepreneurs.

Through exploration of these and other topics, this book will provide insights and best practices for rural community and economic development scholars and practitioners seeking to strengthen the rural innovation ecosystem.

Charlie French, Ph.D. is a Program Leader/Extension Associate Professor, Community & Economic Development at the University of New Hampshire Cooperative Extension.

The Community Development Research and Practice Series

The Heart of Community Engagement
Practitioner Stories from Across the Globe
Patricia A. Wilson

Culture, Community, and Development
Rhonda Phillips, Mark A. Brennan, Tingxuan Li

Community Capacity and Resilience in Latin America
Paul Lachapelle, Isabel Gutierrez-Montes, Cornelia Butler Flora

50 Years of Community Development Vol I
Norman Walzer, Rhonda Phillips and Robert Blair

50 Years of Community Development Vol II
Norman Walzer, Rhonda Phillips and Robert Blair

Community Owned Businesses
International Entrepreneurship, Finance, and Economic Development
Norman Walzer

International Community Development Practice
Charlie McConnell, Daniel Muia and Anna Clarke

Building Rural Community Resilience Through Innovation and Entrepreneurship
Edited by Charlie French

For more information about this series, please visit: https://www.routledge.com/Community-Development-Research-and-Practice-Series/book-series/CDRP

BUILDING RURAL COMMUNITY RESILIENCE THROUGH INNOVATION AND ENTREPRENEURSHIP

Edited by
Charlie French

Routledge
Taylor & Francis Group
NEW YORK AND LONDON

Cover image: © Shutterstock

First published 2022
by Routledge
605 Third Avenue, New York, NY 10158

and by Routledge
2 Park Square, Milton Park, Abingdon, Oxon, OX14 4RN

Routledge is an imprint of the Taylor & Francis Group, an informa business

Library of Congress Cataloging-in-Publication Data
A catalog record for this title has been requested

ISBN: 978-1-032-01421-0 (hbk)
ISBN: 978-1-032-01420-3 (pbk)
ISBN: 978-1-003-17855-2 (ebk)

DOI: 10.4324/9781003178552

Typeset in Bembo
by codeMantra

CONTENTS

FIGURES

TABLES

CONTRIBUTORS

Theodore R. Alter is Professor of agricultural, environmental, and regional economics in the Agricultural Economics, Sociology, and Education Department at Penn State. He is co-director of Penn State's Center for Economic and Community Development and is co-editor of the *Entrepreneurship Research Journal*. In addition, he is an Adjunct Research Fellow in the Australian Center for Agriculture and Law at The University of New England in Australia. Dr. Alter served from 2012 to 2017 as one of the lead researchers for the institutional analysis and community-led action initiative of the Invasive Animal Cooperative Research Centre in Australia. The Victorian Rabbit Action Network, one of the community-led action projects stemming from this initiative, recently received the 2019 United Nations Public Service Award in recognition for its contributions to strengthening working relationships and shared responsibility among citizens and communities, industry, and government. His research, teaching, and community engagement work focus on community and rural development, resource and environmental economics, community engagement in natural resource management, entrepreneurship, behavioral and public sector economics, the practice of public scholarship and civic engagement in higher education, and the political economy of democracy. His work includes the study of public and collective choice, democracy, and innovation, and how paradigms of public discourse have shaped complex societal issues from technology and communications development to entrepreneurship and public-private partnerships.

Douglas Arbogast is West Virginia University Extension Service's Rural Tourism Specialist. He conducts research and delivers training on rural tourism development in destinations across the state and works collaboratively with WVU faculty and students to promote the sustainable development of tourism in West Virginia. His research interests include rural tourism, sustainable tourism development, tourism planning, tourism management, and regional competitiveness.

Alexandra Croteau works on opportunities for others to grow and develop. Currently serving within the George Washington University's Office for Study Abroad, she supports international education opportunities for undergraduate students. As an educator, she has taught in Peru and Costa Rica and incorporates her education experience in the evaluation of programs. Alexandra has a B.S. in Secondary Education Mathematics from the University of Vermont and an M.A. in International Education with specialization in research methodologies from George Washington University.

Molly Donovan is a Community Economic Development State Specialist with the University of New Hampshire Cooperative Extension. Molly works with community volunteers and local leaders to build their capacity for decision-making and change. Her work is focused on community resiliency, revitalizing main street, business retention and community engagement. She is an expert in community development practice and program development. Molly holds a Master's degree in Urban Planning from the University at Buffalo, was a Community Renaissance Fellow at Yale University, and has a B.A. in political science and urban studies from Canisius College. She has worked in the field of community development for over 25 years with experience in New Hampshire, Ohio, Michigan, and New York.

Daniel Eades is an Associate Professor and Extension Specialist with West Virginia University, working in the areas of rural economics and rural development. His research and teaching employ asset-based and data-driven analysis to engage and guide local leaders and community stakeholders in regional economic development decision-making and local planning efforts. Daniel received his B.S. in Environmental Studies from Shepherd University, and Master's in Agricultural and Resource Economics from West Virginia University. He is currently pursuing his Ph.D. in Human and Community Development.

Charlie French leads the University of New Hampshire Cooperative Extension's Division of Community and Economic Development, whose work is focused on empowering communities to engage the public in local decision-making around a range of issues, including economic development, downtown revitalization, and entrepreneurial development. His current work is focused on helping communities build energy resilience leveraging new technologies and innovations. He brings his experience into the classroom as Associate Professor in UNH's Carsey School of Public Policy, where he teaches courses in community and rural development. Charlie has a B.A. in Geography from Dartmouth College, an M.A. in Regional Planning from Western Illinois University, and a Ph.D. in Natural Resources Policy from the University of New Hampshire.

Cornelia Butler Flora is an Emeritus Distinguished Professor in the Department of Sociology at Iowa State University, where she served 15 years as Director of the North Central Regional Center for Rural Development. She is a Research Professor at Kansas State University, where she served as Director of the Population Research Laboratory. Other positions include Program Director for Agriculture and Rural Development for the Andean Region and Southern Cone in Latin America for the Ford Foundation and Chair of the Department of Sociology at Virginia Polytechnic Institute and State University. She has published 13 books, with a 14th co-authored book in preparation. She has served as President of the Rural Sociological Society, the Agriculture, Food and Human Values Society, and the Community Development Society. Her B.A. degree is from the University of California at Berkeley and her M.S. and Ph.D. degrees are from Cornell University.

Michael W.P. Fortunato is an internationally published scholar, researcher, author, entrepreneur, community developer, educator, public speaker, and innovator, and CFO and Founding Partner of Creative Insight Community Development (CICD). Since 2005, Michael's research and practice have focused on developing better strategies to revitalize rural communities and economies and declining cities and towns through more effective collaborative action, community-based entrepreneurship, grassroots and small-scale innovation, and democratic community engagement. He has conducted research and outreach—and been a featured trainer/expert—in well over 100 rural communities and small towns on three continents; and is a frequent speaker at major conferences, on radio shows, guest blogs, and educational/training seminars. Michael received a Ph.D. in Rural Sociology and an M.S. in Community Economic Development from Penn State University's Department of Agricultural Economics, Sociology, and Education, where he still teaches Community and Economic Development online. He is also the founder of Authentic Redevelopment, a development philosophy for community revitalization and affordable housing creation through cooperative action. It is Michael's dream to see every community and region reach their own fullest creative and lifestyle potential.

Roberto Gallardo leads the Purdue Center for Regional Development, which works with regions and communities fostering collaboration and innovation. This work is done through engagement, data analysis and visualization, and technical assistance. His recent work focuses on digital exclusion and its impact in community and economic development. Roberto has widely published on the topic of broadband access and the digital divide. He has an undergraduate engineering degree, a Master's in Economic Development, and a Ph.D. in Public Policy and Administration. He has worked with rural communities and regions for over 15 years.

Stephan J. Goetz is Professor of Agricultural and Regional Economics at Penn State University and Director of the Northeast Regional Center for Rural

Development. He holds Ph.D. and M.Sc. degrees in Agricultural Economics from Michigan State University and an undergraduate degree from the University of Guelph in Canada. His research focuses on the determinants and effects of economic growth and development, with current applications of network science principles to growth, resilience, and innovation. Dr. Goetz has published or presented over 200 professional papers and is the senior co-editor of four books, including *Targeting Regional Economic Development* (Routledge, 2009). He is the principal investigator on external grants valued at over $15 million. He has served as President of the North American Regional Science Council and was a member of the Board of Directors of the Center for Rural Pennsylvania for 21 years.

Yicheol Han (한이철) is a Researcher in the Department of Agricultural & Rural Development Research at Korea Rural Economic Institute, South Korea. His research spans many disciplines and practices, from spatial planning in rural areas and development policy to complex network analysis. His published journal articles are about regional development, economic resilience, and network analysis for local economies. He earned a Ph.D. (engineering) in the College of Agriculture and Life Science at the Seoul National University, and the main topic of his dissertation is an analysis of social phenomena through network theory.

Thomas S. Lyons is the Clarence E. Harris Chair of Excellence in Entrepreneurship and Professor of Marketing & Entrepreneurship in the Gary W. Rollins College of Business at the University of Tennessee at Chattanooga. His research interests are entrepreneurship skills measurement and development, the relationship between entrepreneurship and community economic development, and social entrepreneurship. He is the co-author of 13 books and numerous articles and papers on these subjects, has edited a three-volume set on social entrepreneurship (*Social Entrepreneurship: How Businesses Can Transform Society*, 2012), and has a 15th book under contract. In 2011, Dr. Lyons received the Ted K. Bradshaw Outstanding Research Award from the Community Development Society. Dr. Lyons is currently Co-Editor of the *Entrepreneurship Research Journal*. He is a practicing entrepreneur, who has co-founded two companies. He holds a Ph.D. in Urban and Regional Planning from the University of Michigan, Ann Arbor.

John Mann is an Assistant Professor in the Department of Agricultural, Food, and Resource Economics at Michigan State University, an economist for MSU's Center for Economic Analysis, and a visiting scholar with the U.S. Department of Agriculture's Economic Research Service. His research focus includes topics related to rural innovation creation, rural economic development, and broadband in underserved regions. Additionally, he teaches finance and marketing courses in AFRE. He revived his Ph.D. in Agricultural Economics at Oklahoma State University in 2012.

Devon Meadowcroft is an Extension Instructor for Mississippi State University, based at the Delta Research and Extension Center. Her extension-based work focuses on topics related to rural development and has published works on the opioid epidemic in the rural United States. Devon also has prior experience researching rural business innovation, specifically on how innovation impacts economic outcomes for both firms and regions. Devon received her Ph.D. from Oklahoma State University in Agricultural Economics. Prior to joining Mississippi State University, Devon was a postdoctoral researcher at the Northeast Regional Center for Rural Development at Pennsylvania State University.

Steven Miller is the Director of the Center for Economic Analysis, as a unit of the Michigan State University Product Center, where he specializes in economic modeling for policy, environmental, economic impact assessments, and program evaluations. His evaluation studies focus on approaches for evaluating economic development, environmental and tax policies, as well as around public funded programs on health, education, and environment. He has over 15 years of experience developing econometric and simulation models for regional impact simulation. Dr. Miller received his Ph.D. in Economics from Oklahoma State University in 2005, with a focus on Urban-Regional Economics and Econometrics.

Egbert Ospina is a recent graduate student from the George Washington University Graduate School of Education and Human Development. His research and work focus on monitoring, evaluation, and learning for organizations that work in international sustainable development. He focuses on assessing the impacts of education and extension programs on self-sufficiency and empowerment. He conducted the research on Sustainable Harvest International as his master's thesis project. Egbert has a B.A. in International Development and Economics from the American University and an M.A. in International Education with a specialization in Monitoring and Evaluation from George Washington University.

Cathryn (Casey) Porter is the Community and Economic Development Program Manager at the University of New Hampshire Cooperative Extension. Casey works with communities to build their capacity to gather input, develop strategies, and move to action, resulting in downtown revitalization, community vibrancy, and a strengthened economy. She conducts research and implements programs in the areas of main street revitalization, community engagement and visioning, and community economic resilience. Casey has a B.S. in Environmental Studies with a concentration in community development from the University of Vermont and an M.S. in Natural Resources with a focus on public participation in food systems decision-making from the University of New Hampshire.

Elliott Powell holds the Executive Director role at Sustainable Harvest International (SHI), whose focus promotes working in partnership to create a just and sustainable world through transformative farmer training that nourishes communities and the earth. Elliott leads the organization's operations, administration, and implementation of its multi-year, multi-phase agroforestry-focused extension program. He works directly with the board of directors and staff to set strategic plans and shape SHI's future work. Elliott holds a B.S. in Environmental Management from Indiana University and an M.A. in Latin American Studies from Tulane University.

Jared Reynolds is a Community and Economic Development Field Specialist at the University of New Hampshire Cooperative Extension. He works with communities and organizations to build vibrant and innovative local economies by supporting entrepreneurs, revitalizing main streets, leveraging recreation, and improving quality of life. Jared is the co-founder and President of Making Matters NH and the Concord Makerspace, an innovation space that supports artists and entrepreneurs by providing them with affordable equipment, workspace, education, and collaboration. He also started several events and programs including 1 Million Cups Central NH, Twin State Innovation, and the Community Changemaker Challenge to support and connect entrepreneurs and help to build New Hampshire's entrepreneurial ecosystem. Before joining Extension, Jared worked in community health in rural Alaska, served as a Peace Corps volunteer in Morocco, and worked in economic development in the Midwest. He is a graduate of the University of New Hampshire and holds graduate degrees from the University of Chicago in Public Policy and Social Service Administration.

Sarah Rocker is a research associate with the Northeast Regional Center for Rural Development. Her interests lie at the intersection of food systems, agricultural change, and development. She holds a Ph.D. in Rural Sociology from Penn State University, and her research is focused on regional food value chain coordination as a strategy to connect food and agricultural stakeholders and strengthen local and regional food economies. She holds a Master's degree in Public Administration with a focus on food policy from the Evergreen State College and a Master of Arts from the University of Colorado. Sarah has a diverse background of applied work in food production, farmers' market development, cooperative restaurant/retail management, and food policy and public planning. She is a former co-founding board member of the Cooperative Food Empowerment Directive, a national non-profit committed to empowering students to create cooperatively run food businesses on college campuses.

Shannon Rogers serves as State Specialist of Nature-based Economic Development for the University of New Hampshire Cooperative Extension. She is also an Associate Extension Professor at UNH teaching in the Environmental & Resource Economics program. She has published widely in the field of ecological economics, with a focus on ecosystem services and the nature economy. She holds visiting faculty appointments at Plymouth State and Dartmouth College and is a Senior Fellow in the Environmental Leadership Program. Rogers is on the Board of Granite Outdoor Alliance and graduated with a B.A. from Dartmouth College, an M.S. and a Ph.D. from the University of New Hampshire, and completed her postdoctoral research with the U.S. Army Corps of Engineers' Institute for Water Resources.

Ricardo Romero-Perezgrovas is the Program Manager for the International Tree Foundation, an NGO based in Oxford, United Kingdom, founded in 1922. He has worked on a broad range of topics, including climate change adaptation and mitigation, agroforestry, tropical soils, clean biomass cooking, rural water systems, appropriate technology, and community seed banks. The common thread throughout this work is his engagement with a diverse array of stakeholders in collaborative efforts to regenerate the environment while improving the livelihoods of people in rural communities. Previously, he served as Program Impact Manager for Sustainable Harvest International. His recent research is focused on social and technical innovations that regenerate natural systems while providing economic opportunities and a better quality of life for rural households. Ricardo is a member of the Steering Committee of the Latin American Working Group for Regeneration International, a member of the Advisory Committee of Regeneration Belize, and a collaborator for the Centre for Research and Development of Renewable Energy at EARTH University in Costa Rica.

Geoffrey Sewake is an entrepreneur, brewer, food service and community engagement professional with a diverse set of experiences. He serves as the Community Development Coordinator for the Town of Hardwick, Vermont, during the day and is CEO, Managing Member, and brewer at a small Vermont Brewery by night. Formerly, Geoff served as community and Economic Development Field Specialist for the University of New Hampshire Cooperative Extension, where he provided support to state-wide programs, including the NH First Impressions, a program he co-developed. Before Extension, Geoffrey had a number of unique professional experiences, including managing the community outreach for the City of Los Angeles' Pilot Multifamily Recycling Program, assisting in the draft of investment derivatives at Morgan Stanley, and copy-editing language on the Bing: Jay-Z Decoded project at Droga5. Geoffrey holds a B.A. from the University of Colorado in Geography and Environmental Studies, and a J.D. and Masters of Environmental Law and Policy from the Vermont Law School.

Jodee Smith directs the community engagement efforts for the Sustainable Food Systems Science research group at Indiana University. She has been active in research, education, and outreach in the Indiana Food System for ten years in multiple capacities including farming, extension, research, and implementation projects. Jodee leads the Indiana Value Chain Network and Food Council Network and utilizes an asset-based approach to support community-led initiatives to build more equitable and robust local and regional food systems. Jodee earned a B.A. in Botany from the University of Montana and an M.S. in Plant Biology from the University of California, Davis.

Timothy R. Wojan earned his Ph.D. in Applied and Community Economics from the University of Wisconsin and has devoted his career to developing hard empirical tests of nebulous phenomena thought to be associated with economic prosperity. This work has examined the determinants and impact of the creative class in rural areas, the role of the arts in innovation and economic growth, methods to derive statistical verdicts from null findings, methods to produce reliable estimates of incremental and more far-ranging innovation, and most recently the study of radical innovation by high-tech start-ups. His research has been published in *Research Policy*, *Journal of Economic Geography*, *PLoS ONE*, *Regional Studies*, and the *American Journal of Agricultural Economics* and presented in venues such as the OECD and Harvard Business School. Tim is currently an ORISE Established Scientist Fellow at the National Center for Science and Engineering Statistics within the National Science Foundation.

ACKNOWLEDGMENTS

This book is the result of two years of work contributed by over 30 dedicated scholars and practitioners committed to building economic vitality and resilience in rural places in the United States and beyond. The nucleus of the book was seeded through a generous fellowship awarded to Charlie French by the Northeast Regional Center for Rural Development (NERCRD) at Penn State University. The fellowship facilitated the scoping of the book, and NERCRD provided invaluable backbone support by helping to frame the content, contribute chapters, and edit content. Particular thanks go to Stephan Goetz and Kristen Devlin at NERCRD, whose steadfast support galvanized this research project into a full-blown book compilation. Additional thanks go to the University of New Hampshire Extension for its financial and moral support for this large undertaking. We would be remiss if we didn't recognize the many volunteer chapter reviewers who enriched the quality of the content with their diligent reading and constructive comments to authors. Chapter reviewers include David Foote (UNH), Dev Dutta (UNH), Sarah Rocker (NERCRD), Nancy Franz (Iowa State), Kristen Devlin (Penn State/NERCRD), and Jada Lindblom (UNH). We are also grateful for our colleagues at Routledge/Taylor & Francis—Kate Schell, Sean Speers, and Jyotsna Gurung for their excellent editorial work and guidance—and Dr. Rhonda Phillips, Purdue University, who serves as the Series Editor of this Community Development Research and Practice Series. Lastly, we appreciate you, the reader, for your interest in rural innovation and entrepreneurship and for your continued work to support and raise awareness of innovation in rural places.

FOREWORD

Building Rural Community Resilience Through Innovation and Entrepreneurship

Mark D. Partridge, The Ohio State University

Rural communities face unprecedented and daunting challenges, whether they be the result of a global pandemic, wildfires, floods, a recession, loss of a major industry, or restructuring of the regional economy. Further exacerbating the plight of rural places is climate change, highlighting the need for economic development. Given the many challenges facing rural communities, this book—*Building Rural Community Resilience Through Innovation and Entrepreneurship*—is a timely addition to the growing work on how rural places can thrive.

The challenges facing rural places reflect both persistent and long-term trends, as well as new or emerging threats such as climate change and land degradation. Let us briefly turn to the historic challenges and trends to provide the context for the need to adopt the systems of supports for innovation and entrepreneurship that are espoused in this book. Since the 1920s and 1930s, rural America has faced unremitting economic restructuring of its key industries. Foremost, labor-saving technological change radically altered agriculture and other primary-sector industries in rural America. Agriculture, which accounted over one-third of U.S. total employment in 1900, barely accounts for 1% of total employment today. Similarly, coal mining employment fell by over 95% in the last century, primarily due to mechanization. The typical story that is echoed in rural places is that the industries that built rural America and supported the expansion of cities in the early 20th century are no longer relevant today.

Just how has economic development responded to the structural changes facing rural America? Early efforts to revive rural places typically entailed a "doubling-down" of effort, whether that was through increased promotion of a town's historic assets or ramping up farm and food-related activities. Likewise, the path to saving a coal-country town was to dig more coal, regardless of the environmental costs or the demands placed on labor to increase production. Such strategies invariably failed. Simply put, attempts to increase employment in an industry that is rapidly shedding jobs have not proven to be a viable road to creating employment over the long term.

Another common economic development strategy dating back to the late 1930s is industry recruiting, or "smokestack chasing," which entails the use of tax breaks and other subsidies to lure industry. Such efforts are often referred to as a race to the bottom, as each community competes to offer the most attractive package to said industry. Typically, for communities that are successful with their recruitment, the gains from new jobs created are offset by lost tax revenues and/or reduced ability to provide public services.

Rather, the last 30 years of rural economic development research suggest that the most sustainable route to community economic prosperity is to draw upon a community's existing assets and resources. Rural communities facing economic challenges are best served by leveraging the capacity of their residents, businesses, and local institutions. The most sustainable way for rural communities to thrive and enhance their resiliency to unpredictable events is for local residents to launch new enterprises or expand existing business. In doing so, the profits stay local and the likelihood that firms will relocate to Asia or other parts of the world is reduced. Skeptics who are not persuaded by this argument should visit places like Holmes County, Ohio, which does not have a major community with a town center, let alone proximity to a highway or larger cities. Yet, Holmes County has somehow managed to thrive as a cluster of small rural manufacturers that produce for niche markets. These small manufacturers have managed to turn what appeared to be a near hopeless case into a relatively stable and prosperous county. They did it by leveraging their local assets, resources, and talent.

Of course, it should be noted that innovation goes hand-in-hand with entrepreneurship. Innovation leads to new products that expand niche markets and new processes that lower prices. A common public misconception is that innovation must be "high-tech" and mainly occur in growing metropolitan areas like Silicon Valley. Such misconceptions have led to countless failed efforts. For example, rural communities that have sought to attract "high-tech" firms, even though the town lacks the basic resources to support them, typically ended up expending scarce resources without success. And communities that focused on retraining displaced workers such as farmers or loggers to become computer coders found that the skillsets didn't match. The reality is that innovation is nuanced and there is no quick fix, which might explain why so many innovations are informal and not even patented.

Effective rural economic development is about understanding psychology. The first step is for rural communities to realize that their best asset is themselves and that they too can be entrepreneurial and innovative. And once an entrepreneurial community emerges, it can be self-sustaining, leading to growth that does not need constant government handouts.

Indeed, *Building Rural Community Resilience Through Innovation and Entrepreneurship* comes at an excellent time when climate change, a global pandemic, and never-ending economic restructuring represent some of the biggest threats ever experienced by rural America. The collection of authors that contributed to this book are key thought leaders in modern rural development. As such, they provide the best tools for helping rural places move forward. Every rural economic development practitioner would benefit from reading this volume.

1

RURAL INNOVATION REDEFINED

Charlie French

Introduction

Communities across rural America face a plethora of socioeconomic forces that have contributed to their social and economic decline over the past several decades. Places once dependent on agriculture, forestry, and mining—as well as certain manufacturing subsectors like paper production—have been impacted by global economic forces such as cross-border trade, downward pressures on wages, and workforce automation (Ziliak, 2019). These and other factors have contributed to job losses in sectors that once predominated rural areas, resulting in population decline in many rural regions.

Transformations impacting rural America were greatly exacerbated by the Great Recession, as many of the jobs that were shed between 2007 and 2009 did not return. Adding to the plight of rural places is a global pandemic. While it is unclear what the long-term economic impacts of the COVID-19 pandemic will be on rural America, it will likely permanently reshape communities: the types of business and industry that survive and thrive in rural places, their sociodemographic makeup, how people access human and social services, and what opportunities abound for people of all ages (Mueller, Burow, Pofahl, Merdjanoff & Farrell, 2020).

Compounding these challenges is the fact that the median age is seven years higher in rural America as compared to metropolitan areas. This is attributed in part to brain drain, as rural youth are more likely to leave their communities post high school in search of opportunity than their more urban counterparts (Segel, Ross, Edwards, Braun & Davis, 2020). On the other end of the age spectrum, many older rural workers, as well as retirees with limited incomes, find themselves unable to leave their community or region due to lack of resources and social and familial networks in places where they might otherwise move to.

DOI: 10.4324/9781003178552-1

This can put additional strain on their families, who often end up taking care of them, and it pushes to the brink the system of social and human support for aging rural residents.

Beyond the sociodemographic and economic challenges, rural America also faces human health and health care-related challenges. Epidemics like obesity, diabetes, and substance misuse hit people in rural places disproportionately harder than their urban and suburban counterparts. These issues are often exacerbated by the relative lack of access to health services in rural communities, many of which have lost their hospitals or health clinics due to consolidation in the health-care industry. Even if health services do exist in rural places, many individuals and families lack health insurance to pay for care (Cosby, McDoom-Echebiri, James, Khandekar, Brown & Hanna, 2019). It does not help that many rural places are situated in food deserts that have very limited access to affordable, healthy food. These factors together can lead to poor health outcomes in rural places.

Lastly, a growing digital divide is contributing to stagnant economic growth in large swaths of rural America. Although broadband access is expanding in some rural places, it is overall not keeping pace with broadband expansion in more urbanized places and there is a growing gap between rural and urban with respect to affordable broadband access. With slower relative upload and download speeds, rural places struggle to attract new enterprises, let alone retain existing ones, in sectors such as financial and legal services, communications, information technology, health services, and advanced manufacturing. Lack of affordable broadband access also limits learning opportunities for people of all ages and further reduces the likelihood that young people in rural communities will go on to college or gain the skills needed to secure good-paying jobs (Gallardo, Whitacre, Kumar & Upendram, 2020). Yet, it is not merely lack of broadband access that limits learning and career development opportunities but also lack of digital literacy in many rural, broadband-underserved places regarding how to use broadband and broadband-enabled applications.

Given the array of challenges facing rural places, it would be easy for state and national political leaders to write off rural America as not worthy of investment and instead focus resources and policies on urban and peri-urban areas. Yet, some scholars believe that rural America is perhaps more relevant than it has ever been since World War II. According to a recent Pew poll conducted after the start of the COVID-19 pandemic, rural places are experiencing a recent population influx as urban dwellers seek opportunities to settle in less crowded places, a reversal from decades of population decline. Young people and families appear to be moving to internet-connected rural places, bringing with them a wealth of talent, ideas, and new enterprises. While it is unclear if this trend will continue, it has raised hope for many rural communities.

Furthermore, rural America continues to play a critical role to the growth and sustenance of the country by continually adapting to economic social change: it remains the breadbasket of the nation's food supply, it supports a multitrillion dollar recreation economy, it provides ecosystem services necessary for sustaining life like clean air and water, and it is home to around 60 million hearty residents. Rural places across the United States have figured out how to adapt to continual change and innovate in unexpected ways that make them more vibrant and attractive to people and to businesses, as well as more resilient to social, economic, and environmental change.

The question that has long intrigued rural scholars is what makes certain rural places adaptive and resilient? Part of the answer to that question is innovation: that creative milieu that is brought to life as people work together across sectors to find creative solutions to problems and adapt to change. In this book, we discuss the various forms of innovation, how they manifest themselves in rural places, and how communities can cultivate a system of supports that enable innovation and entrepreneurship to thrive, ultimately leading to community resilience (Thiede, Greiman, Weiler, Beda & Conroy, 2017).

Characterizing Rural Innovation

Throughout human history, rural places have undergone dramatic changes emanating from an array of events and phenomena such as the introduction of new technologies, changing resource consumption patterns, ever-increasing global interconnections, natural and human disasters, new discoveries, changing natural resource demands, and socioeconomic shocks. Despite the torrent of forces continually exerting pressure on rural places, some have demonstrated their resilience time and time again by bouncing back from adversity.

A key attribute that distinguishes thriving rural places from those that run the risk of becoming economically stagnant and lacking in vitality is their ability to adapt to change and overcome adversity by working across sectors to leverage assets and resources in innovative ways to tackle problems and capitalize on opportunities. Innovation is one of the most important ingredients to forging resilient, thriving rural economies (Lichtenstein & Lyons, 2010). Without innovation, rural communities lack the tools and resources to adapt to socioeconomic forces of change or disruptive events and shocks such as the loss of an industry or a natural disaster.

The term "innovation" is used in this text in a community context to refer to the introduction of a new idea, method, technology, or system that adds economic or social value to the people, institutions, organizations, or businesses residing in a place such as a city, town, or region. We refer to this form of innovation as place-based innovation, as it occurs when people in a community or a place draw from local resources, ideas, and talent—often borrowing from solutions or ideas implanted in other places—to generate alternative approaches to addressing community problems and capitalizing on opportunities (Maddock, 2010).

So much emphasis in the literature has been placed on innovation in the business sector, but we assert that innovation can emanate from *any* sector in a community or a geographic place. For instance, innovation may be introduced by community decision-makers seeking to manage public works more effectively and efficiently; by a nonprofit organization seeking to adapt its service delivery model in a new way to reach underserved clients; a group of local residents seeking more effective ways to engage people in community action, or by a social entrepreneur seeking a groundbreaking approach to effecting societal change around systemic issues like poverty and public health. Innovation can indeed emerge from any individual or group of individuals working together to solve a problem or create economic or social value. What brings innovation to life in rural places is the system of supports that help communities, entrepreneurs, civic and municipal leaders, and others come together to solve problems and add value in new and creative ways. We refer to this system as the "Innovation Ecosystem," which will be discussed in depth in Chapter 3.

While the focus of this text is on innovation at the community scale, it draws on the field of business innovation to characterize distinct forms of innovation that impact rural places. The following are four types of innovation that manifest in rural places:

- **Sustaining innovations** comprise a significant improvement(s) to a product, service, or social enterprise to ensure that it is still relevant to those benefitting from it such as a community's or organization's adoption of an emerging web-based technology platform to enhance connections with stakeholders.
- **Incremental innovations** entail gradual improvements to a product or service over time such as continual changes to policies that incorporate web-based tools for holding virtual public meetings to make them more accessible to the public.
- **Disruptive innovations** are those that introduce a new way of delivering a product or service by incorporating a new technology such as the development of a novel, ubiquitous, web-based platform for social networking.
- **Radical innovation** is what gives birth to a whole new way of solving problems and providing value, often by creating a new market. An example is the formation of Grameen Bank, which forged a new financial model for providing critical microcredit to rural poor around the world.

Lastly, we incorporate a fifth distinctive form of innovation that bears relevance to rural places: **social innovation**. Social innovation refers to the process by which civic, social, environmental, and other leaders work across sectors to develop solutions to systemic issues such as poverty, homelessness, inequities in education, or climate change. The goal of social innovation is to meet human and social needs more effectively than existing solutions. Furthermore, social innovation can occur at any scale, from local to global. An example of social innovation is how the Mayor of a struggling upstate New York town created a new financial mechanism to enable people to invest in—and ultimately own a stake in—revitalizing Main Street buildings. This model of community capital helped to revive the community. We argue that social innovations like this are prevalent in rural communities, simply because rural places are continually challenged to adapt to socioeconomic and other forces of change.

While there are no doubt examples of disruptive and radical innovation in rural places—particularly considering that electrification, telephony, and mechanized agriculture are three groundbreaking innovations that helped shape rural America in the last century—the contributions to this book focus largely on sustaining, incremental, and social innovations because they often go underrecognized and underappreciated. Yet, they are critical to rural community vitality. Sustaining, incremental, and social innovations in rural places may come about as a result of new forms of collaboration; adaptive policies that leverage rural assets and address critical service or product gaps; novel strategies for accessing financial capital; creative infusion of the arts into diverse aspects of community life; or the cultivation of knowledge and resource networks that bridge entrepreneurs, organizations, and institutions.

Debunking the Myth that Rural Places Don't Innovate

What distinguishes this book from other scholarly works on innovation is our primary focus on rural places. We do so because the vast majority of scholarly literature focuses on innovation in and around urban places with dense clustering of firms that facilitates knowledge spillover, greater relative access to financial capital, large relative pools of educated or skilled labor, presence of postsecondary research institutions, and strong public support for research and development. Moreover, the body of research on innovation as an economic driver tends to focus on disruptive and radical innovation—the rare breakthrough innovations that have relatively large economic impacts—but fails to characterize the smaller-scale, often subtle forms of innovation that occur frequently in rural places.

The so-called "innovation gap" between rural and urban places—the notion that the per capita rate and volume of innovations emanating from urban places exceeds that of rural places—is partly skewed because the specific indices of innovation commonly measured and cited in the literature by think tanks and academic institutions are at a scale that is not conducive to rural places such as venture capital investment, rate of commercialization of intellectual property, rates of job creation in emerging industry sectors, and number of patents. By and large, rural places do not have access to the scale of resources or infrastructure needed to enable the above activities, at least at the same level as urban places. Thus, there is an inherent measurement bias towards urban places that have the infrastructure and resources to spawn disruptive and radical innovation. The resulting picture is one that fails to recognize the unique forms of innovation that take place in rural places.

Yet, rural places *do* innovate, and many are thriving as a result. In fact, a number of innovation-related characteristics and practices correlate to economic vibrancy in rural places such as the positive relationship between the presence of art-focused institutions and local economic performance (Wojan & Nichols, 2018), higher relative economic performance in rural places that leverage recreational assets (García-Sánchez, Siles & Vázquez-Méndez, 2019), and linkages between economic vibrancy and the presence of value chain integrated food systems in rural places (Barrett, Reardon, Swinnen & Zilberman, 2019).

That is not to say that all rural places across America have been able to successfully leverage innovation to thrive and remain resilient. The economic reality is that many rural communities—even those with effective leadership and creative and engaged individuals, businesses, and institutions—continue to struggle because of factors that are out of their control such as national trade policies, geography, and the onset of human and natural disasters. Likewise, it would be inaccurate to say that there is not an innovation gap between rural and urban places. Overall, urban and suburban places economically outperform rural places with respect to wages, number of jobs created, goods produced, and many other key economic indices. We simply argue that the innovations that take place in rural places often go unnoticed, albeit they are important to the resiliency of rural places and the people living there. Furthermore, with challenges like pollution, congestion, housing affordability, and an increasing ability for people to work remotely, it is highly likely that rural places will continue to play an important function in the foreseeable future.

The Link between Innovation, Entrepreneurship, and Rural Resiliency

Innovation does not occur in a vacuum in rural places. It begins with an individual or a group that has the foresight to conceive of an idea, product or service that addresses a compelling problem or need facing rural communities. Whether the innovation has potential for deployment is contingent upon an agent to turn that idea into a tangible solution: hence the need for the entrepreneur. Entrepreneurs and entrepreneurial institutions are the ones that take the innovation the last mile, often at considerable financial or other risk (Lichtenstein & Lyons, 2010). Without entrepreneurs, and entrepreneurial institutions, innovations are mere ideas.

We define entrepreneurship as the process by which individuals, or a group of individuals, provide value to people by providing them with a product, service, or experience or by solving a problem such as homelessness. Entrepreneurs, by and large, rely on innovation to spur new or more effective ways of providing value to customers or constituents. As such, entrepreneurship and the process of innovation are inextricably linked. Furthermore, entrepreneurship can emanate from any sector or cut across sectors: government, institutions, organizations, businesses, and/or individuals (Johannisson & Nilsson, 1989).

While one hallmark of a successful entrepreneur is their ability to incorporate innovation into the development and implementation of an idea, it is important to note that not all entrepreneurs are inherently innovation driven

(Blundel, Lockett & Wang, 2017). Replicative entrepreneurs, for instance, seek to implement business or service models that already exist for a given product or service in an existing market such as a Mexican restaurant or flower shop. Provided that there is a market for a given product or service, certain enterprises can theoretically be replicated anywhere. In the context of a rural communities and institutions, replicative entrepreneurship might entail the adoption of telemedicine or telepsychiatry by a rural health association in the absence of medical facilities to increase access to critical services. Or it might entail a community leveraging existing broadband infrastructure to expand high-speed internet access to underserved businesses and residents. The model of implementation already exists and can be adopted from other places.

That is not to say that replicative entrepreneurs are not innovative or do not incorporate innovation, as they may indeed incorporate innovation into various aspects of their enterprise and their processes. Rather, the distinction is that replicative entrepreneurs are not solely driven by innovation.

Innovative entrepreneurs, on the other hand, rely on new ideas, creative thinking, technology solutions, prototyping, and customer-focused iteration to develop new products, services, and societal benefits, or deliver them in new ways that meet the changing needs of customers. From a business perspective, innovative entrepreneurship is an important driver to the creation of new jobs and is critical to the growth of the economy. It can also have its downsides. In the context of business and industry, innovative entrepreneurship is a primary source of creative destruction, whereby the formation of new industries can potentially eliminate sectors of the economy that existed prior to the introduction of the disruptive innovation, thus potentially resulting in job losses. Furthermore, if not managed well, disruptive innovations can lead to unintended consequences such as the demise of important industries or services once critical to rural places, or it can lead to socioeconomic inequities if access to the innovation is restricted to certain segments of the population such as those with high purchasing power (Aghion, Akcigit, Deaton & Roulet, 2016).

With these caveats aside, innovative entrepreneurship can be harnessed in positive ways and has led to rural communities and businesses finding creative solutions to pressing problems and adapting to change. As an example, during March-April 2020, the COVID-19 pandemic forced many Main Street restaurants to limit their indoor seating spaces to maintain social distancing. This put major financial stress on restaurants dependent on turnover and many were forced to close. It also placed economic strain on communities dependent on the service sector. Yet, in some communities, restaurant owners and managers were able to work with municipal and state leaders to find creative ways of expanding dining spaces such as by modifying local ordinances to allow for temporary outdoor seating on municipal property, setting aside parking and street frontage for curbside pickup, or by allocating public resources to pay restaurants to prepare food kits for community kitchens. Communities also found creative ways of utilizing web-based technologies that enabled crowdsourcing up-to-date information on where and how to access food, including from restaurants, grocery stores, farm stands, and food pantries.

The point is both replicative and innovative entrepreneurship help rural communities build resilience: the ability of a place to bounce back after a threat or shock such as a destructive storm event, the loss of a major industry, or a pandemic. In the context of rural places, the term community resilience characterizes how nimbly a place can adapt to change. Resilience does not necessarily mean that a community will bounce back to the exact state that it was in prior to the shock or event, or that all the negative impacts will be completely mitigated. Rather, resilient communities find ways to rebuild strength, often incorporating innovative solutions to solve problems or emerge from the crisis in a manner that leverages assets (Aldrich & Meyer, 2015). One example is how a Maine town repurposed its abandoned papermill—once the town's main economic engine—into an aquaculture production site, or how an Illinois farming town redesigned and rebuilt its main street after it was destroyed by a tornado, ultimately enabling it to attract more visitors and accommodate new enterprises that otherwise would not have emerged.

In sum, resilient communities have several characteristics in common that enable them to adapt to change. Foremost, they are willing to work across sectors towards a common purpose. Second, they leverage people, ideas, and resources in innovative ways that enable them to tackle problems and capitalize on opportunities. Most important, they maintain the infrastructure, systems, and processes necessary for fostering entrepreneurship and innovation at the community scale. In addition to physical infrastructures such as business incubators and high-speed internet, they also maintain "soft" infrastructures that are critical to fostering entrepreneurship and innovation. Those include educational institutions that teach problem-solving, supportive local government institutions that create effective policies and programs, engaged community volunteers that work to improve the community and support local business, and well-networked institutions and organizations that coordinate education, technical assistance, financing, mentoring, and peer networking (Roundy, Brockman & Bradshaw, 2017). These systems, structures, and processes all together comprise the innovation ecosystem.

The Innovation Ecosystem

Some rural places have been more resilient than others in the wake of major social and economic changes because they were able to weave together the various stakeholders and resources necessary to stimulate innovation. Communities that focus on fostering an innovation ecosystem—as opposed to grasping for single solutions such as providing costly incentives to catalyze economic growth—are better able to weather shocks such as devastating storm events, loss of a major industry, or even a global pandemic. Much like a resilient ecological ecosystem rebounds from a natural disturbance, an innovation ecosystem enables communities to restore balance after a shock or disruptive event. The ecosystem

FIGURE 1.1 Community innovation ecosystem components.

components necessary to support innovation and resiliency are diverse, integrated, and span multiple sectors and levels of geography (see Figure 1.1).

Key values that facilitate an innovation ecosystem—and ultimately strengthen a community's ability to adapt to change—are as follows:

- Ability to leverage community assets by working across sectors (e.g., businesses, educational institutions, and government)
- Focus on cultivating human capital (e.g., education and training)
- Commitment to cultural norms of openness (e.g., willingness to explore new ideas)
- An eye towards leveraging local and regional assets (e.g., natural and cultural amenities)
- A problem-focused mentality that is market- and value-driven
- Strong networks that enable people to connect and share ideas and solutions

Furthermore, the types of solutions that an innovation ecosystem spawns need not reside solely within the business sector. They span sectors and therefore lead to collaborative solutions to a wide range of problems facing communities, from lack of key infrastructures such as public transportation and broadband access to systemic issues such as substance misuse among young people. Communities that exemplify the above characteristics are not guaranteed to thrive, since factors such as geography, demographic change, and globalization can have an overpowering influence, but they are more resilient because they plan for the future, they seek to empower and mobilize the collective assets of the community or region, and they are open to change and to trying new things. Most important, they have institutions, businesses, and citizens that come together to find collective solutions to current challenges and capitalize on future opportunities.

Examples of rural communities that have focused on building an innovation ecosystem include a coastal Maine town that fell into decline following the closure of its seafood cannery, but was able to forge a new vision and recreate itself into a tourist destination and a regional hub for the arts; a small Vermont town that was struggling to sustain its farms in the wake of a dairy crisis, but managed to turn itself around by shifting its focus from commodity agriculture to developing high-quality, value-added products by sharing resources and integrating the value chains for products ranging from cheese to baked goods; and an Pacific Northwest town that depopulated after the decline of its timber industry, but found novel ways of attracting overnight visitors, in spite of limited lodging options such as by developing and leveraging Air BnB rental properties.

The point is, without an innovation ecosystem, rural communities are overly dependent individuals to craft solutions to challenges. More than likely, sustainable solutions to the more complex challenges facing communities do not lie within the reach of any one individual. They require people to come together and leverage the network of assets and resources that every community maintains. That can only happen if there is a structure to weave together all the supports available to a community.

Synthesis and Conclusion

Rural communities across America face a plethora of socioeconomic forces of change that are forcing them to adapt. Places once dependent on agriculture, forest products, mineral mining, and manufacturing have experienced global transformations that have resulted in job losses, and ultimately, population decline. To add to these stressors, rural places overall are aging, they have relatively poor access to health services, and they maintain inadequate infrastructure—let alone skilled workers—to compete fully in today's global economy. Thus, it should come as no surprise that when there is a major shock to the social and economic system, such as the great recession of 2007–2009 or the COVID-19 pandemic, rural communities are disproportionately negatively impacted.

In spite of these dynamics, some rural communities have been extraordinarily resilient in the face of major social and economic changes because they have cultivated an innovation ecosystem: the system of supports that enable communities, entrepreneurs, civic and municipal leaders, and others come together to solve problems and add value in new and creative ways. Much like a natural ecosystem, an innovation ecosystem has certain characteristics that give it resiliency and enable it to adapt to change. Characteristics of resilient communities with an innovation ecosystem include embracing of diversity, which increases the pathways for a community to adapt to a change or shock to the system; cultivation of networks and social capital, whereby connections amongst diverse stakeholders lead to greater ability to leverage resources and ideas; cultivation of relationships, which enables disparate partners to work towards common goals; supportive institutions, which contribute human, financial, political, and knowledge capital to support solutions and entrepreneurs; and forward-thinking political leaders who are willing to try new things and remove policy barriers to enable ideas to take root.

Innovation has been undervalued and appreciated in rural places, largely because traditional measures of innovation fail to characterize the various forms of innovation that occur in rural communities. As such, the purpose of this book is to elucidate the processes by which innovation occurs in rural communities, where it is taking place, and examples of how rural communities have leveraged community capitals to adapt to change and address community challenges. The book will close with a set of best practices that rural communities and regions can draw from to cultivate innovation ecosystems. The fact is that rural places do innovate and there has never been a more important time to recognize the role of innovation as rural communities seek to rebuild their economies in the wake of COVID-19.

Chapter Overview

The goal of this edited volume is to provide diverse scholarly perspectives on innovation in rural places and its connection to entrepreneurship and community resilience. Drawing from empirical analyses, case studies, and a synthesis of best practices, chapter authors explore various forms and facets of innovation with the goal of characterizing how innovation manifests itself in rural places and how it contributes to entrepreneurial development and resilience. Geographically, this compilation focuses on places that lie outside of urban and urban-adjacent areas, given the dearth of scholarly literature dedicated to innovation in rural places.

The book is divided into three sections. The first section seeks to define rural innovation and lays the context for where innovation is occurring and what components lead to an effective innovation ecosystem. Section 2 focuses on the dynamics of rural innovation, specifically looking at the process of innovation creation in rural places, the role of social capital, and innovation in the face of uncertainty. The final section of this book explores how specific innovation-related characteristics relate to rural economic vibrancy such as a strong connection to the arts, adaptive and sustainable use of natural resources, value-chain integrated food systems, robust bridging social capital networks, creative leveraging of technology, and presence of innovation-focused entrepreneurs. Through exploration of these and other topics, we hope this book will provide insights and best practices for rural community and economic development scholars, local and state community leaders, extension educators, and economic development practitioners seeking to strengthen the rural innovation ecosystem. This first chapter lays the context, and the remaining chapters are summarized here.

In Chapter 2, Goetz, Meadowcraft, and Han explore county-level measures of innovation often overlooked in rural places, as conventional measures of innovation are urban centric, suggesting that only large cities foster new ideas. They look at "hidden innovation," which is the effect of knowledge spillover on firms, which can lead businesses to make incremental improvements to their business, as well as products and processes. Their measures suggest innovation is widespread in rural places, though not well documented in the scholarly literature. They lay forth new aspects of innovation that decision-makers should consider and how they can support it.

In Chapter 3, Reynolds discusses the components of an innovation ecosystem: the resources, physical infrastructure, institutions, policies, capital, and other supports critical to helping people transform ideas into action. Because entrepreneurs in rural areas often face challenges getting their ideas off the ground, this chapter seeks to identify existing barriers, challenges, benefits, opportunities to innovation and entrepreneurship and how rural places can weave together people, programs, and resources to make it easier for entrepreneurs and innovators to get their ideas off the ground and cultivate small businesses and social ventures that provide value and solve community problems.

In Chapter 4, Mann and Miller explore many of the assumptions underlying how innovation occurs in rural places and how government policies may not accurately reflect rural firms or the regions in which rural firms operate. Data from the Rural Establishment Innovation Survey (REIS) are used to reveal important distinctions between rural and urban firms such as the intellectual property (IP) strategies used and the types of industries in which the firms operate and develop innovations. This chapter also looks more closely at innovation creation through the lens of the Small Business Innovation Research (SBIR) program. The goal is to improve our understanding and framework regarding rural innovation, and thus, inform rural-focused polices that could catalyze innovation in rural places.

In Chapter 5, Lyons discusses the critical importance of networks and social capital in enabling rural entrepreneurs to reach beyond their local communities for the resources they need to thrive and grow. Rural places typically have relative geographical isolation, a dearth of financial capital, fewer venture development organizations, a lower-skilled workforce, and underpopulation. As such, they rely on creating and maintaining networks to overcome these challenges. This chapter will explore bridging (versus bonding) social capital, and its advantages to fostering entrepreneurship. It will examine the ways in which bridging social capital is built and maintained within the entrepreneurial ecosystem.

In Chapter 6, Flora explores rural communities' creative and innovative use of local assets or capitals—specifically natural, cultural, human, social, political, financial, and built capital—to address poverty that often goes underrecognized in rural communities, thus leading to greater economic security for the most economically vulnerable rural residents. In particular, Flora explores the potential of local food systems as a vehicle for unleashing rural assets in a manner that not only helps sustain rural farmers struggling to make a living but also provides jobs and needed resources to community residents.

In Chapter 7, Alter and Fortunato discuss one potential, albeit significant, negative connotation of innovation on rural communities, which is risk. While it is understood that risk is essential to return, a great deal of effort is given to reducing risk through the institutionalization of economic action; from systematizing innovation processes to creating universal "best practices" for success. Some of these best practices and efforts can have the unintended consequence of exposing communities to black swan events: rare events with outsized, totally unexpected outcomes. As such, Alter and Fortunato discuss how communities can organize themselves to benefit from, rather than suffer from, uncertainty and disorder by embracing shocks and stressors as the necessary fuel for productive and creative new ideas. They refer to this concept as antifragility—those characteristics of a system that increase a place's ability to thrive in the face of stressors and shocks—which stands in stark contrast to the idea of resilience.

In Chapter 8, Gallardo posits that rural communities are innovative and, more importantly, have the same or even greater capacity to innovate as urban and suburban places. He demonstrates how an enhanced capacity to innovate can be unleashed as sophisticated, digital age applications and mindsets expand. The digital age offers new opportunities and challenges, particularly for rural communities. However, for innovation to fully lead to prosperity in rural places, a series of barriers have to be overcome, which are: (1) lack of awareness of the digital age; (2) the need to address digital parity issues (around connectivity, mindset, and skills); and (3) digital inclusion or exclusion. This chapter will discuss these barriers in an effort to identify opportunities for unleashing the true innovative potential of rural communities in this nascent digital age.

In Chapter 9, Wojan draws important linkages between the arts, creativity, and economic resilience in rural places by investigating the possible role that imagination plays in rural innovation. The predominant thought has been that the concentration of scientific and engineering resources makes large cities the privileged location for innovative activities, relegating rural places with less capability for producing new knowledge to routine manufacturing, logistics, service provision, and the production of food and fiber. Wojan draws on empirical evidence to illustrate an alternative view of how rural innovation is conceived, assessed, and fostered. This alternative view, espoused by John Dewey, is that innovation is dependent on two essential inputs: science and imagination. Science is required for a firm grounding in what is, while imagination is required to envision the full realm of future possibilities. Wojan explores the role of imagination—and what he refers to as "imaginariums"—as the creative spark that stimulates the innovation process in rural places.

In Chapter 10, Rocker and Smith elucidate the importance of "social" infrastructure to support and coordinate regional, values-based food supply chains and regional economies. In particular they focus on the role of value chain coordination, which includes market matchmaking, convening stakeholders, and providing technical assistance to emerging and existing businesses in local food chains. A case study of Indiana, which developed a statewide value chain coordination network, illustrates a novel organizing framework for bringing together value chain coordination professionals who are developing the capacities of producers and food businesses in various regions across the state. Rocker and Smith conclude with examples and considerations for future development of value chain coordination networks as a place-based development strategy that could be applied to other regions and sectors beyond food.

In Chapter 11, Arbogast and Eades discuss the innovative responses of three West Virginia communities to the challenges of destination management and the successes and challenges rural Destination Management Organizations (DMOs) face as they seek to balance economic development, sustainable tourism, and residents' quality of life. They argue that DMOs and Convention and Visitor Bureaus play a key role in cultivating innovative solutions to rural tourism challenges. They also demonstrate how university outreach initiatives can help DMOs develop innovative responses to tourism development issues in their community, with particular attention paid to Cooperative Extension's role in co-creating knowledge with rural DMOs, sharing research and best practices, and translating tacit knowledge and learned experiences to explicit knowledge that can be shared within the state and across the nation.

In Chapter 12, Rogers, Donovan, Porter, and Sewake discuss how rural communities that are rich in natural assets can leverage those assets in innovative ways to generate local economic activity and created community vibrancy connected to economic centers. They share a case study of a rural New Hampshire community that trained community volunteers, mapped local assets, and developed an action plan to build connectivity between the area's natural assets and the town's Main Street. The program catalyzed a series of projects and actions that have contributed to the town's vibrancy.

In Chapter 13, Romero-Perezgrovas, Ospina, Croteau, and Powell provide an international context by illustrating how Sustainable Harvest International (SHI)—a development organization focused on Central America—simultaneously addresses rural poverty and climate through the creation of local innovation ecosystems in rural, Honduran communities where the environmental crisis and lack of economic opportunity are intertwined. The authors provide a case study from the Yoro District of Honduras to illustrate how SHI's long-term, participant-centered training program has helped rural farming families sustain their livelihoods while also stewarding the environment through regenerative agriculture, an innovative adaptation to changing environmental conditions aimed at meeting and sustaining human needs. Participating families have each incorporated new regenerative agriculture techniques, doubled their conservation initiatives, and accessed local finance. Outcomes resulting from these actions include enhanced well-being, better access to life-sustaining resources, and enhanced ecosystem integrity.

In Chapter 3, Reynolds outlines the characteristics and best practices that communities need to develop and incorporate to foster innovation and entrepreneurship. Such characteristics and practices include an emphasis on weaving together a network of people and resources to solve problems, creative leveraging of financial capital, strong linkages with educational institutions, forward-thinking political leaders who are open to new ways of doing business, and an inclusive and community-engaged approach to solving problems. Communities that effectively leverage their assets and weave together the network of supports and resources are more readily capable of innovating and adapting to change, thus making them more resilient. As such, this closing chapter will outline the characteristics and practices that communities need to develop and implement to foster innovation and entrepreneurship.

References

Aghion, P., Akcigit, U., Deaton, A., & Roulet, A. (2016). Creative destruction and subjective well-being. *American Economic Review, 106*(12), 3869–3897.

Aldrich, D. P., & Meyer, M. A. (2015). Social capital and community resilience. *American Behavioral Scientist, 59*(2), 254–269.

Barrett, C., Reardon, T., Swinnen, J., & Zilberman, D. (2019). *Structural transformation and economic development: insights from the agri-food value chain revolution.* Working paper, Dyson School of Applied Economics and Management, Cornell University.

Blundel, R., Lockett, N., & Wang, C. (2017). *Exploring entrepreneurship.* Newbury Park, California: Sage.

Cosby, A. G., McDoom-Echebiri, M. M., James, W., Khandekar, H., Brown, W., & Hanna, H. L. (2019). Growth and persistence of place-based mortality in the United States: the rural mortality penalty. *American Journal of Public Health, 109*(1), 155–162.

Gallardo, R., Whitacre, B., Kumar, I., & Upendram, S. (2020). Broadband metrics and job productivity: a look at county-level data. *The Annals of Regional Science, 66*(1), 1–24.

García-Sánchez, A., Siles, D., & Vázquez-Méndez, M. D. M. (2019). Competitiveness and innovation: effects on prosperity. *Anatolia, 30*(2), 200–213.

Johannisson, B., & Nilsson, A. (1989). Community entrepreneurs: networking for local development. *Entrepreneurship & Regional Development, 1*(1), 3–19.

Lichtenstein, G. A., & Lyons, T. S. (2010). *Investing in entrepreneurs: a strategic approach to building a stronger regional and community economy.* Santa Barbara, CA: Praeger/ABC-CLIO, p. 3.

Maddock, S., & Robinson, B. (2010). *Place based innovation.* London: National School of Government.

Mueller, J. T., McConnell, K., Burow, P. B., Pofahl, K., Merdjanoff, A. A., & Farrell, J. (2020). Impacts of the COVID-19 pandemic on rural America. *Proceedings of the National Academy of Sciences, 118*(1), 1–6.

Roundy, P. T., Brockman, B. K., & Bradshaw, M. (2017). The resilience of entrepreneurial ecosystems. *Journal of Business Venturing Insights, 8*, 99–104.

Segel, J. E., Ross, H. I., Edwards, J. L., Braun, K. A., & Davis, L. A. (2020). The unique challenges facing rural providers in the COVID-19 pandemic. *Population Health Management, 24*(3), 304–306.

Thiede, B., Greiman, L., Weiler, S., Beda, S. C., & Conroy, T. (2017). Six charts that illustrate the divide between rural and urban America. *The Conversation*. Retrieved from http://ruraljobscoalition.com/clientuploads/toolkit/Six%20charts%20that%20illustrate%20the%20divide%20between%20rural%20and%20urban%20America.pdf

Wojan, T. R., & Nichols, B. (2018). Design, innovation, and rural creative places: are the arts the cherry on top, or the secret sauce? *PLoS One, 13*(2), e0192962.

Ziliak, J. (2019). Restoring economic opportunity for "the people left behind": employment strategies for rural America. *The Aspen Institute Economic Strategy Group, 34*, 100–128.

2

THE GEOGRAPHY OF RURAL INNOVATION AND ENTREPRENEURSHIP IN THE UNITED STATES

Stephan J. Goetz, Devon Meadowcroft and Yicheol Han

Introduction and Overview

Together with growth in capital and labor stocks, innovation is critical to the long-term increases in economic productivity that are at the heart of rising standards of living in any nation. Conventional wisdom suggests that new ideas are primarily spawned in large cities or metropolitan areas when in fact even rural places that are not typically viewed as innovative also can be home to new ideas and insights, as well as significant entrepreneurial energy. These less obvious or hidden forms of innovation and entrepreneurship can also benefit rural workers and communities, but new and broader ways of thinking about innovation and entrepreneurship are required, if they are to be better understood and fostered to the benefit of rural residents. In particular, rural businesses sometimes make incremental but strategic improvements to the goods or services they provide, and these can be critical to keeping the businesses profitable and resilient. These improvements based on innovative or entrepreneurial thinking can be just as important to the vitality of rural areas as to major metropolitan cities.

This chapter explores and documents these broader measures of innovation, beyond those reported by agencies such as the National Science Foundation (NSF), while also showing where they occur across the nation. As such, the chapter provides a context for subsequent chapters that seek to understand how rural innovation and entrepreneurship can be enhanced in different communities.

Rural counties generally lag behind urban areas on the typical NSF-type measures of innovation such as patents, research and development expenditures and Science and Engineering workforce. Yet these NSF measures are narrowly conceived and ignore more general types of innovation, a number of which also occur in rural areas (Wojan & Parker, 2017). Innovation or innovative entrepreneurship covers a broad range of activities, extending from marginal changes to

DOI: 10.4324/9781003178552-2

existing goods and services to fundamentally new products that spawn entire new industries, including software development as in the case of Microsoft's Bill Gates, or electronic payment systems, as in the case of PayPal and Jeff Bezos. Not all types of entrepreneurship are thus necessarily genuinely *innovative*—for example, some authors distinguish between innovative vs. replicative entrepreneurship (e.g., Baumol, 2010). Even *simple* or replicative innovation is essential, however, to the extent that it allows existing business to survive and even flourish and grow when they otherwise would not.

The United States has a history of producing genuinely *new* goods and services in rural areas (e.g., Loveridge, 2006); these are products that have not existed before and can potentially spawn completely new industries. Often their production sites eventually move to more urbanized counties to benefit from scale economies by accessing deeper markets such as those for skilled labor. Li et al. (2016) examine locations of the fastest growing firms by total revenue, as reported by *INC5000* magazine, and find that such firms also are found in rural counties, although their overall share is declining over time. Rapid revenue growth can be a key indicator of innovation as it suggests a new product, process, or service that is capturing a growing market share.

In general, firm growth and related indicators of entrepreneurship can serve as measures of innovation that are occurring even in rural areas. One such indicator is the presence of performing arts institutions, which Wojan and Nichols (2018) have found to be positively related to local economic growth via a hypothesized link through innovation and related underlying creative processes. More recently, Goetz and Han (2020) developed a measure of hidden innovation that is based on proximity spillovers in production and process innovation among firms and found that such innovation also occurs in rural communities. This kind of innovation occurs when ideas and insights are generated and exchanged among business owners and workers, and when these flows then give rise to new ways of producing or selling a product or service. At its core, the measure is based on the notion that insights are sparked primarily when individuals talk with others, rather than working by themselves. We elaborate on this measure below.

In this chapter, we map and describe the geography of the specific and related types of innovation that are occurring in rural U.S. counties to provide an empirical context for the book. These types of innovation include patent activity as a conventional measure of innovation that is tracked by the federal government; growth in firms or establishments per existing population as a measure of economic vibrancy and, indirectly, economic innovativeness; self-employment rates as a measure of how entrepreneurially driven the local workforce is; and, finally, hidden or *latent* innovation, which is a new measure that was only recently developed. We also examine the relationship between rural innovation activity and other predetermined county characteristics, such as the USDA/ERS amenity index and the rural urban continuum code. In general, we hypothesize to see less innovation in more remote areas depending on the measure used, but we also expect a pattern whereby innovation does occur even in some rural areas;

for example, rural areas with higher levels of natural amenities or those adjacent to metro areas, are expected to demonstrate more innovation activity than those not meeting these criteria, to the extent that they are able to attract footloose creative class workers.

Measuring Entrepreneurship and Innovation

Researchers have considered different measures of entrepreneurship and innovation, sometimes facing challenges distinguishing between the two (e.g., Motoyama, 2019). Perhaps the most common measure of creative innovation is that of patenting activity. Yet, as Wojan and Nichols (2018) and Goetz and Han (2020) point out, not all patents are truly innovative, and not all innovations are inherently patentable. Thus, patents are, at best, one proxy measure of innovation, albeit a commonly used one.

A key feature of patents is that whoever is seeking a new one has to cite related work that has preceded his or her own; this creates interesting patenting networks of authors. An important phenomenon with patent citations, first identified by Jaffe et al. (1993), is the importance of proximity. Authors of patents are more likely to cite other authors who are nearby than authors across the country, thus leading to important density and agglomeration effects. The United States is a global leader in per capita patent-granting activity, although other nations are catching up, and this is commonly pointed to as one of the reasons for this nation's strong performance in terms of productivity-enhanced economic growth and associated rising standards of living over time.

A commonly used measure of entrepreneurship, with implicit consideration of innovation, is new firm or business formation in a community. This idea gained broader recognition with the groundbreaking book, *Entrepreneurship, Geography, and American Economic Growth*, by Acs and Armington (2006). In addition to presenting a comprehensive treatment of where entrepreneurship was occurring across the United States, in the form of establishment growth, these authors made an important contribution by spawning a broad set of studies examining how entrepreneurship contributes to subsequent local economic growth (e.g., Rupasingha & Goetz, 2013; Shrestha et al., 2007). A key drawback of this study, for present purposes, is that the Acs and Armington (2006) study uses labor market areas as the unit of observation rather than counties. As such, it does not shed any light on rural and urban differences, as we endeavor to do here. In other words, we use a conceptually similar measure but apply it to counties rather than labor market areas.

Other studies have focused on self-employment as a measure of entrepreneurship (e.g., Goetz & Rupasingha, 2009), largely because the data were readily available and found to be good proxies for the measure as well as for innovation. More refined studies also consider differences in male- and female-originated self-employment (e.g., Patrick et al., 2016). Importantly, these studies have documented that local economic growth in terms of both employment and jobs increased with a more robust self-employed sector. The latter also tended to be more resilient to the impacts of the 2008 Great Recession (Han & Goetz, 2019) as well as less vulnerable to international trade shocks (Liang & Goetz, 2016).

Most recently, Goetz and Han (2020) explored the possibility that latent or hidden innovation, which is by definition difficult to measure, in fact exists in many rural communities. They find that such activity does exist, and we report the data below in a map. Moreover, they find their measure to be associated in a statistically significant and positive manner with subsequent income and job growth in local economies; it is highly correlated at the county level with patenting activity, a human capital and knowledge creation index, as well as with a business dynamic index (see Appendix B and C in their paper). In the next section we discuss our four selected measures in more detail while also providing maps to provide a sense of how these measures are dispersed across space.

The Geography of Innovation and Entrepreneurship

Patent Activity

We start with the number of patents granted. While the highest rates not surprisingly are found in urban or metro areas, where they average 279.4/capita 100,000, it is surprising to find that patenting activity also occurs in more rural counties across the nation, including especially in the nation's heartland. High rates are also granted in selected New England counties as well as in the Rocky Mountain states (Figure 2.1).

Despite this overall positive picture shown in the map, it is also true that patenting activity declines with distance from urban areas as well as with declining overall population size. In this context the USDA ERS's Rural Urban Continuum Code is a useful measure of rurality that is also correlated with declining

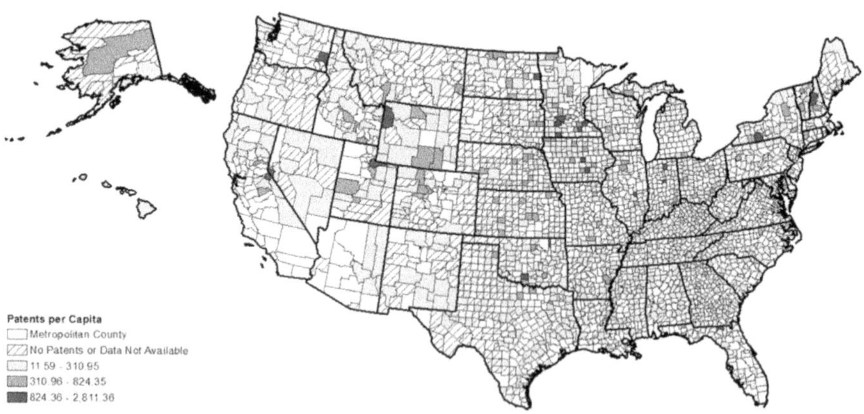

FIGURE 2.1 Patents granted per capita for nonmetropolitan counties.
Source: Authors using US Patent and Trade Office data.

population density and greater agricultural activity. Codes 4, 6, and 8 are counties with successively smaller populations that are adjacent to metro areas and thus benefit from urban spillovers, while code 5, 7, and 9 counties are the same in terms of population size that are not adjacent to metro areas. In the RUCC code 4 counties, patents were granted at a rate more than 3 times higher than was the case in RUCC code 9 counties: for each of the county types, shown in square brackets, the rates per 100,000 population are 163.0 [4]; 114.5 [5]; 84.6 [6]; 76.1 [7]; 80.0 [8]; and 48.3 [9]. Alternatively, the least amount of patenting activity occurs in the smallest rural counties that are also not adjacent to a metropolitan area.

This finding is consistent with the common perception that rural areas are less innovative than urban areas, and this is truer for areas that are most remote and have the smallest populations. The declining trend of patenting activity in more rural communities is also consistent with the fact that R&D spending also is lower in those communities, and the generally smaller research infrastructure both in terms of labs and scientific facilities as well as the share of scientists in the local workforce. Using patents as a measure of innovation is consistent with the idea of having clusters or agglomerations of research activities, with mutually beneficial spillovers of ideas among scientists, for example, through casual interactions around water coolers but also at scientific conferences. As we have argued, while patenting activity is important as a measure of innovation, it is only one option.

Net Change in Establishments Per Employee

Following in the spirit of Acs and Armington [AA] (2006), we next examine the net change in establishments per 1,000 employees as a measure of county entrepreneurship and innovation. Specifically, this is aggregate net change in establishments averaged over the years 2014–2015 and 2015–2016 (to obtain a more representative picture) per 1,000 employees [in 2015 and 2016], respectively. While AA used confidential LEEM data to examine gross firm formation (see p. 12, *ff*), which tracks new business startups, business survival and expansion, we instead use the net change in total establishments from the U.S. Census County Business Patterns, as these can be accessed with fewer restrictions. Our use of publicly available secondary data also facilitates replication of this work.

This firm formation measure we use is not without problems, in that the net change in establishments could simply reflect the splitting up of one firm into two or more smaller firms, which may or may not represent entrepreneurial vigor within a community. As this is a rate per 1,000 workers in the industry, the net formation rate would drop even if the net change in total establishments remains constant as the number of employees in a county grows. On the other hand, the measure is intuitively appealing in that it can be interpreted as the net number of new establishments that arise from an existing workforce (i.e., the employees). This is sometimes referred to as an ecological model of entrepreneurship

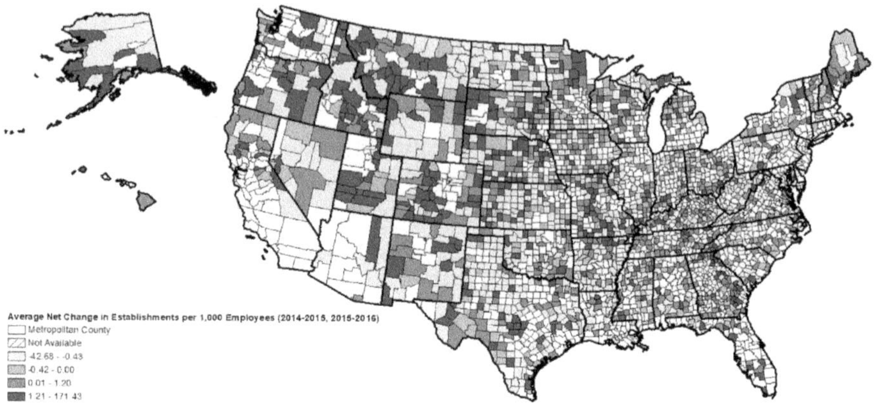

FIGURE 2.2 Average net change in establishments per 1,000 employees between 2014 and 2015 and 2015 and 2016 for nonmetropolitan counties.

Source: Authors using US County Business Patterns data.

(Audretsch et al., 2019; Manolova et al., 2017). It also reinforces the idea that a greater number (or cluster) of firms is associated with more competition (and possibly collaboration) and thus more pressure on firms to innovate in order to survive (citation).

Even more importantly, the measure is highly appropriate for communities experiencing rapid population change, as is the case for many rural areas. Establishment growth over time could just reflect population (and worker) growth. Measuring the number of firms per worker as the denominator should more accurately capture underlying innovativeness and entrepreneurial energy within a county (Figure 2.2).

Many high-growth or innovative counties are visible on this map, especially in the Central Plains states which have a long history of outmigration but also in the high amenity areas of the Rocky Mountains (Wyoming, Idaho, Montana). Remarkably, a number of these remote counties—also classified as Frontier and Remote Areas by the ERS—are home to one or more artistic and performing institutions (Wojan & Nichols, 2018, Fig. 1). The same is true of the rapidly growing frontal mountain range of Colorado, which also stands out in the map with rapid establishment growth relative to employees. In addition, however, there are pockets of counties with high growth throughout the Northeast as well as the Southeast Census areas. As suggested in the legend, the maximum value for this firm formation is 171 net establishments created per 1,000 workers.

Importantly, however, many counties experienced net declines in the number of establishments, suggesting a shrinking local economy and a lack of dynamic entrepreneurship or growth. Such declines are generally associated with population outmigration caused by declining overall employment opportunities, associated with the consolidation of economic activity, as well as innovation and entrepreneurship, in metropolitan areas. A key task for researchers is sorting out why some rural areas continue to flourish while others decline, and what if anything can or should be done about it.

More specifically, the relationship between new firm or establishment and employment growth is important and closely related to whether innovation and entrepreneurship ultimately lead to new job growth, including jobs that are well paid. One way of assessing this relationship is to graph the two variables against one another. This will show whether a given increase in new firms is associated with a large or small increase in new employment, and vice versa; note that we discuss this as an association and not necessarily causation.

AA also plot the relationship between their firm formation rate and employment growth at the Labor Market Area level (Figure 1.3, page 17). They find a tightly clustered relationship, indicating a very close fit of a line through the data points, whereby a higher rate of employment growth is strongly associated with a higher rate of firm formation (with an R-square value of 0.58). They also show a much wider range in employment growth, from about -5% to 48%, compared to firm formation where the rate is between 2% and 10%. In other words, the range in variation of job growth is much greater than the range of variation in firm growth in their data set. Or, a relatively small increase in new firms in a labor market can be associated with a relatively large range in employment increases.

With our county-level data, and using the rate of change in establishments rather than new firm formations, we obtain a weaker relationship or fit of the data to the line through the points (an R-square value of only 10%). We also find the differences in employment growth rates across counties are only about twice as large as the establishment growth rates, where in the case of AA the differences were much greater, at about five times for job growth vs. firm start-ups. This means that a given range of net establishment growth rates is associated with a similar range in the rate of employment growth rates (in the case of AA, the latter was much greater). Our data points also are very tightly clustered around the origin (0,0) of the graph, showing less variation. It is also important to note that many of our data points reflect either a loss of establishments, a loss of employment, or both. In general, LMAs, which are centered on metro areas, tend to be more robust in terms of economic growth, as well as entrepreneurship and innovation.

A more refined analysis by RUCC indicates that the relationship between establishment growth and employment growth is always stronger in metro-nonadjacent rural counties than is true in metro-adjacent rural counties. We show this below for the RUCC = 5 counties, where the R-square value is highest of all the RUCC codes, with a value of 24.9%. This suggests that not being adjacent to a metro county somehow insulates the rural county from metro spillover effects, so that the relationship between employment growth and establishment growth is stronger. Or counties that are adjacent to metro areas benefit more from economic growth in those metro areas than from new firm formations with the counties themselves. Another interpretation of this finding is that investing in

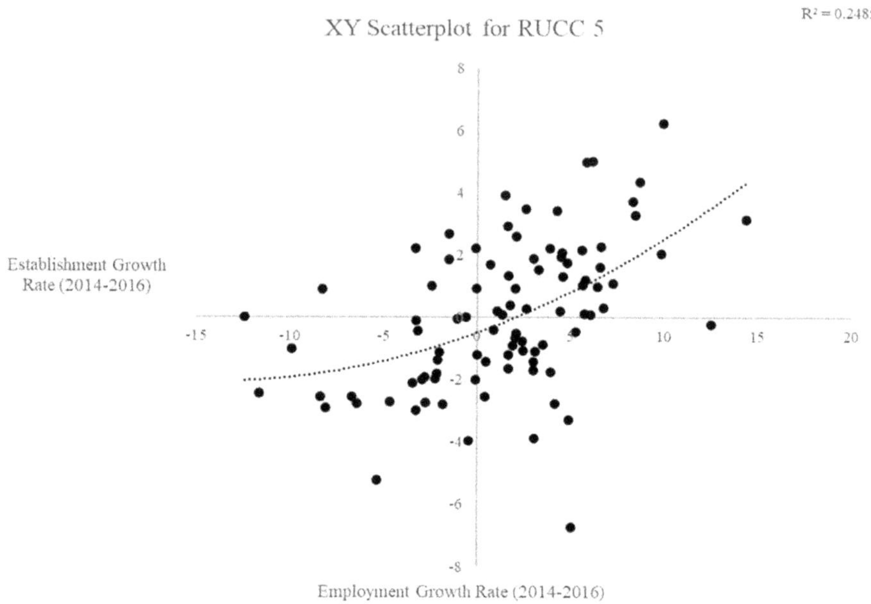

FIGURE 2.3 X-Y scatterplot for counties in RUCC code 5 showing establishment growth rate (2014–2016) and employment growth rate (2014–2016).

Source: Authors using USDA Economic Research Service and US County Business Patterns and Bureau of Labor Statistics data.

new firm formation through appropriate economic policy to achieve job growth is likely to have a higher payoff in counties that are not adjacent to metro areas than in those that are adjacent (Figure 2.3).

In supplementary maps [now shown in this book] we also examine net establishment growth separately for the manufacturing, retailing, and service industries. Net increases in manufacturing establishments per 1,000 employees are especially noteworthy in counties of the intermountain states, but also in other rural areas of the nation. In follow-up research it would be interesting to determine what kind of manufacturing is involved (e.g., food or high-technology related) and what roles, if any, local economic conditions and related factors have played in their emergence.

A different image appears for retail establishments per 1,000 workers, where high growth rates proliferate especially in the Great Plains states. It is not obvious why this is occurring given the general trend towards consolidation in retailing across the United States, with Big Box stores, etc. Again, it would be important to follow up in future research to assess what kinds of operations these are, such as perhaps speciality retailers, purveyors of local products or services, or tourism-related goods. We also examined net change in service-related establishments and again found that high rates occur in counties scattered across the nation.

Perhaps most remarkable here is that the counties with high formation rates in the three industries—manufacturing, retailing, and services—all differ; in other words, high formation rates in one industry do not predict higher rates in other industries. Or, different, industry-specific local factors appear to play a role in supporting the emergence of firms in certain industries but not in others. Again, this could be investigated in future research, including delineating what these factors are in the different industries, and if there are opportunities for cross-fertilization. In a general sense, the diverse and inconsistent patterns we detect in net establishment growth across the U.S. counties confirm that each county is unique, and above all that one-size-fits-all solutions will not work. Rapid growth in one set of industries (e.g., retailing) does not predict rapid growth in another one (e.g., manufacturing). Understanding whether or not common factors can be identified to enhance rural firm formation through innovation and entrepreneurship to stimulate employment growth is a a critical research question. Alternatively, different local factors and their interactions are likely to be important in different county types, and it is important to identify these factors.

Self-Employment

Self-employed individuals or sole proprietors are required to file payments for their services on Internal Revenue Service Schedule C (Form 1040 or 1040-SR), Profit or Loss From Business (Sole Proprietorship). The rate of self-employment, that is, the share of all workers who are self-employed based on this filing is commonly used as a measure of entrepreneurial spirit within a local economy. Here it is important to separate true business innovation from mere replication, which is difficult to do in practice. Even so, as Goetz et al. (2012) and others argue, individuals who enter into some form of self-employment when faced with a lack of opportunities to work for someone else can be considered more entrepreneurial than those who choose unemployment instead. Moreover, a substantial body of evidence suggests that self-employment is associated with more robust local economic growth (e.g., Fleming & Goetz, 2011; Rupasingha & Goetz, 2013; Shrestha et al., 2007), and it has also helped communities mitigate adverse effects of imports (Liang & Goetz, 2016).

Often the distinction is made between self-employment of *necessity* and *opportunity*, where the latter is sometimes measured by the returns to such activity (Low & Weiler, 2012). Higher earnings from self-employment in a county suggest the presence of business owners who supply goods and services that are highly rewarded in the marketplace, or who face fewer competitors because what they sell is unique. Our map shows high instances of this type of entrepreneurship in general in the Rocky Mountain states of Idaho, Montana, and Wyoming. These high-amenity places attract workers from across the country, including film stars whose presence may distort the overall picture of local rural innovation to a degree, to the extent that they earned their basic wealth elsewhere through entrepreneurial activities (Figure 2.4).

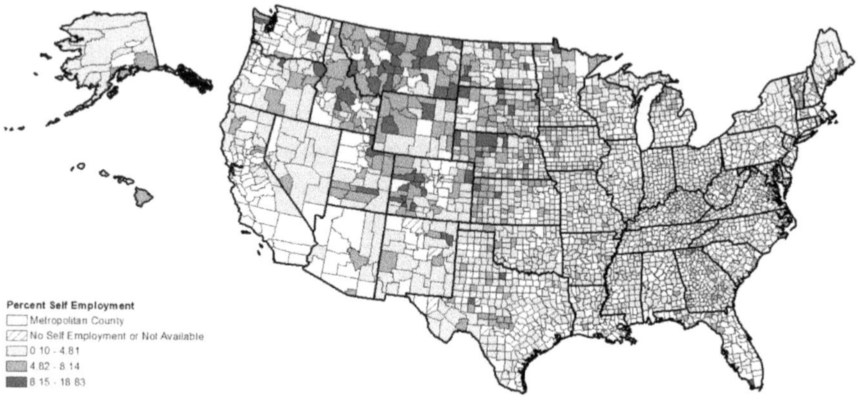

FIGURE 2.4 Percentage of employees who are self-employed for nonmetropolitan counties.

Source: American Community Survey 2020, U.S. Census Bureau.

Interestingly, self-employment rates rise noticeably with the rural status of a county: the smallest and most remote counties also have the highest rate of self-employment on average, which may largely represent independent and smaller rural business owners. The self-employment rate across the RUCC is as follows: 3.1 [4]; 3.3 [5]; 3.2 [6]; 3.7 [7]; 3.9 [8]; and 4.6 [9]. Again comparing metro-adjacent and nonadjacent rural counties we observe that the latter tend to have higher self-employments. In other words, the smaller and more remote rural counties have higher self-employment rates, which is a pattern similar to but the reverse of that observed for patenting. One interpretation is that, the smaller the population of a county, the greater the desire for and perhaps opportunity for self-employment, and this relationship is always greater if the county is adjacent to a metro area than if it is not.

Hidden Innovation

A novel measure of hidden (or latent) innovation was recently proposed by Goetz and Han (2020). It has long been known that insights and innovation often come about through chance encounters among individuals, who may exchange ideas and observations that, in turn, lead to new products or services and ways of producing them. This is also sometimes referred to as serendipitous innovation, which is more likely to occur when individuals are close to one another in space. Another source of innovation can be the result of frustration with a product or service, that induces an individual to set out and develop an improvement. Until recently it has not been possible to measure this kind of impetus to innovation because such chance encounters and spillovers are almost by definition impossible to observe and capture in practice except, for example, at conferences or in seminars, etc.

The newly devised measure captures opportunities for knowledge spillovers in measuring whether or not the conditions for them to arise exist. This is accomplished by using the input-output matrix to track product flows among industries, which in principle are accompanied by flows of ideas. This is done both on the purchasing (input) and the selling (output) sides, where opportunities exist for process improvement (how better to build products, or do so more efficiently) –and for product improvement (how to improve the product so that it better meets the needs of the end user). Thus the measure captures opportunities in both process and product innovation, and it is structured so that the greater the diversity of industries among which the flows occur, the greater the potential for innovation; this follows from the idea that greater diversity produces more novel thinking and inspiration than does less diversity, in this case the industries involved in the transaction. In addition, the measure takes into account the spatial proximity of the different economic actors, that is, how far apart they are; with greater distance in space, opportunities for knowledge and information spillovers decline. Importantly, Goetz and Han (2020) show that their measure predicts both income and job growth within communities, after holding constant other relevant explanatory factors.

The map again shows a surprising density of such activity in many parts of the Great Planes as well as throughout the rural United States more generally. This kind of innovation arguably is not captured in official NSF-type statistics, and yet it may be critical to the economic survival of many of the communities in which it is found. Understanding in greater detail how this innovation comes about, and how it can be made more transparent and more widespread, is an important problem and potential opportunity for policymakers concerned with revitalizing rural communities (Figure 2.5).

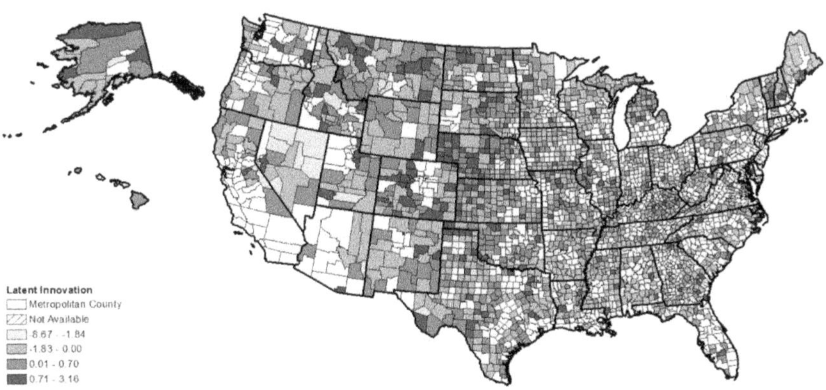

FIGURE 2.5 Latent innovation values for nonmetropolitan counties.

Source: Authors using data from Han and Goetz (2019) available at: https://aese.psu.edu/nercrd/community/latent-innovation

Conclusion and Future Research

This chapter has provided a few alternative county-level measures of entrepreneurship and innovation and mapped them to provide an idea of how they are distributed over geographic space, with an emphasis on rural areas. We find that various forms of these activities do occur in rural areas as well, but there are no systematic patterns in terms of the particular counties where innovation activity occurs and where it does not. Beyond this general finding, we saw that NSF-type innovation relative to the population base does decline with county size and distance from metro areas. At the same time, certain types of counties, especially those offering attractive natural amenities, are home to individuals who are more likely to work for themselves. For the association between net establishment growth rates and employment growth rates, we find a positive trend in general, but there are significant differences in the relationships over space and also according to the sector, whether it is retailing, manufacturing, or other. Sorting out this key relationship between new firm formation and job growth across space and rural areas especially, as measures of innovation and entrepreneurship, is critical.

An important next step, explored in subsequent chapters of this volume, is to understand why these differences exist. More specifically, research is needed to better understand why some communities, and their residents, are more entrepreneurial and innovative than others. This could be a question of having the correct mix of local supporting businesses in the supply chain or local ecosystem—from accountants to tax lawyers and business coaches—or the correct form of social capital which enhances community support for local businesses where applicable. Or it could be that a single, forward-looking individual in a community has the right idea at the right time and is able to pull together the resources needed to establish a flourishing enterprise. Sam Walton, the legendary founder of Wal-Mart, started out with a modest "nickel and dime" store in what was then rural Arkansas, and built a domineering global business powerhouse that continues to innovate and evolve. In principle, the chain could have emerged from any county in the United States, and any one individual could have started the same kind of company. Another important dimension for researchers and policymakers to understand better is gender differences in self-employment formation. This is an area of great research opportunities, building on the seminal work of Patrick et al. (2016).

This leaves us with the broader question—in many ways the holy grail of local economic development: Is it a matter of pulling together the right combination of factors to make a place innovative and entrepreneurial, or is it a matter of having an energetic and resourceful individual with the right idea in the right place and at the right time, or both. And, most importantly, what can and what cannot be transported and replicated in other communities? The present volume seeks to shed light on these important questions.

Acknowledgments

This work was supported by USDA NIFA grants 2019–51150-29876 and 2018–67023-27638 as well as the College of Agricultural Sciences at Penn State University. Any opinions are strictly those of the authors. We also appreciate valuable discussions with Dr. Timothy Wojan.

References

Acs, Z. J. and C. Armington (2006). *Entrepreneurship, Geography, and American Economic Growth*. New York, NY: Cambridge University Press.

Audretsch, D. B., J. A. Cunningham, D. F. Kuratko, E. E. Lehmann and M. Menter (2019). Entrepreneurial Ecosystems: Economic, Technological, and Societal Impacts. *The Journal of Technology Transfer*, 44(2): 313–325.

Baumol, W. J. (2010). *The Microtheory of Innovative Entrepreneurship*. Kauffman Foundation Series on Innovation and Entrepreneurship. Princeton, NJ and Oxford: Princeton University Press, p. 246.

Fleming, D. and S. J. Goetz (2011). Does Local Firm Ownership Matter? *Economic Development Quarterly*, 25(3): 277–281.

Goetz, S. J., D. A. Fleming and A. Rupasingha (2012). The Economic Impacts of Self-Employment. *Journal of Agricultural and Applied Economics*, 44(3): 315–321.

Goetz, S. J. and Y. Han (2020). Latent Innovation in Local Economies. *Research Policy*, 49(2). doi:10.1016/j.respol.2019.103909.

Han, Y. and S. J. Goetz (2019). Predicting U.S. County Economic Resilience from Industry Input-Output Accounts. *Applied Economics*, 51(19): 2019–2028.

Jaffe, A., M. Trajtenberg and R. Henderson (1993). Geographic Localization of Knowledge Spillovers as Evidenced by Patent Citations. *Quarterly Journal of Economics*, 108(3): 577–598.

Li, M., S. J. Goetz, M. Partridge and D. Fleming (2016). Location Determinants of High Growth Firms. *Entrepreneurship and Regional Development*, 28(1–2): 97–125.

Liang, J. and S. J. Goetz (2018). Technology Intensity and Agglomeration Economies. *Research Policy*, 47(10): 1990–1995.

Loveridge, S. (2006). "Getting Started in Community-Based Entrepreneurship," Ch. 13 in Norman Walzer, ed., *Entrepreneurship and Local Economic Development*. Plymouth, UK: Lexington Books, pp. 255–274.

Low, S. A. and S. Weiler (2012). Employment Risk, Returns, and Entrepreneurship. *Economic Development Quarterly*, 26(3): 238–251.

Manolova, T. S., C. G. Brush, L. F. Edelman, A. Robb and F. Welter (2017). *Entrepreneurial Ecosystems and Growth of Women's Entrepreneurship: A Comparative Analysis*. Northampton, MA: Edward Elgar Publ. Ltd.

Motoyama, Y. (2019). *From Innovation to Entrepreneurship: Connectivity-based Regional Development*. Northampton, MA: Edward Elgar Publ., p. 176.

Patrick, C., H. Stephens and A. Weinstein (2016). Where Are All the Self-Employed Women? Push and Pull Factors Influencing Female Labor Force Decisions. *Small Business Economics*, 46: 365–390.

Rupasingha, A. and S. J. Goetz (2013). Self-Employment and Local Economic Performance: Evidence from U.S. Counties. *Papers in Regional Science*, 92(1): 141–161.

Shrestha, S. S., S. J. Goetz and A. Rupasingha (2007). Proprietorship Formation and U.S. Job Growth. *Review of Regional Studies*, 37(2): 146–168.
Wojan, T. and T. Parker. September 2017. Innovation in the Rural Nonfarm Economy: Its Effect on Job and Earnings Growth, 2010–2014, ERR-238, U.S. Department of Agriculture, Economic Research Service.
Wojan, T. R. and B. Nichols (2018). Design, Innovation, and Rural Creative Places: Are the Arts the Cherry on Top, or the Secret Sauce? *PLoS One*, 13(2): e0192962. doi:10.1371/journal.pone.0192962.

3

BUILDING AN ENTREPRENEURIAL ECOSYSTEM TO CATALYZE INNOVATION IN RURAL PLACES

Jared Reynolds

Understanding Your Entrepreneurial Ecosystem

Entrepreneurship is a vital component of economic development in rural areas, and it is what gives life to innovation: the introduction of a new idea of a product or solution to a problem in a rural place. Entrepreneurs start businesses, create jobs, and launch products and services that serve their communities and create dynamic and innovative economies. This has led to a shift in contemporary economic development strategy from a focus on recruiting businesses to a recognition that entrepreneurs should be center stage in growing rural economies and creating vibrant communities. This strategy necessitates the cultivation of an entrepreneurial ecosystem: the environment, community, resources, amenities, infrastructure, and people that support entrepreneurs and innovators in identifying opportunities, launching new ideas, growing their endeavors, and reaching their goals. Successful ecosystems support entrepreneurs and innovators but also build vibrant communities that offer a high quality of life and attractive places to live.

Building entrepreneurial ecosystems differs from approaches that focus on business attraction and retention, industrial development, and a traditional approach on improving the general business environment. Supporting entrepreneurship and innovation and developing an entrepreneurial ecosystem is about breaking down barriers for new businesses and ideas. These entrepreneurial initiatives can sometimes take place even at the expense of existing and incumbent businesses (Auerswald, 2014).

This chapter looks at what an entrepreneurial ecosystem is comprised of, as well as how building a rural entrepreneurial ecosystem differs from an urban and suburban context. The chapter lays out key elements to consider when building an entrepreneurial ecosystem. It looks beyond just the provision of direct services and resources to support entrepreneurs and explores how to build a community

DOI: 10.4324/9781003178552-3

with the amenities, infrastructure, and quality of life features that welcome, support, and encourage entrepreneurship and innovation. Building your entrepreneurial ecosystem is not an easy task. Effective ecosystem building necessitates a long-term commitment but investing time, energy, and resources will pay off and offer significant benefits.

This chapter places communities at the center of the entrepreneurial ecosystem. As was introduced in the introductory chapter, this chapter uses a broad definition of community. A community may be your town city, county, or some other geographic area that has the common goal of supporting entrepreneurship.

Keys to Building a Rural Ecosystem

Before one begins to build out the components of an entrepreneurial ecosystem, communities should first step back and think about how they are building their ecosystem, what they are identifying as priorities, and who is being included. Entrepreneurial ecosystem are not top-down or hierarchical structures, and they are complex, messy, and disorganized. They are so often comprised of networks of organizations and individuals with different interests and priorities that come together to create a support structure that encourages entrepreneurship and innovation.

Although leadership is important, an ecosystem cannot be built or controlled by a single organization or individual. Rather, building and improving an entrepreneurial ecosystem entails understanding the resources that are available and those that are needed, fostering collaboration, and encouraging a degree of coordination. What it does not do is attempt to tame what is a messy and complex process or create a hierarchy or strictly managed structure where it does not belong. The following are some key points for a community to consider when building or strengthening its entrepreneurial ecosystem.

Use a Broad Definition of Entrepreneurship

Entrepreneurs fall within different categories, have different motivations, and exist with a range of different sectors. There are *lifestyle* entrepreneurs interested in developing a business to serve their local community and *high-growth* entrepreneurs that have a vision to grow and sell in distant markets. Individuals also choose to become entrepreneurs for different reasons. *Necessity* entrepreneurs may have experienced a recent job loss or are suffering due to an economic downturn and have limited employment opportunities in their community. *Opportunity* entrepreneurs, on the other hand, are those who saw a market opportunity and pursued a new idea or innovation to fill a gap. Opportunity entrepreneurs are known to create jobs and economic growth and spur further entrepreneurship, whereas necessity entrepreneurs often emerge due to greater economic challenges (Acs, 2006).

In rural areas, necessity and lifestyle entrepreneurs tend to predominate (Lyon, Miller, & Mann, 2016). Rural communities have fewer high-growth entrepreneurs and often struggle to support these entrepreneurs in the same way they support lifestyle businesses (NCOE, 2001). However, rural ecosystems benefit from taking a big tent approach to entrepreneurship. They should welcome and encourage all types of entrepreneurs to be a part of their ecosystem, whether they be a main street retailer or the next big technology company. Rural ecosystems benefit from the increased entrepreneurial density, from bringing in individuals with new ideas, and building energy and excitement for the ecosystem. With the right resources and support, necessity entrepreneurs can hone their skills and identify further opportunities, and lifestyle entrepreneurs may see an opportunity to grow beyond their immediate community.

Engage Entrepreneurs and Innovators

Entrepreneurial ecosystems are designed to support entrepreneurs as they develop and grow their ideas and businesses. Despite that important tenet, entrepreneurs themselves are so often left out of the planning, design, and implementation of the ecosystem components. Local government, universities, and nonprofits, with good intentions and wanting to develop their economies and support entrepreneurs, design initiatives and programs without consulting the entrepreneurs that are operating in their communities. When the voices, views, and insights of entrepreneurs are not considered, the impact of entrepreneurial initiatives and the ecosystem may be far more limited. Entrepreneurs themselves need to not only be consulted and engaged but also should be leaders in the ecosystem. Entrepreneurs understand the challenges they face and where opportunities lie to develop and improve the ecosystem. Entrepreneurs need to be consulted, included, and placed in leadership positions to ensure that the ecosystem effectively serves and supports them.

Map the Ecosystem and Measure Progress

Communities need to know where they are starting and what resources they have in order to build and improve their ecosystems. Mapping the ecosystem helps one to understand the current state, what assets the community has, and where the gaps and opportunities lie. In rural areas, many individuals and organizations work to support and increase entrepreneurship and innovation but may not be thought of as traditional resource or service providers or even think of themselves as participants in an entrepreneurial ecosystem. Such an ecosystem may be diffuse, with libraries and coffee shops serving as coworking spaces; high schools and community colleges providing education; and informal events being hosted by local businesses or nonprofits with broad missions. Mapping the ecosystem helps one to identify connections, or a lack of thereof, between diverse entities, and visualizes where these connections could potentially be developed.

There is no single approach to categorizing or visualizing an ecosystem map. The purpose of the map is to help the community understand the ecosystem and support entrepreneurs in navigating and connecting with it. Maps might include a picture of funding, available workspaces, existing events and competitions, workshops, and mentorship opportunities (Renando, 2017). There are many organizations that can potentially work with communities to help them map their ecosystems. They provide a framework, help with data collection, and develop the map itself, but that framework is no substitute for getting out and interacting with organizations and individuals that make up the ecosystem.

Lastly, ecosystem mapping helps to provide a baseline for measuring progress, and it serves as a guidepost to continually refer to as the ecosystem grows. Understanding where you started and where you are today helps your ecosystem to tell its story to your community, entrepreneurs, and potential funders and supporters. As noted below, building an entrepreneurial ecosystem is an iterative, ongoing process that requires a long-term commitment. Having a map to refer to and measure progress against helps communities to reflect and to continue to improve.

Foster Collaboration and Partnerships

Entrepreneurial ecosystems should be comprised of networks of people, organizations, and institutions and not hierarchies (Feld & Hathaway, 2020). They should seek to encourage collaboration and partnerships. Mapping and building your ecosystem should demonstrate the important roles that different organizations, individuals, and initiatives play and produce opportunities for those organizations for collaboration and growth. So often, territorial organizations are committed to only their own development or their specific role in the ecosystem, which inadvertently makes it more challenging to develop a successful and impactful ecosystem. In essence, ecosystems should encourage collaboration among entrepreneurs, not serve as a barrier to it.

Develop and Support Leaders

Leadership is essential to building an impactful and sustainable entrepreneurial ecosystem. Many ecosystems are cultivated and launched because of the vision, leadership, and energy of a single individual or organization. They saw an opportunity, brought key stakeholders together, helped to establish a vision, and charted a path forward to develop the ecosystem and support entrepreneurship and innovation.

While such individuals and organizations can catalyze an entrepreneurial ecosystem, it is critically important to focus on developing and encouraging an array of leaders. Individuals come and go from the ecosystem and choose to move on and direct their time to new initiatives. Successful ecosystems encourage and foster a range of leaders that connect, support, and develop entrepreneurs and the ecosystem as a whole. Feldman and Zoller refer to some of these leaders as *dealmakers* and find that they are one of the most important components in creating a connected, vibrant, and successful ecosystem (Feldman & Zoller, 2016).

Many rural ecosystems struggle to develop and support strong leaders. Rural communities tend to be more tightly knit and often define roles in ways that can make it difficult for new leaders to emerge and new and innovative approaches to be pursued (Flora & Flora, 1993). As such, focusing on entrepreneurial and ecosystem development is a new economic and business development approach in many rural communities for those used to traditional approaches. It can bring into question long-held beliefs and approaches and may challenge the roles of existing organizations and leaders. That is why focusing on and developing an ecosystem requires competent, strong leaders that welcome and encourage entrepreneurs and employ new leadership approaches.

Key Components of Rural Entrepreneurial Ecosystems

There is no single path or blueprint for communities to follow to build their entrepreneurial ecosystem. However, communities do have agency in determining whether they are welcoming and supportive of entrepreneurs and innovators. Building a community's entrepreneurial ecosystem may seem overwhelming and at times unattainable, but there are concrete and actionable steps communities can take to support, encourage, and build entrepreneurship (Feldman, 2014). And there are systems and values that need to be in place in the community and the broader region to enable entrepreneurship to thrive (See Figure 3.1).

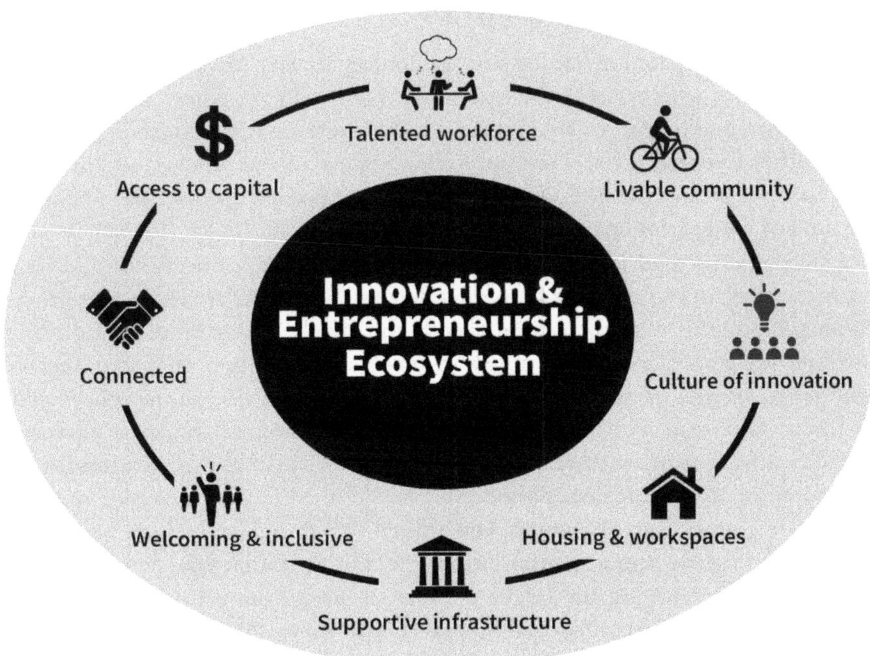

FIGURE 3.1 Components of an innovation and entrepreneurship ecosystem.

Rural entrepreneurs face unique challenges that their urban and suburban counterparts do not but also have unique assets that bring about opportunity to support entrepreneurs and build a thriving ecosystem. Rural entrepreneurs have limited access to markets and capital; infrastructure constraints that can make production more expensive and reaching consumers more difficult; they may be isolated from other entrepreneurs and vital support systems; and the entrepreneurial culture often does not support growth and innovation. As a result of these and other challenges, rural entrepreneurs tend to experience slower growth rates and contribute less to job creation compared to their urban peers (Markey, Pages, Scruggs, & Miller, 2012).

Despite these challenges, rural communities offer many benefits. Top among these benefits is the high quality of life and relative affordability of living in rural areas. The recreation and natural amenities make rural communities attractive places to live, and they provide opportunities to balance both work and play. Furthermore, technology is allowing many rural communities to bridge the innovation divide, which is currently making rural places even more attractive to young professionals and families. Considering these and other factors, this chapter focuses on the components that make up a vibrant innovation and entrepreneurial ecosystem, as well as where rural communities may struggle and where there are opportunities to continue to grow and improve rural ecosystems.

Connected and Networked Ecosystem

Social networks and connections between entrepreneurs play an important role in determining whether they are successful. Networks are where entrepreneurs access capital and resources, find mentors, talk with potential customers, and find many other opportunities. The more connections an individual and entrepreneur has, the greater likelihood opportunities will present themselves. That said, the type of connection matters.

Entrepreneurs tend to develop both strong and weak connections, and both types can play an important role in their success. *Strong ties* are those that an individual maintains with their close friends and family. These close relationships and trust are important for entrepreneur success as it is where they may receive funding, a business partner, and important support. *Weak ties*, on the other hand, are those that exist between acquaintances and occasional business partners. These connections provide access to expanded networks and opportunities for collaboration, as well as new perspectives and critical feedback outside of one's immediate connections (Elfring & Hulsink, 2004). Rural individuals tend to be successful in developing a smaller number of strong connections but face more challenges in developing the larger number of weak connections that are also important to their entrepreneurial success (Freire-Gibb, 2004).

There are steps that entrepreneurial ecosystem builders can take to foster both strong and weak connections. Long-term and intensive initiatives, such as business incubation and acceleration, build deeper connections and stronger relationships. These may lead to business partnerships or financial investments that require deeper, more trusting relationships. Ecosystems can build weak connections by hosting events, happy hours, pitch competitions, and other initiatives that bring entrepreneurs together, develop new connections, and bridge existing networks. They introduce entrepreneurs to new partners and markets and provide feedback from outside individuals and different perspectives.

Rural communities around the country are promoting events and utilizing technology to foster connectivity to strengthen their entrepreneurial networks. For example, many rural communities, as we do here in New Hampshire, host the Kauffman Foundation's 1 Million Cups. This event brings together entrepreneurs and the community in a welcoming and supportive environment to share their stories and visions and to collaboratively solve challenges. In New Hampshire, this event generates new ideas, develops new resources, and infuses much needed energy into the entrepreneurial ecosystem.

In Vermont, an initiative called the *Vermont Startup Collective* is using a mobile and web-based application to connect entrepreneurs. Through this initiative, entrepreneurs can ask questions and connect with resources on various forums. They can join discussions around key topics or seek expert advice to grow their idea. Classes and workshops are available for education, and there is a central calendar function that enables sharing of upcoming events. This initiative is a great example of how rural areas can leverage technology to connect and support entrepreneurs when they are distant and do not have the same access to physical spaces and in-person collaboration.

Welcoming and Inclusive

Communities and ecosystems benefit from being welcoming and inclusive of all types of entrepreneurs and individuals, whether from within the community, a neighboring town, a larger city, or a distant country. Creative people of different backgrounds bring unique skillsets and viewpoints to communities that results in the generation of new ideas and the development of new businesses (Lee, Florida, & Acs, 2004). Additionally, effective rural ecosystems encourage entrepreneurship and innovation from within their own community. They bring neighbors to events, support risk-taking, and welcome and encourage their young people to remain in their rural communities and become the next generation of entrepreneurs and innovators.

Rural communities would especially benefit from being open and welcoming to new immigrants. Many rural places have struggled to diversify their communities, and the proportion of immigrants that make up rural communities is far lower than in metropolitan areas (Parker, Horowitz, Brown, Fry, Cohn, & Igielnik, 2018). Immigrants bring different life experiences and new ideas. Many large successful businesses were started by immigrants, and this business success plays out at the local level as well. Immigrants both start and own businesses at higher rates than nonimmigrants (Fairlie, 2012). There are several potential reasons for this, including higher risk-taking among immigrant communities and a lack of social networks and connections, which leaves entrepreneurship as one of the few economic opportunities for immigrants. As a result, immigrants often bring important innovation and entrepreneurial skillsets that are missing in rural places.

Many rural communities are recognizing the important role that immigrants and new residents play in not only building their entrepreneurial ecosystems but also strengthening their entire communities. Welcoming America is a nonprofit organization that is working to create more welcoming and inclusive communities. They are working with rural communities to provide information, technical assistance, and a peer network that is providing a guide to rural communities on how they can effectively welcoming new immigrants. Although not rural, St. Louis Economic Development Partnership created the Mosaic Project, an initiative that includes a range of resources and initiatives to support immigrant entrepreneurs. One such resource is an ecosystem map to help immigrant entrepreneurs navigate their ecosystem of resources. The map includes entrepreneur and business development resources, as well education, health, housing, and so much more. They recognize the important role that immigrants play in creating a more innovative and entrepreneurial community and the positive impact that a support system can have on their success.

A Culture of Innovation and Entrepreneurship

Successful entrepreneurial communities build a culture of entrepreneurship that encourages innovative thinking and new ways of solving problems; fosters trust between entrepreneurs and within the community; and encourages risk-taking and supports both success and failure.

Entrepreneurial ecosystems that foster trust are better able to support and develop entrepreneurs (Muldoon, Bauman, & Lucy, 2018). Although some degree of trust is solidified in our systems through laws, contracts, and legally binding agreements, trust is also socially and intentionally forged within communities. Trust makes it easier for entrepreneurs to collaborate and share and support each other's ideas. In trusting communities, entrepreneurs see others as supporters and feel more comfortable talking about the challenges they face and asking for help when they need it. Trust is also important for key resources, like funding. Banks and investors are more likely to get involved in the ecosystem and offer financial support to new and high-risk ideas and initiatives.

Entrepreneurs take risks with their time, money, and social standing to launch and grow an idea that may not ultimately succeed. Entrepreneurs come up with new ideas and new ways of thinking about markets or addressing social challenges. Entrepreneurial ideas may challenge existing ways of thinking as well as incumbent businesses, industries, and institutions that currently exist within the community.

Empirical evidence suggests that entrepreneurs find it more difficult to take risks in rural communities (Foster, 2001). That is because rural entrepreneurs often have strong connections and relationships with their communities and the individuals in them. They have long-term commitments to their communities, particularly since they may have grown up there and plan to spend their lives there. That can make it difficult to risk failure. Rural communities need to overcome this challenge to support innovative businesses. They need to support risk-taking and celebrate failure as an important step in pursuing an entrepreneurial endeavor.

Rural communities should encourage entrepreneurs and innovators to challenge their traditional institutions, sectors, economic approaches, and ways of solving problems. Many traditionally rural sectors, such as resource extraction and agriculture, are experiencing slow if not negative growth in recent years (Goetz, Partridge, Deller, & Fleming, 2010). Some rural communities have struggled to transition their economies to growing industry sectors or to challenge the role of incumbent businesses. In most rural communities, small, family-owned businesses play a pivotal role in the local economy. They have been around for generations and are pillars of the community, supporting local initiatives and serving as hubs for community activity. While there are many benefits to family-owned businesses, a family approach to business can also hinder entrepreneurship and innovation. Family businesses typically grow at slower rates than non-family-owned businesses because they are less likely to lever external sources of capital or take risks because they see the family business as central to maintaining a family income and certain lifestyle (Hamelin, 2009).

That is why rural communities need to strike a balance in their economic and innovation approach. They can support small family-owned businesses and recognize the important role many historic incumbent businesses play in a small community. However, this should not occur at the expense of new ideas. Rural communities must be open to change, supportive of new approaches, and welcoming to those challenging traditional economic approaches.

Capital and Financial Resources

Accessing capital to launch and grow one's enterprise is often cited as the biggest challenge for entrepreneurs. To some degree, there will always be some challenges for entrepreneurs to access limited pools of capital. Investors are careful about how and where they invest dollars, and most entrepreneurs think their idea is worthy of receiving what is always limited amounts of funding. However, rural entrepreneurs do face unique challenges in funding their ideas. Additionally, they tend to access capital in different ways than their urban and suburban peers that is important to understand in order to effectively support rural entrepreneurship.

Understanding how rural entrepreneurs leverage funding to start their businesses is important in designing programming and resources that meet their needs. Although venture capital and angel investors are often a focus in entrepreneur funding, they are quite rare in rural communities, as well as urban areas. Only a small percentage of entrepreneurs ever receive investments from venture capital. The majority of financing for entrepreneurs comes from personal savings or loans, family and friends, banks, and/or credit cards (Annual Survey of Entrepreneurs, 2016). In rural areas, entrepreneurs depend on debt financing from local banks at higher rates than urban and suburban entrepreneurs (Markey, Pages, Scruggs, & Miller, 2012). This can be a challenge, as many rural banks have a more conservative approach in their lending practices compared to urban areas, don't offer many of the financial packages that urban and suburban banks do, and depend more on relationships and connections in their lending decisions.

Considering the financial challenges facing entrepreneurs, and the lack of pathways to access capital, entrepreneurial ecosystems can help by increasing coordination between the various funding agencies and institutions. A critical ecosystem function is to create connections between entrepreneurs, banks, credit unions, Community Development Financial Institutions (CDFIs), and an array of local funding programs. This allows entrepreneurs to understand their funding options and the ecosystem players to understand where gaps exist to getting funding to entrepreneurs when they need it.

Following are a few recommendations for how rural ecosystems can work with local banks and CDFIs to increase access to capital for their entrepreneurs:

- Build connections between local banks and entrepreneurs. Local banks and credit unions are committed to their communities and should be included as key players in the ecosystem. When they are engaged and included in the ecosystem and understand the important role they play they are more likely to be part of the solution in getting needed capital to rural entrepreneurs.
- Help banks to understand the value of investing in innovative local businesses and hone their lending practices so they make those investments. Leverage CDFIs, who provide needed funding and create a bridge between entrepreneurs and local banks when it is needed.
- Work at the state and community level to enact policies and programs that increase bank lending in rural areas. Policies have been successful at increasing bank liquidity and offering protection to banks that are lending to emerging entrepreneurs to make financing more likely and lending practices less conservative.

Although not often used, there is an opportunity to increase venture capital, angel funds, and other financing opportunities for innovative and higher risk businesses. People are deeply invested in their rural communities and want to support local businesses, especially with growth potential, and develop guidance, resources, and encouragement for individuals that may be interested in making equity investments in local businesses. Angel investment groups that introduce people to this practice and provide guidance do not exist in rural communities to the same degree that they do in more populated areas. West Slope Angels in an example of an angel fund that serves rural Western Colorado. The group is welcoming and inclusive: it breaks down barriers for rural residents to invest in local businesses and has a lot of success and innovative businesses to show for it. This could be a model for other rural places.

On the innovation front, several rural communities are adapting technology to increase crowdsource funding—or crowdfunding—to support new start-ups. Crowdfunding is becoming much more popular, and there are a range of different platforms to facilitate it. Local organization have combined crowdfunding's success with their own connections with rural communities and technical support for entrepreneurs to create successful programs. Vital Communities, a nonprofit that serves the Upper Valley region of New Hampshire and Vermont, launched a community crowdfunding initiative called The Local Crowd to help connect new businesses with funding from residents. This initiative allows a select number of businesses to get posted and promoted on the community platform and fundraise to launch their business.

A Trained and Talented Workforce

A trained and talented workforce means that the entrepreneurs themselves have the necessary skills to grow their ideas and launch them, and that they have access to a workforce with the skills they need. Successful entrepreneurs cite access to a talented workforce as the most important factor in determining where they start and grow their business (Endeavor Insight, 2013). All types of entrepreneurs, but especially those with innovative ideas, require access to a skilled workforce in order to grow and thrive. Innovation-focused entrepreneurs, for instance, need workers with specialized skills in the sciences, technology, and engineering.

Access to a trained and talented workforce is a challenge for many rural communities. Rural residents overall have lower rates of college attainment and less exposure to key disciplines such as computer science in schools (Google, 2016). As a result, rural communities often have a hard time attracting and retaining entrepreneurs and innovation-focused businesses. Many rural communities send their young students off to college or elsewhere to continue their education and struggle to bring them back to the community. Building a community that retains and attracts educated individuals is key to building a vibrant and successful entrepreneurial ecosystem.

Most rural communities do not have access to a major university or research institution that they can leverage for new talent and training. That said, there are other approaches they can take to ensure they have the talented workforce they need to support an innovative local economy. Foremost, they can leverage their local community college and other workforce training centers and encourage them to develop programming focused on the innovation economy. To succeed—and effectively leverage limited resources—rural communities need to think regionally. This begins with forging partnerships with neighboring communities and regions to develop the workforce development resources that they need.

Rural communities also need to provide resources and education to entrepreneurs themselves so that they have the skills they need. Mentorship plays an important role in entrepreneur success (Bosma, Hessels, Schutiens, Praag, & Verheul, 2012). Mentor programs connect entrepreneurs with more experienced individuals who provide valuable feedback and guidance as they get started and grow. Mentoring programs build entrepreneur networks and offer technical advice in their field of focus. Entrepreneurs that receive mentorship can then become mentors themselves as they build their skills, offering the same valuable mentorship that they received.

Lastly, rural areas should focus on developing entrepreneurial skills among their young people and encouraging individuals to see entrepreneurship as a viable career path. Many organizations around the country implement youth entrepreneurship programs. These programs introduce young people to the concept of entrepreneurship, teach them the skills they need to develop an enterprise, and often support them in launching a business with greater likelihood of succeeding. New Hampshire recently launched the *Community Changemaker Challenge*, a program targeted at high school students that teaches them entrepreneurial skills and innovative thinking. The program also guides them through a process of launching an entrepreneurial endeavor that has a positive impact on their community. The goals are to instill new skills and innovative thinking, introduce the concept of entrepreneurship, and develop economic connections between students and the community to increase retention.

Quality of Life, the Arts, and Creativity

The high quality of life rural communities offer residents, visitors, and potential entrepreneurs is one of their biggest assets. Rural communities often provide an attractive work-life balance, access to recreational and natural amenities, a lower cost of living, vibrant downtowns, and an overall lifestyle that many entrepreneurs and innovators seek. In surveys, successful entrepreneurs report that a high quality of life is one of the most important factors in determining where they choose to live (Endeavor Insights, 2013). Recognizing this, many rural communities are focusing less on attracting businesses through tax incentives and easing regulations and placing emphasis on attracting people by building trails, revitalizing downtowns, and supporting the development of local amenities.

A focus on quality of life is a good investment for rural communities that seek to build a more vibrant entrepreneurial ecosystem. For example, retired and pre-retired workers are often attracted to rural communities towards the end of their careers because of the better work-life balance and the amenities they offer. They bring with them a wealth of knowledge and career experience. Studies show that attracting retired and near-retired individuals improves the entrepreneurial environment in rural communities. Not only do the new residents start businesses, but they increase entrepreneurship across all ages by mentoring other entrepreneurs, investing in emerging initiatives, and spending their money locally (Deller, Kures, & Conroy, 2019).

One challenge that rural communities face is that many entrepreneurs and individuals want access to the recreation and natural amenities of rural areas, while also having access to urban amenities, supportive infrastructure, and larger markets. For example, Headwaters Economics found that when rural western counties provided access to an airport they fared as well economically as urban communities (Rasker, Gude, Gude, & Nort, 2009). Since communities cannot alter their geographic location—and investments in airports, rail, or other infrastructure are often too costly to be feasible—it is key that communities identify innovative and entrepreneurial ways to improve local cultural, retail, and restaurant amenities.

Honesdale, Pennsylvania, is a good example of a community that strived to accomplish this balance. Honesdale is a small community of around 4,000 residents located 2.5 hours from New York and Philadelphia and adjacent to the Poconos Mountains. Honesdale has become an attractive place to live for people from New York and Philadelphia seeking a more relaxed lifestyle, while still being close to the city. To spur entrepreneurship, Honesdale built a shared workspace and business incubator that offer access to technology, prototyping equipment, and education and workshops. However, Honesdale also focused on revitalizing their downtown, recognizing that the key to attracting and retaining innovators and entrepreneurs was to offer local amenities, a vibrant economy, and a community that residents want to live and spend time in.

Additionally, the arts and creativity are integrally interconnected, and the creative milieu of the two coming together in the community help to spur innovation and entrepreneurship (Wojan, Lamber, & McGranahan, 2007). As discussed, the arts are a key component to a community's quality of life and help makes it an attractive place to live (Duxbury, Campbell, & Keurvorst, 2011). But artistic and creative culture supports entrepreneurship in additional ways. Artistic and creative people are themselves entrepreneurs. Creativity is about looking at the world in new ways, thinking innovatively, challenging existing structures, and imagining new possibilities. This has significant crossover with entrepreneurship, which is also about thinking of new and creative ways to solve problems or meet a community or market need. Rural communities that support the arts and creativity improve their quality of life, attract a more talented workforce, and develop innovative and entrepreneurial thinkers (Lee, Florida, & Acs, 2004).

Supportive Infrastructure

The remoteness of rural communities presents challenges and opportunities. On one hand, entrepreneurs are attracted to rural communities because of their remoteness, quality of life, affordable cost of living, and recreational amenities, as we discussed. The challenge for rural communities is providing entrepreneurs, especially those who are growth oriented, with meaningful connections to outside resources and larger markets so they can grow. Increasing infrastructure does not necessarily mean building a new highway or port. Those types of investments are typically cost prohibitive and may take away from what makes a rural community attractive. However, there is a balance that rural communities can find. For instance, they can maintain their rural charm while expanding access to broadband internet, building affordable and quality housing, ensuring that entrepreneurs have access to workspaces, and better connecting the community to the outside world.

Broadband internet can be a relatively expensive investment for rural communities, which is part of the reason why they continue to lag behind urban and suburban areas in access to high-speed internet. Low population density makes building out broadband networks expensive to take on. Houses and buildings are dispersed, and it costs more money per user to connect rural areas. However, recent years have seen successful broadband expansion take place in rural areas. Communities that provide broadband see an increase in both the number of businesses as well as the growth rates of businesses, which contributes to the local economy and the tax base (Whitacre, Gallardo, & Strover, 2014).

Broadband does not just benefit technology companies and large industries. It allows main street business to process credit card payments. It enables remote entrepreneurs to provide services from their home. It expands a business's marketplace to a global audience. For example, with access to broadband internet, a local retailer can grow by shifting a portion of their sales online and selling in new markets. That encourages them to refine their product and their approach as they compete with new businesses outside their immediate community. In fact, 30% of the Etsy retailers that sell their goods online are based in rural areas (Erickson, 2017). Broadband internet allows rural artisans to sell their crafts to new customers and encourages new artisans to launch. Broadband benefits businesses across industries and all types of entrepreneurs.

If there is a silver lining to the COVID-19 pandemic, which deeply impacted individuals, communities, and families, it may be that it helped to bring the importance of broadband internet to the forefront. For instance, high-speed internet enabled many students to shift to homeschooling and to continue to learn by engaging with teachers and peers. But broadband expansion also made rural communities hubs for remote workers looking for a break from cities and showed the further potential for rural entrepreneurship, thus drawing new people and ideas to communities. This migration from the city occurred as urban residents began to seek out the natural amenities and quality of life that rural communities provide, all the while staying connected to amenities, like internet, which enabled them to shift to remote work. It is premature to say whether this trend will continue, but there may be potential for rural communities to leverage this new interest in rural places as more and more companies test the waters with shifting to remote work to attract educated and innovative workers.

Communities across rural America have taken unique approaches to expanding broadband access, particularly in areas where private sector investment has not occurred due to the small number of customers. For instance, some communities have utilized tax dollars to kick-start broadband expansion, or they have started cooperatives to fill the private sector void. Cooperatives have helped rural America solve infrastructure challenges throughout history, bringing telephone and electricity to many towns (Trostle, Kienbaum, & Mitchell, 2019). Furthermore, the U.S. Department of Agriculture and Federal Communications Commission both have grant and loan programs designed to bring broadband to rural communities. Communities are tapping into these and other grants and loans to increase the feasibility of expanding broadband access.

Housing and Workspaces

Entrepreneurs and innovators, like everyone, need a range of affordable and quality housing and workspace options to live, work, collaborate, and connect. A lack of housing options in rural communities makes it challenging to attract and retain talented workers and entrepreneurs. However, housing can be an asset for rural communities to leverage if they have available housing stock, or the potential to expand and upgrade housing. The cost of housing is approximately 30% less in rural compared to urban communities (Hawk, 2013). This has proven to be a key factor in making rural communities more attractive in relation to their more expensive urban peers.

With that said, many rural communities have struggled to keep up with booming housing demand, particularly in places like New Hampshire, Colorado, and Alabama, all of which have experienced threefold increases in second home purchases (Ford, 2021). Furthermore, it can be expensive to build modern housing in rural areas where developers and construction companies cannot leverage economies of scale. When communities lack modern and affordable housing, it becomes a challenge to attract entrepreneurs and innovators, as well as the talented workforce they need to sustain existing enterprises (Raice, 2018).

Along with a place to live, entrepreneurs require affordable and flexible spaces to work from. Such workspaces might include traditional offices, coworking spaces, local libraries, coffee shops, business incubators, and accelerators. As is the case with housing, the lower cost of office space in rural communities makes it comparatively more affordable to launch and grow businesses. However, the challenge is that many rural communities are not able to offer the same availability of specialty office space, as compared to more urban environments, that innovative businesses need in order to launch and grow, such as wet and dry lab space.

Shared workspace has become much more popular in recent years across all types of communities. These workspaces typically offer affordable and flexible office space, or desks that businesses and entrepreneurs of all types can rent. They also provide an environment that promotes collaboration and connections, and may provide resources to support entrepreneurs. Surveys show that entrepreneurs, small businesses, and remote workers do find coworking spaces beneficial and impactful. Members of coworking spaces report improved work success, greater networks and social connections, greater ability to acquire valuable new skills, and that they are happier and more productive workers (GCUC, 2017). Having a workspace where you can connect and build collaboration can make a big difference to an entrepreneur seeking to bring a new idea forward or grow a small business. Additionally, coworking space can serve as a base to build energy in an entrepreneurial ecosystem and develop additional resources that serve local entrepreneurs.

It can be challenging to launch and sustain a coworking space in a rural community simply because there is not the same critical mass of entrepreneurs, remote workers, and small businesses that bring consistent energy and income to the space and make the initiative financially feasible. Despite these challenges, rural communities find creative ways to offer the benefits and impact of coworking in a way that works for them. Some rural communities with limited resources have effectively used existing community spaces, such as libraries, coffee shops, or community centers, for coworking. They host coworking get-togethers at dedicated hours a few times a week and welcoming local entrepreneurs to join, connect, and build collaboration. Such spaces offer many of the key components that make coworking an impactful part of an entrepreneurial ecosystem.

Meanwhile, other communities are effectively leveraging underused space in existing organizations that they can use for coworking. This includes partnering with local nonprofits with a similar mission, or collaborating with an economic development organization, makerspace, or even establishing a permanent location in a local coffee shop. This provides coworking and may even benefit an existing organization that could use an additional revenue stream.

Conclusion

Entrepreneurship and innovation are key to building strong rural communities and vibrant economies. To succeed, entrepreneurs need communities that welcome them and ecosystems that support them. There is no blueprint or step-by-step guide to building an entrepreneurial ecosystem. Entrepreneurship and the systems that support it are comprised of unique individuals and encompass complex interactions. Building an ecosystem requires a long-term commitment and an understanding that there will be no single investment that will result in sudden and dramatic change. However, communities have agency and can make decisions and take steps that make a difference. They can engage entrepreneurs, foster collaboration, and lay out a vision to build a community that welcomes and supports entrepreneurs and innovators.

This chapter highlights key components that exist in successful rural entrepreneurial ecosystems and provides communities with ideas to get started. Successful ecosystems are welcoming and inclusive of all entrepreneurs and foster connections and networks between entrepreneurs and within the community. They create a culture that fosters trust, encourages risk-taking, and challenges traditional problem-solving and economic systems. They value a quality of life and create a community where entrepreneurs and talented individuals want to live. Lastly, they provide infrastructure, whether housing, offices, or broadband internet, that provide entrepreneurs with affordable places to live and work and the resources they need to grow.

References

Acs, Z. (2006). How is entrepreneurship good for economic growth? *Innovations: Technology, Governance, Globalization*, 1(1), 97–107.

Auerswald, P. Enabling Entrepreneurial Ecosystems (2014). Forthcoming in David the Oxford Handbook of Local Competitiveness. Oxford, UK: Oxford University Press., GMU School of Public Policy Research Paper No. 3.

Bosma, N., Hessels, J., Schutjens, V., van Praag, M., & Verheul, I. (2012). Entrepreneurship and role models. *Journal of Economic Psychology*, 33(2), 410–424.

Deller, S., Kures, M., & Conroy, T. (2019). Rural entrepreneurship and migration. *Journal of Rural Studies*, 66, 30–42.

Duxbury, N., Campbell, H., & Keurvorst, E. (2011). Developing and revitalizing rural communities through arts and culture. *Small Cities Imprint*, 3(1), 111–122.

Elfring, T., & Hulsink, W. (2004). The strong versus weak tie effect on entrepreneurial processes: ICT-Start-ups in the Netherlands. Paper for 20th EGOS conference, 1–24.

Endeavor Insight. (2013). What do the best entrepreneurs want in a city? February Issue, 1–16.

Erickson, A. (2017). Data show Etsy sellers driving a new economy. March issue, 1–2.

Fairlie, R. W. (2012). Immigrant entrepreneurs and small business owners, and their access to financial capital. *Small Business Administration*, 396, 1–46.

Feld, B., & Hathaway, I. (2020). *The startup community way: Evolving an entrepreneurial ecosystem*. Hoboken, NJ: John Wiley & Sons.

Feldman, M. P. (2014). The character of innovative places: Entrepreneurial strategy, economic development, and prosperity. *Small Business Economics*, 43, 9–20.

Feldman, M. P., & Zoller, T. D. (2016). Dealmakers in place: Social capital connections in regional entrepreneurial economies. In Westlund, P., & Larsson, L. (Eds) *Handbook of social capital and regional development*. Northampton, MA: Edward Elgar Publishing, 141–165.

Flora, C. B., & Flora, J. L. (1993). Entrepreneurial social infrastructure: A necessary ingredient. *The Annals of the American Academy of Political and Social Science*, 529(1), 48–58.

Ford, C. (2021). *Why vacation-home markets are booming in Alabama and New Hampshire*. Market Watch.

Foster, N. (2001). *Entrepreneurship in rural communities: An emerging strategy presents opportunities and challenges*. Federal Reserve Bank of Minneapolis.

Foster, L., & Norman, P. (2016). The annual survey of entrepreneurs: An introduction. *US Census Bureau Center for Economic Studies Paper No. CES-WP-15-40R*, 1–73.

Freire-Gibb, C. (2014). Entrepreneurship within urban and rural areas: Creative people and social networks. *Journal Regional Studies*, 48(1), 139–153.

GCUC. (2017). The 2017 global coworking survey. Retrieved from https://gcuc.co/wp-content/uploads/2019/02/GCUC-2017-Global-Coworking-Survey.pdf

Goetz, S. J., Partridge, M., Deller, S. C., & Fleming, D. A. (2010). Evaluating US rural entrepreneurship policy. *Journal of Regional Analysis & Policy*, 40(1), 20–33.

Google. (2016). Computer science learning: Closing the gap. Retrieved from https://services.google.com/fh/files/misc/computer-science-learning-closing-the-gap-girls-brief.pdf

Hamelin, A. (2009). Do small family businesses have a peculiar attitude toward growth? Evidence from French SMEs. Working Paper, 1–33.

Hawk, W. (2013). *Expenditures of urban and rural households in 2011*. US Bureau of Labor Statistics.

Lee, S. Y., Florida, R., & Acs, Z. (2004). Creativity and entrepreneurship: A regional analysis of new firm formation. *Regional Studies*, 38(8), 879–891.

Lyons, T. S., Miller, S. R., & Mann, J. T. (2018). A new role for land grant universities in the rural innovation ecosystem? *Journal of Regional Analysis & Policy*, 48(2), 3775.

Markey, D., Pages, E., Scruggs, P., & Miller, K. (2012). Access to capital in rural America: Supporting business startup, growth, and job creation in the wake of the great recession. *Rural Policy Research Institute*, April, 1–8.

Muldoon, J., Bauman, A., & Lucy, C. (2018). Entrepreneurial ecosystem: Do you trust or distrust? *Journal of Enterprising Communities: People and Places in the Global Economy*, 12(2), 158–177.

NCOE. (2001). Embracing innovation: Entrepreneurship and American economic growth, 1–11

Parker, K., Horowitz, J. M., Brown, A., Fry, R., Cohn, D., & Igielnik, R. (2018). *Demographic and economic trends in urban, suburban and rural communities. What unites and divides urban, suburban and rural communities.* Pew Research Center.

Raice, S. (2018). Rural America has jobs. Now it just needs housing. *Wall Street Journal*. May 30, 2018.

Rasker, R., Gude, P., Gude, J., & Van den Noort, J. (2009). The economic importance of air travel in high-amenity rural areas. *Journal of Rural Studies*, 25(3), 343–353.

Renando, C. (2017). Supporting Australian entrepreneurship and innovation. Mapping innovation ecosystems.

Trostle, H., Kienbaum, K., & Mitchell, C. (2019). *Cooperatives Fiberize Rural America: A trusted model for the internet era*. Institute for Local Self-Reliance.

Whitacre, B., Gallardo, R., & Strover, S. (2014). Broadband's contribution to economic growth in rural areas: Moving towards a causal relationship. *Telecommunications Policy*, 38(11), 1011–1023.

Wojan, T. R., Lambert, D. M., & McGranahan, D. A. (2007). Emoting with their feet: Bohemian attraction to creative milieu. *Journal of Economic Geography*, 7(6), 711–736.

4

EXPLORING INNOVATION CREATION IN RURAL PLACES THROUGH RURAL ESTABLISHMENTS

John Mann and Steven Miller

Introduction

Innovations—new products, processes, or services—play key roles in economic competitiveness and are critical for economic growth. Economic growth, driven by innovation, in some cases under the Schumpeterian framework of "creative destruction," provides a means of sustainable job creation and wage growth (Mann & Shideler, 2015; Romer, 1990; Shumpeter, 1942). However, the innovative process does not occur in a vacuum. New ideas are synthesized within the broader environment which includes multiple actors, such as competing firms and entrepreneurs, higher education, and local and national policies (Ander, 2006; Lyons, Miller, & Mann, 2018; Porter, Ketels, Miller, & Bryden, 2004). These innovation ecosystems may span multiple boundaries, for example, connecting firms with stakeholders across different industries and geographies (Aryal, Mann, Loveridge, & Joshi, 2020; Lyons, Miller, & Mann, 2018; Porter, Ketels, Miller, & Bryden, 2004). Therefore, policies directed at sustaining economic growth should incorporate innovation into the process, making innovation creation a central theme. Further, policies intended to encourage innovation creation should also be innovative in their approaches, for example, widening their lens in terms of geography and metrics. More specifically, an argument is made in this chapter that polices could be designed to be more inclusive of rural areas and consider a broader array of what innovation in rural areas may look like (Mann & Loveridge, 2020; Whitacre, Meadowcroft, & Gallardo, 2019).

One challenge impacting this argument is that many of our assumptions about innovative rural firms are derived from our understanding of the behaviors, characteristics, and motivations of innovative urban firms. This may result in misconceptions or, at a minimum, an incomplete picture in terms of innovation in rural areas, which can be conflated by other factors (Aryal, Mann, Loveridge, &

DOI: 10.4324/9781003178552-4

Joshi, 2020; Wojan, Dotzel, & Low, 2015). For example, much of the innovation literature is derived from research in urban settings and reflects data and observations on firms operating in agglomerated economies (Aryal, Mann, Loveridge, & Joshi, 2018; Lyons, Miller, & Mann, 2018). Plus, many innovation studies only consider narrow measures of innovation, such as patents or R&D investments (Mann & Loveridge, 2020). Further hampering our understanding of rural innovation is the dearth of data and measures of innovation in rural areas (Wojan & Parker, 2017). Another challenge is that much of US rural policy has historically been focused on agriculture, but has been ineffective in supporting Rural America's resiliency, self-sufficiency, and competitiveness (Acs & Malecki, 2003; Markley, 2001; Stauber, 2001). This may contribute to a broader misperception about Rural America's innovation potential, as rural economies have not been dominated by farming and agriculture sectors for many years. Combined, these concerns and challenges contribute to outcomes and policy recommendations that often assume urban-based strategies in terms of encouraging future innovations.

The main point is this, while significant literature across multiple disciplines is focused on different aspects of innovation exits, the majority is urban- or metro-centric and results may not accurately reflect rural firms or rural business environments. This is also a primary motiving factor for developing the Rural Establishment Innovation Survey (REIS), a data set uniquely focused on rural innovation. In this chapter, we explore innovation creation by examining the REIS and how the data have been applied in research on the innovation process in rural communities.

Understanding Innovation Creation

Innovation creation leads to technological change which, in turn, drives economic growth (Acs & Audretsch, 2005; Romer, 1990, 1996). Technological change is born from a range of innovative activities, from radical innovations that disrupt marketplaces to evolutionary innovations, which, aggregated over a longer period of time, also contribute to measurable changes (Acs & Audretsch, 2005; Aryal, Mann, Loveridge, & Joshi, 2018; Wojan, Crown, & Rupasingha, 2018). Innovative firms and entrepreneurs provide new opportunities for less innovative firms while also creating incentives for competitors to be innovative (Goetz, Partridge, Deller, & Fleming, 2010). Incorporating Schumpeter's views into this framework, sustained economic growth can result from this innovative process where the "new" replaces the "old" and leads to opportunities throughout an economy (Aghion & Howett, 1990; Goetz, Partridge, Deller, & Fleming, 2010; Mann & Shideler, 2015). In other words, the impact of opportunities exploiting innovation is a key consideration regarding sustained growth as innovation-based entrepreneurship and growth-oriented firms lead to more innovation-based entrepreneurship and growth-oriented firms (Aghion & Howitt, 1990; Goetz, Partridge, Deller, & Fleming, 2010; Shane, 2008).

A major obstacle to innovation that may be more pronounced in rural settings is the ability of firms (and entrepreneurs) to recognize opportunities when they arise and position themselves to lead or capitalize on them. Historically, this is one area where the urban-rural divide comes into play. More specifically, agglomeration economies have the benefit, by definition, of concentrated resources and information flows, making it easier to identify and respond to new opportunities (Lyons, Miller, & Mann, 2018; Porter, 1996). In this context, firms operating in rural areas are at a clear disadvantage. At the same time, the urban-centric nature of existing innovation data and studies make it difficult, if not impossible, to understand the innovation process for rural firms. It begs the question, can rural firms or regions thrive in the global marketplace in the absence of agglomeration economies, and under what conditions might we expect them to thrive? It may also be that the question itself is incomplete. That is, to be able to anticipate firm and community development through innovation, we must first understand the process of innovation in rural areas. These and other similarly framed questions drive the need to develop new data, allowing the exploration of innovation creation by firms operating in Rural America.

The Rural Establishment Innovation Survey

The REIS was implemented in 2014 (after the 2007–2009 recession), using a multimodal data collection approach: online survey access, postal mail, and phone calls to collect data (Moore, 2015; Wojan & Parker, 2017). Overall, 10,911 responses were collected (22.4% response rate), targeting establishments found in the Business Registry of the Bureau of Labor Statistics. The establishments of interest were in the following "tradeable" industries, mining (NAICS 21), manufacturing (NAICS 31–33), wholesale trade (NAICS 42), transportation and warehousing (NAICS 48; NAICS 49 not included), information (NAICS 51), finance and insurance (NAICS 52), professional, scientific, and technical services (NAICS 54), management of businesses (NAICS 55), and arts, entertainment, and recreation (NAICS 71). Surveys were restricted to establishments with at least five employees and included oversampling in rural areas. The data set targeted and is made up of about 75% rural and 25% urban establishment responses.[1]

One of the most interesting features of the survey is that it includes over 40 different measures of innovation, ranging from traditional metrics, such as patents and in-house R&D to an array of alternative measures. The importance of this feature is that the REIS data allow researchers a first look at how broadly defined measures of innovation activity occur in establishments across urban and rural geographies. We highlight this feature in two tables below showing a selected list of 12 potential innovation measures by geography or industry.

Table 4.1 (above) shows the percentages broken down by the nine Rural-Urban Continuum Codes (RUCCs)[2] of establishments surveyed utilizing selected innovative activity measures. These codes range from urban (metropolitan) core counties (RUCC=1) to the most rural counties (RUCC=9). For

TABLE 4.1 Selected Innovation Measures in REIS By RUCC

Variable Name		*RUCC*								
		2 (%)	*3 (%)*	*4 (%)*	*5 (%)*	*6 (%)*	*7 (%)*	*8 (%)*	*9 (%)*	
Input-new knowledge	In-house R&D	41	40	39	39	35	33	31	38	31
	In-house design	34	30	30	32	28	27	25	26	21
	Innovation plan	35	33	33	34	31	29	27	33	26
	Train staff	47	45	49	44	42	41	39	43	38
IP protection	Licensed patent(s)	9	8	5	8	6	6	6	6	5
	Patent application	7	7	8	7	5	5	4	5	3
	Industrial design	5	2	2	3	2	2	2	3	1
	Trade secret	30	24	28	20	17	15	15	13	15
Output	New good	40	41	38	41	35	41	37	41	38
	New service	58	55	62	58	58	54	56	54	61
	Manufacturing method	39	34	37	41	33	37	35	37	36
	Marketing method	48	47	48	47	43	39	37	43	41

additional context, the metrics were further divided into three groups based on the innovation creation process, input-new knowledge (initial input to the innovative process), IP protection (intermediate output from the innovative process), and output (final output such as new product, process, or service).[3] As shown in Table 4.1, a traditional measure of innovation, like patenting and undertaking in-house R&D, tends to be lower for firms in rural counties than those in urban counties. This is consistent with prior literature and indicates that the more rural an establishment, the less likely it is to participate in traditional or standard innovative activity measures (Wojan, Dotzel, & Low, 2015).[4] On the other hand, alternative measures such as produced a "new good" or "new service" are flat in comparison. In other words, there are similar rates of many alternative measures for establishments regardless of geography. In only a few cases, such as with creating new or improved "manufacturing method," do any rural areas outperform any urban areas in terms of the share of firms participating in the innovative activity.

The picture changes slightly when we look at these metrics by industry. In Table 4.2, the list of selected measures from Table 4.1 are categorized by 2-digit NAICS industry codes, and each industry is further broken out into two geographic categories: urban (defined as RUCCs 1–3) and rural (RUCC 4–9). For example, manufacturing sectors have a long tendency to migrate toward rural economies (Blackley, 1986). Looking under NAICS 33, we see slightly higher percentages of rural establishment participation across many innovative activities compared to urban establishments. This includes traditional measures like patents and in-house R&D, as well as some alternative measures of innovation activities. Rural firms in key sectors (notably those in NAICS 31, 33, and 71), appear to favor traditional means of IP protection like patenting or licensing a patent compared to urban firms. On the other hand, in industries like NAICS

55 and 54, urban establishments tend to patent more frequently than their rural counterparts. For in-house R&D, rural establishments in the NAICS 33 industry have the highest overall percentage across all urban and rural establishments. However, urban firms in other industries outpace rural firms in the same or similar industries in terms of participating in in-house R&D activities. Also evident in Table 4.2, rural manufacturing firms (NAICS 31–33) compare most closely to their urban counterparts with few exceptions. The largest gaps appear between rural and urban firms in NAICS 48, 51, 52, 54, and 55. This is especially true for in-house R&D and trade secrets. In fact, urban firms appear to use trade secrets much more frequently than rural firms.

REIS Literature: Measures of Innovation

Building on the observations in Tables 4.1 and 4.2, Wojan (2019) explored selected intellectual property (IP) practices in detail. He reported that urban establishments are about twice as likely to use IP strategies than rural establishments. However, with respect to substantive innovators (defined as patenting establishments), the differences between rural and urban establishments are much smaller. The findings suggest that using a broad array of IP tactics as innovative measures may be an effective strategy for comparing urban and rural substantive innovators. Results also revealed that using mixed IP strategies (ranging from technological, such as patenting, as well as nontechnological, such an informal IP like first-mover advantage) may be beneficial to identify substantive innovators in rural areas from other data sets. The broader implication of this study was that rural firms may experience a greater benefit, compared to urban firms by pursuing mixed IP strategies.

To explore this in more detail, Mann and Loveridge (2020) used the REIS data and compared the drivers of 39 firm-level (alternative) innovative activity measures to those of patents. Additionally, they considered rural and urban subsamples with the goal of: (1) understanding how drivers of alternative innovation measures may differ from those of patenting and (2) seeing how drivers may vary across urban and rural firms. The findings suggest patents do not capture innovation for rural establishments in the same way that the measure does for urban establishments. In other words, while patents may work for measuring innovation in urban areas, the study implications are that they do not work as well for measuring innovation in rural areas.

Using a wide range of traditional and nontraditional measures of innovation contained in the REIS, Whitacre, Meadowcroft, and Gallardo (2019) developed an innovation index with the goal of more accurately reflecting innovative activity across urban and rural geographies. For their analysis, they developed firm-level and regional-level models that included the index as an independent variable. At the firm level, their results indicated the index has a strong positive relationship with wages and market growth. At the regional level, they found a strong positive relationship with median household income, a positive

TABLE 4.2 Selected Innovation Measures by 2-Digit NAICS for Rural and Urban Areas

Variable Name		*2-Digit NAICS/Region*																			
		31		*32*		*33*		*42*		*48*		*51*		*52*		*54*		*55*		*71*	
		Urban (%)	*Rural (%)*	*Urban (%)*	*Rural (%)*	*Urban (%)*	*Rural (%)*	*Urban (%)*	*Rural (%)*	*Urban (%)*	*Rural (%)*	*Urban (%)*	*Rural (%)*	*Urban (%)*	*Rural (%)*	*Urban (%)*	*Rural (%)*	*Urban (%)*	*Rural (%)*	*Urban (%)*	*Rural (%)*
Input-new knowledge	In-house R&D	52	48	47	43	48	59	33	25	28	14	44	39	32	15	40	27	39	28	44	42
	In-house design	53	50	37	39	43	44	30	21	12	8	48	33	16	19	27	17	34	16	46	42
	Innovation plan	38	40	40	41	53	57	28	21	18	12	44	31	25	10	31	19	30	26	35	31
	Train staff	46	42	44	36	49	47	43	40	26	26	61	59	48	38	49	43	49	45	51	45
IP protection	Licensed patent(s)	5	6	10	9	12	12	8	6	3	2	5	7	4	5	8	4	15	6	4	5
	Patent application	4	6	10	10	14	15	6	4	2	1	2	0	4	2	7	2	9	1	0	1
	Industrial design	4	3	5	5	7	7	3	2	1	0	1	0	2	0	4	1	7	1	0	1
	Trade secret	32	25	33	22	33	32	24	12	11	5	27	11	29	10	31	14	33	12	10	5
Output	New good	75	74	64	58	61	71	46	34	16	10	41	41	21	18	25	17	31	23	35	38
	New service	48	48	46	42	46	48	53	59	53	49	79	80	70	67	65	63	59	62	76	77
	Manufacturing method	59	60	62	56	62	66	33	28	19	18	32	34	23	16	27	24	33	22	24	15
	Marketing method	52	46	36	35	45	39	51	47	33	25	63	55	54	50	47	39	48	47	72	71

relationship with the share of creative class, and a negative relationship with poverty. Interestingly, they also found that for establishments in rural areas, the positive relationship between the innovation index and wages is smaller compared to establishments located in urban areas. On the other hand, the relationship between the index and market growth is larger for establishments in rural areas compared to those in urban areas. One implication from this study is that innovation activity is occurring in rural areas and provides important benefits to the local economy.

In a study categorizing establishments as noninnovators, incremental innovators (minor changes in methods or process), and substantive innovators (patenting establishments), Wojan and Parker (2017) reported that innovation rates in manufacturing were more similar, than different, across rural and urban regions. This is consistent with the observations of rural and urban firms in NAICS 31–33 from Table 4.2. However, the types of manufacturing industries where substantive innovators operate differed in rural and urban areas. In rural areas, for example, these were mostly manufacturing in pharmaceuticals, chemicals, computers, plastics, and textile mills. The only nonmanufacturing industries with substantive innovators in rural areas were telecommunications and wholesale electronic markets. On the other hand, substantive innovative establishments in urban areas include a much wider range of industries in addition to manufacturing, such as broadcasting, data processing, web hosting, air transportation, and business management. In rural areas, impacts of substantive innovative establishments did not broadly affect the region in terms of employment growth, but these establishments did impact employment at the establishment level.

Wojan, Crown, and Rupasingha (2018) used the same innovation activity intensity framework as Wojan and Parker (2017) to examine the influence on manufacturing establishment survival in rural and urban areas. In a similar fashion to Whitacre, Meadowcroft, and Gallardo (2019), they discovered that manufacturers in rural areas gain a greater positive benefit to survival from substantive and incremental innovations compared to urban manufacturers. They also reported that innovation is not more important to survival of urban manufacturers compared to their rural counterparts. In other words, the "innovate or die" aphorism applies equally to manufacturing establishments in both rural and urban regions. Additionally, they explained that while incrementally innovative manufacturers in rural areas had a higher probability of survival compared to noninnovative manufacturers, substantive innovative manufacturers were likely the most resilient.

REIS Literature: Information Sources

There are two studies that used the REIS data to explore the influence of information sources on innovation creation. In one, Demircioglu, Audretsch, and Slaper (2019) considered how sources of information broadly impacted innovation activity as well as the specific types of innovation—namely, on product, process, or marketing. Their model combined rural and urban establishments, controlling for the rural establishments using a rural index measure. In general, the estimated parameters for the rural index indicated that innovation output, such as product, process, or marketing, was about 10% smaller than for urban establishments. They reported that younger establishments with more employees and those in urban areas had greater degrees of all three innovation types. Additionally, establishments tended to create more product-type innovations compared to process or marketing innovations. They also reported that the extent and mode of innovation depended on the industry in which the establishment operates (or type of organization). More specifically, they reported that transportation and management establishments have low level of innovative activity relative to other industries.

In the second study, Dotzel and Faggian (2019) also considered knowledge and information sources, but their model separated data into rural and urban samples. Additionally, they expanded the list of information sources and included a measure for location, distinguishing between local, regional, and global locations of information. While results were similar to Demircioglu, Audretsch, and Slaper (2019), using the subsampled data for rural and urban establishments provided additional nuanced outcomes. More specifically, they reported that the sources or information appeared to be more important for rural establishments compared with urban ones for some innovation creation activities.

To better understand the results from both studies, outcomes were combined into a new, single table shown below (Table 4.3). The terms "strong," "moderate," or "none" indicate the intensity of the impact from the information or knowledge source on the type of innovation. Here, results from Dotzel and Faggian (2019) appear in the rural and urban columns under each innovation type, while the results from Demircioglu, Audretsch, and Slaper (2019) appear in the combined columns under each innovation type. The primary differences between the two studies are the influence of universities on the innovation type, and the influence of customers on marketing innovations.

REIS Literature: Small Business Innovation Research

New research (Mann, Miller, & Malone, 2021) is exploring the REIS data in the context of external government R&D funding. More specifically, this research is exploring the influence of the Small Business Innovation Research (SBIR) program on innovation creation by establishments in rural and urban areas. The SBIR program provides millions of R&D dollars annually to small, innovative businesses in the United States. The program is managed by the Small Business Administration (SBA) but administered through the 11 federal agencies with external research budgets greater than that of $100 million annually (SBA, 2020). SBIR awards are competitive and based on each administering agency's priorities. Since its inception in the early 1980s, the program has awarded over $59 B to over 30,000 small businesses.

TABLE 4.3 Influence of Information and Knowledge Sources on Innovation

Information and Knowledge Source	*Innovation Type*										
	Product			*Process*			*Marketing*			*Green*[a]	
	Rural	*Urban*	*Combined*	*Rural*	*Urban*	*Combined*	*Rural*	*Urban*	*Combined*	*Rural*	*Urban*
Suppliers	Strong	Moderate	Moderate	None	None	None	None	None	None	None	Moderate
Customers	Moderate	Moderate	Strong	Strong	None	Strong	None	None	Strong	Strong	Moderate
Others in industry	None	None	None	None	Moderate	Moderate	None	Moderate	Moderate	None	Strong
Employees	-	-	Strong	-	-	Strong	-	-	Strong		
Universities	None	None	Strong	None	None	Strong	Moderate	None	Strong	Moderate	None
Others outside industry	None	None	-	Strong	None	-	Moderate	None	-	None	None
Business/trade association	None	None	-	None	None	-	Moderate	None	-	Moderate	None
Media	None	None	-	None	None	-	None	None	-	None	None
Location											
Local	None	None	-	None	None	-	None	None	-	Moderate	Moderate
Regional	None	None	-	Moderate	None	-	None	None	-	Strong	Strong
Global	Moderate	None	-	None	None	-	Moderate	Moderate	-	None	Moderate

Source: Summarized results are from Dotzel and Faggian (2019) for rural and urban columns, and Demircioglu, Audretsch, and Slaper (2019) for combined columns.
[a] *Innovation type only considered in the Dotzel and Faggian (2019) study.*

Historically, only a small portion of firms operating in rural areas receive SBIR awards, but the SBA has also included rural outreach as part of its mission (Cooper, 2003). In fact, the USDA has a specific topic area designated for rural and community development. However, SBIR award data for the period 2000–2015 reveal that firms located in the largest urban areas (RUCC=1) accounted for about 66.0% of all awards in the period 2000–2015, while firms in smaller regions (RUCC 4–9) received about 3.5% of all SBIR awards in the same period (Mann, Miller, & Malone, 2021). Additionally, the number of awards that firms located in rural areas received varies considerable by agency. For example, at one extreme during the same 2000–2015 period, rural firms accounted for about 19.1% of awards from the USDA (agency with the highest share of awards to rural firms), but only 2.1% of awards from the US Department of Health and Human Services (agency with the lowest share of awards to rural firms).[5]

In preliminary work exploring the relationships between rural establishment innovative activity and SBIR awards, Mann, Miller, and Malone (2021) matched the REIS data to SBIR data using DUNS numbers included with each data set. Their modeling considered the influence of phase II SBIR awards on 15 different innovative activity outcomes, such as applying for patent applications or using trade secrets (as well as potential alternative measures like producing a new product or starting to export). Their results showed that the SBIR parameters for rural firm models were about 1.5–2 times the size of the same parameters in urban models. Further, results were statistically significant for rural establishments for a wide array of measures, including many alternative measures (such as producing a new product or starting to export). This was not the case, however, for urban firms. The implication is that SBIR awards appear to be more impactful in terms of innovation creation for rural establishments compared to their urban counterparts.

In the context of the SBIR program, while far fewer rural firms ever receive awards, the program does provide rural establishments with important R&D capital necessary to innovate. Based on the broader SBIR literature (which is primarily focused on urban firms), businesses with SBIR awards have higher rates of obtaining private equity after the awards, and they experience faster growth (Lerner, 1996). Further, Link, Ruhm and Siegel (2014) reported that firms that receive private equity have a higher probability of licensing and selling their technology. Thus, efforts to increase the number of qualified rural small businesses that pursue SBIR awards could also improve the innovation creation landscape in Rural America.

Policy Implications and Conclusion

The new body of literature that used the REIS to explore innovation creation in rural regions in the United States has a number of important policy implications. The first and most substantial is that the manifestation of innovation in rural and urban regions surpasses traditional measures, such as in-house R&D expenditures or patents (grants or applications). This is especially true when measuring the innovative activity of firms operating in rural regions. Further, the absence of or lower rates of traditional metrics like patenting do not mean that firms in rural areas are not innovating. In fact, firms in rural areas are engaged in innovation creation, but in many cases at different levels and in different ways compared to firms in urban areas. Additionally, the industry makeup of innovative firms in rural areas appears different from urban areas which may impact the types of innovation-related resources firms pursue. Therefore, innovation measures need to be much broader in scope to effectively capture the innovative process in Rural America. While the REIS data provide an important tool for better understanding innovation, additional data as well as data that can regularly be updated are necessary to understand how the innovative process in rural and urban areas is evolving. For example, the USDA provides five-year updates to the Census of Agriculture (in years ending in 2 and 7). Similarly, the REIS could be expanded to include a larger number of firms and industries as well as updated on a regular schedule. Doing so would establish a longitudinal database beneficial for exploring innovation across all US geographies.

A second important policy implication is that while innovative firms in urban areas appear to be able to better capitalize on regional resources compared to firms in rural areas (a potential benefit of agglomeration economies), the influence or impact of innovation creation on the firms themselves appears to be more potent on rural firms compared to urban ones. For example, Whitacre, Meadowcroft, and Gallardo (2019) made the following observation and recommendation: "regional innovation policies that are geared towards improving wages may find more success in more urban locations, while those focused on growing a specific market might accomplish more in relatively peripheral areas" (p. 946). In other words, the outcomes of policies encouraging innovation creation will fundamentally differ in urban and rural areas—that is, growth in wages (urban) versus growth in the market (rural). Additionally, the preliminary findings of Mann, Miller and Malone (2021) are that the SBIR program appears to have a stronger influence on the creation of new innovations for rural firms compared to urban ones. They also found that the SBIR program influenced rural firms to start exporting. Combined, the findings in these two studies suggest that a unique focus of rural innovation policy should encourage establishing new and growing existing markets for new products, processes, and services. Such policies might be focused on local or regional markets or could include exporting nationally or globally.

Finally, rural firms appear to benefit more from a wider range of information sources about or leading to innovation creation. In particular, Dotzel and Faggian (2019) demonstrated that the influence of information from suppliers and universities, and, in some cases, others outside industry or businesses and trade associations has a greater influence on rural establishment choices to innovate and how they innovate. Thus, for more effective innovation creation in rural areas, policies must allow for a diversity of innovation metrics to be considered combined with a strategy that includes a diversity of information and communication paths. Following Lyons, Miller and Mann (2018), universities, especially the Extension system of Land Grants, could play key roles in helping facilitate these information and communication pathways. Additionally, mechanisms that can enhance or augment the flow of information and communication, namely, broadband, are also crucial. At the same time, more research is needed to understand how rural firms may best benefit from and utilize existing infrastructure and how they may capitalize on advances in these areas.

Notes

1 The survey and detailed summary statistics for each survey variable are available through the Office of Information and Regulatory affairs, Pilot Study: National Survey of Business Competitiveness Appendix D.
2 RUCC are from the by USDA's Economic Research Service.
3 The categorization strategy is based on the innovative process described by Aghion and Howitt (1990) and was expanded by Mann and Loveridge (2020) and Mann, Miller, and Loveridge (2020) to incorporate the wider range of innovation measures include in REIS.
4 Metropolitan (urban) counties: 1 = counties in metro areas of one million population or more; 2 = counties in metro areas of 250,000 to one million population; and 3 = counties in metro areas of fewer than 250,000 population. Nonmetropolitan (rural) counties: 4 = urban population of 20,000 or more, adjacent to a metro area; 5 = urban population of 20,000 or more, not adjacent to a metro area; 6 = urban population of 2,500–19,999, adjacent to a metro area; 7 = urban population of 2,500–19,999, not adjacent to a metro area; 8 = completely rural or less than 2,500 urban population, adjacent to a metro area; and 9 = completely rural or less than 2,500 urban population, not adjacent to a metro area (Parker, 2013).
5 This table is not shown, but calculations are based on the same data as in Table 4.3.

References

Acs, Z. J., & Audretsch, D. B. (2005). Entrepreneurship, innovation, and technological change. *Foundations and Trends in Entrepreneurship, 1*(4), 149–195.

Acs, Z. J., & Malecki, E. J. (2003). Entrepreneurship in rural America: The big picture. *Federal Reserve Bank of Kansas City*, 21–29.

Adner, R. (2006). Match your innovation strategy to your innovation ecosystem. *Harvard Business Review, 84*(4), 98.

Aghion, P., & Howitt, P. (1990). *A model of growth through creative destruction* (No. w3223). National Bureau of Economic Research.

Aryal, G., Mann, J., Loveridge, S., & Joshi, S. (2018). Exploring innovation creation across rural and urban firms: Analysis of the National Survey of Business Competitiveness. *Journal of Entrepreneurship and Public Policy,* 7(4), 357–376.

Aryal, G. R., Mann, J., Loveridge, S., & Joshi, S. (2020). Drivers of differences in inventiveness across urban and rural regions. *Journal of Urban Affairs, 43*(5), 1–18.

Blackley, P. R. (1986). Urban-rural variations in the structure of manufacturing production. *Urban Studies, 23*(6), 471–483.

Cooper, R. S. (2003). Purpose and performance of the Small Business Innovation Research (SBIR) program. *Small Business Economics, 20*(2), 137–151.

Demircioglu, M. A., Audretsch, D. B., & Slaper, T. F. (2019). Sources of innovation and innovation type: Firm-level evidence from the United States. *Industrial and Corporate Change, 28*(6), 1365–1379.
Dotzel, K. R., & Faggian, A. (2019). The impact of external knowledge sourcing on innovation outcomes in rural and urban businesses in the US. *Growth and Change, 50*(2), 515–547.
Goetz, S. J., Partridge, M., Deller, S. C., & Fleming, D. A. (2010). Evaluating US rural entrepreneurship policy. *Journal of Regional Analysis & Policy, 40*(1), 20–33.
Lerner, J. (1996). *The government as venture capitalist: The long-run effects of the SBIR program* (No. w5753). National Bureau of Economic Research.
Link, A. N., Ruhm, C. J., & Siegel, D. S. (2014). Private equity and the innovation strategies of entrepreneurial firms: Empirical evidence from the small business innovation research program. *Managerial and Decision Economics, 35*(2), 103–113.
Lyons, T. S., Miller, S. R., & Mann, J. T. (2018). A new role for land grant universities in the rural innovation ecosystem? *Journal of Regional Analysis Policy, 48*(2), 32–47.
Mann, J., & Loveridge, S. (2020). Measuring urban and rural establishment innovation in the United States. *Economics of Innovation and New Technology,* 1–18. https://doi.org/10.1080/10438599.2020.1846248
Mann, J., Miller, S., & Malone, T. (2021). Can targeted government investment in rural establishments induce innovative activity?. *Economic Development Quarterly,* forthcoming.
Mann, J., & Shideler, D. (2015). Measuring Schumpeterian activity using a composite indicator. *Journal of Entrepreneurship and Public Policy, 4*(1), 57–84.
Markley, D. (2001). Financing the new rural economy. *Exploring Policy Options for a New Rural America, 69*, 80.
Moore, D. (2015). Data report 14–56 National Survey of Business Competitiveness. Social and Economic Sciences Research Center Pullman, Washington State University.
Parker, T. (2013). Rural-urban continuum codes. Economic Research Service, United States Department of Agriculture.
Porter, M. E. (1996). Competitive advantage, agglomeration economies, and regional policy. *International Regional Science Review, 19*(1–2), 85–90.
Porter, M. E., Ketels, C. H., Miller, K., & Bryden, R. (2004). Competitiveness in rural US regions: Learning and research agenda. *Institute for Strategy and Competitiveness, Harvard Business School,* 1–17.
Romer, P. (1996). Why, indeed, in America? Theory, history, and the origins of modern economic growth. *American Economic Review, 86*, 202–207.
Romer, P. M. (1990). Endogenous technological change. *Journal of Political Economy, 98*(5, Part 2), S71–S102.
Schumpeter, J. A. (1942). *Socialism, capitalism and democracy.* Harper and Brothers.
Shane, S. A. (2008). *The illusions of entrepreneurship: The costly myths that entrepreneurs, investors, and policy makers live by.* Yale University Press.
Small Business Administration (SBA). (2020). Leveraging America's Seed Fund. Washington, DC: U.S. Small Business Administration. Available at: https://www.sbir.gov/about
Stauber, K. N. (2001). Why invest in rural America—and how? A critical public policy question for the 21st century. *Economic Review-Federal Reserve Bank of Kansas City, 86*(2), 57.
Whitacre, B. E., Meadowcroft, D., & Gallardo, R. (2019). Firm and regional economic outcomes associated with a new, broad measure of business innovation. *Entrepreneurship & Regional Development, 31*(9–10), 930–952.

Wojan, T., & Parker, T. (2017). *Innovation in the rural nonfarm economy: Its effect on job and earnings growth, 2010–2014*. U.S. Department of Agriculture, Economic Research Service (ERR-238, No. 1477–2017–5393). doi: 10.22004/ag.econ.264596

Wojan, T. R. (2019). Geographical differences in intellectual property strategies and outcomes: Establishment-level analysis across the American settlement hierarchy. *Regional Studies, Regional Science, 6*(1), 574–595.

Wojan, T. R., Crown, D., & Rupasingha, A. (2018). Varieties of innovation and business survival: Does pursuit of incremental or far-ranging innovation make manufacturing establishments more resilient? *Research Policy, 47*(9), 1801–1810.

Wojan, T. R., Dotzel, K. R., & Low, S. A. (2015). Decomposing regional patenting rates: How the composition factor confounds the rate factor. *Regional Studies, Regional Science, 2*(1), 535–551.

5

SOCIAL CAPITAL BUILDING FOR RURAL INNOVATION

Thomas S. Lyons

Introduction

Creativity can be defined as invention. Innovation is the implementation of that invention—getting it to the market that needs it (Baldacchino, 2009; Govindarajan, 2010). Thus, any community's principal innovators are its entrepreneurs, whether they are the inventors of what they bring to the market or not. Encouraging rural innovation is, at its core, about fostering entrepreneurship. Rural entrepreneurs face numerous challenges to acquiring the financial, human, and physical capital they require to start, grow, and sustain their businesses. As discussed in this chapter, these include relative geographical isolation, a dearth of financial capital, fewer venture development organizations, a lower-skilled workforce, and underpopulation that lessens the serendipitous encounters that foster innovation, among others.

The ability to create and maintain networks is crucial to overcoming these challenges. Networks are the product of social capital building, particularly the creation of bridging social capital. This type of social capital allows rural entrepreneurs to reach beyond their local communities for the resources they need. It is a variety of informal social capital that permits interactions among individuals and groups that do not necessarily know each other well. This chapter explores bridging (and bonding) social capital, and their advantages in fostering entrepreneurship. It begins with an accounting of the challenges to rural entrepreneurship. The relationship between entrepreneurship and social capital is then detailed. It examines the ways in which bonding and bridging social capital are built and maintained, and how they can be used to address rural entrepreneurship challenges. An example from the rural context is used to illustrate these concepts, and a set of recommendations for social capital building in support of successful entrepreneurship is provided.

DOI: 10.4324/9781003178552-5

Challenges to Rural Entrepreneurship

The literature on rural entrepreneurship is replete with discussions of the challenges that entrepreneurs face to successfully starting and growing their businesses in rural communities. Some of these trials stem from the spatial isolation of rural places in the United States, which have been found to be even more isolated than those in Europe (Besser & Miller, 2013). This remoteness tends to make the resources necessary for successful entrepreneurship—physical, human, immaterial, financial, and social—less available locally and more difficult to obtain from external sources (Muller & Korsgaard, 2017). These resources tend to be concentrated in urban areas, making them more expensive to acquire as well, due to higher transportation costs (Lamb & Sherman, 2010).

It has been widely observed that rural areas suffer from low population density and increasing population aging and outmigration (Besser & Miller, 2013; Frazier et al., 2013; Lamb & Sherman, 2010; Leung & Murray, 2009; Shields, 2005). In addition, household incomes tend to be lower than in urban areas (Shields, 2005; Mickiewicz et al., 2016; Yu & Artz, 2019). Because of this lack of "economic critical mass" (Lichtenstein & Lyons, 1996), rural entrepreneurs are less likely to enjoy financial success, as their immediate markets are smaller, have less disposable income, are less budget elastic, and are less educated (Shields, 2005; Yu & Artz, 2019). Local markets are crucial in the retail and service economy, in particular, created by the shift from manufacturing perpetuated by globalization (Frazier et al., 2013; Robinson & Finley, 2007; Rupasingha & Contreras, 2014). As a result of all of these deficiencies, rural entrepreneurs have diminished access to financial capital (Mickiewicz et al., 2016; Lyons et al., 2020). This is exacerbated by the fact that small rural banks are more risk averse in their business lending, and equity capital is relatively scarce (Robinson, 2006; Lamb & Sherman, 2010). This tends to discourage the scaling of enterprises that are formed in rural areas, reducing the number of high-growth businesses (HGBs), which create more jobs (Lamb & Sherman, 2010). It also helps to explain why necessity and lifestyle businesses are much more common in rural areas than are opportunity-based enterprises (Lyons et al., 2018; Miles & Morrison, 2018).

Rural areas are often dominated by a single industry (Lichtenstein & Lyons, 1996). In many cases this is agriculture, which has been steadily declining in its importance to U.S. GDP. Yet, rural policy has not caught up to this fact and continues to focus on supporting agriculture at the expense of entrepreneurship in other industries (Lyons et al., 2018). Dominance by one industry is never healthy for an economy, as it stifles creativity and innovation and limits economic diversity (Lichtenstein & Lyons, 1996). It should be noted, however, that a growing number of rural communities are embracing entrepreneurship as an economic development strategy and have been since the beginning of this century (Drabenstott et al., 2003).

Using focus groups, Leung and Murray (2009) found that a lack of information and communication infrastructure was a frequently cited obstacle to entrepreneurship in rural areas. This dearth of technology makes it difficult to both do business on a daily basis and to attract needed talent into the community (Leung & Murray, 2009; Robinson & Shah, 2004).

A lesser known and cited challenge to rural entrepreneurs is regulation, which can be more stringent than that affecting urban entrepreneurs (Deakins et al., 2016; Frazier et al., 2013). Rural regulation can also be highly industry-specific and complex, in that it comes from multiple levels of government. Rural entrepreneurs often lack the skills needed to manage this regulation, nor do they have the networks to help them compensate for their own lack of skill (Deakins et al., 2016; Lyons et al., 2020).

Along these lines, rural entrepreneurs often lack the education and skill, in general, to be successful businesspeople. This is particularly true for rural women (Bauer, 2010). Whereas urban entrepreneurs have access to a sophisticated collection of entrepreneurship support organizations (ESOs) to provide business and technical knowledge and help with developing skills, rural entrepreneurs have little or none of this type of support (Lamb & Sherman, 2010). As Lichtenstein et al. (2004: 15) expressed it, oftentimes "…no one in the community is responsible for the community's supply of entrepreneurs."

Some scholars have found that a major obstacle to entrepreneurship in rural areas is psychological in nature or having to do with mindset. Many prospective rural entrepreneurs lack self-efficacy—they tend not to believe their business will ultimately be profitable (Liang & Dunn, 2014). Despite this, some will press forward with starting a business, which demonstrates research findings that economic gain is not the principal driver of entrepreneurial behavior (Carter et al., 2003; Liang & Dunn, 2014); however, these businesses, as a result, are more vulnerable to the other challenges already described and ill-prepared to handle them.

All of the trials noted to this point contribute to another challenge to creativity and innovation—the lack of a creative class in rural places. The concept of the "creative class" was popularized by researcher Richard Florida (2003) and refers to a collection of individuals who are artists and professionals who bring fresh perspectives, knowledge, and skills to the community in which they reside and work. This can change the mindset of a community from what psychologist Carol Dweck (2006) calls "fixed" to one of "growth." A fixed mindset receives things as they are, accepting viewpoints, traditions, policies, and relationships as being immutable, whereas a growth mindset is open to learning, self-improvement, and progress. McGranahan et al. (2011) posit that the in-migration of a creative class can be a major boon to creating a successful entrepreneurial ecosystem in a rural region. Lyons et al. (2018) take this a step further by arguing that creativity has become the purview of urban areas, leaving rural communities without the ideas needed to fuel entrepreneurship: the so-called "urban-rural innovation gap."

A challenge to rural entrepreneurship that is particularly relevant to this chapter has to do with social capital. The issue is not a lack of social capital but, perhaps, an overemphasis on one type: bonding social capital, or what sociologists call "strong ties" (Lyons et al., 2020). It has been argued that bonding social capital—close connections between members of a community—tends to make that community more insular and less open to developing relationships outside the community, including the pursuit of entrepreneurship skill development (Campopiano et al., 2016; Levitte, 2004; Lyons et al., 2020). This issue is discussed in more detail in the following section.

Social Capital and Entrepreneurship

Social capital has been closely linked to entrepreneurship in the academic literature (Flora et al., 1997; Grisham, 1999; Lichtenstein & Lyons, 1996; Lyons, 2002a; Lyons et al., 2012, 2020; Neck et al., 2018; Servon, 1998; Tolbert et al., 1998). There appears to be a consensus that it is crucial to successful entrepreneurship; however, there is some disagreement as to what type(s) of social capital is the most efficacious.

Social capital is a difficult concept to pin down, in part because it is intangible (Bhandari & Yasunobu, 2009). There is no single accepted definition because scholars have approached the topic from different perspectives and areas of interest, from urban policy (Jacobs, 1961; Seely et al., 1956) to income distribution (Loury, 1977). It can be said, however, that all definitions of social capital share an emphasis on social interactions that create value for the participants (Bhandari & Yasunobu, 2009).

There are three scholars whose work is credited with providing a contemporary understanding of social capital and popularizing it: Bourdieu, Coleman, and Putnam. Pierre Bourdieu, a sociologist, defined social capital as "the aggregate of the actual and potential resources which are linked to possession of a durable network of more or less institutionalized relationships of mutual acquaintance and recognition" (Bourdieu, 1983: 249). For Bourdieu, this meant that social capital was an asset owned by a community that afforded economic and social advantages to its members (Bhandari & Yasunobu, 2009).

Unlike Bourdieu, who focused on how social capital benefited the economic and social elite, sociologist James Coleman argued that social capital benefited the working class as well (Smith, 2000–2009). This caused him to broaden its definition,

> Social capital is defined by its function. It is not a single entity, but a variety of different entities, having two characteristics in common: they all consist of some aspect of social structure, and they facilitate certain actions of individuals who are within the structure.
>
> *(Coleman, 1994: 302)*

Arguably, Harvard political scientist Robert Putnam did the most to bring social capital into the popular vernacular through his book *Bowling Alone* (Bhandari & Yasunobu, 2009; Smith, 2000–2009). Putnam argues that,

> Whereas physical capital refers to physical objects and human capital refers to the properties of individuals, social capital refers to connections among

> individuals – social networks and the norms of reciprocity and trustworthiness that arise from them. In that sense social capital is closely related to what some have called 'civic virtue.' The difference is that 'social capital' calls attention to the fact that civic virtue is most powerful when embedded in a network of reciprocal social relations. A society of many virtuous but isolated individuals is not necessarily rich in social capital.
>
> *(Putnam, 2000: 19)*

These definitions give us a broad understanding of what social capital is, but how does it work? Lin (1999: 30) has succinctly described the essence of how social capital functions as "...investment in social relations with expected returns." When people interact, they have expectations of each other. If I do something for you, you will do something for me (Lyons, 2002a). When social capital is built, this is intentional, not serendipitous. Coleman (1988) has described this as a system of credits and debts. When these obligations are consistently fulfilled, trust is established between the parties and social capital is built.

Building social capital has several benefits. It facilitates increased awareness among community, or organization, members as to who each other is, what they have to offer, and how their interests and fortunes are intertwined (Putnam, 2000). This prevents what cultural geographers call "distance decay"—the breakdown of interactions among people who share common characteristics, interests, etc. due to physical and/or social separation—resulting in the collapse of the society (Hanks, 2011). Conversely, increased awareness through social capital building can facilitate action that likely would not otherwise have happened.

Social capital also permits members of a community or organization to resolve disputes. This is because it enables cooperation (Putnam, 2000). It can reduce the transaction costs of daily business and societal interaction by its ability to establish trust among participants. In this way it is a lubricant for community or network progress (Putnam, 2000; Smith, 2000–2009).

It should be noted that social capital has its negative aspects. It has been argued that it serves to provide advantages to the members of a community or organization that are unavailable to those outside this group (Portes, 2014), thereby perpetuating inequality. It has also been criticized for fostering a herd mentality and a closed mindset that impede creativity and innovation (Lichtenstein & Lyons, 1996; Portes, 2014) as well as a lack of self-sufficiency and motivation (Gomez et al., 2015). These criticisms, however, tend to focus on bonding social capital, for which bridging social capital can be an antidote, a distinction that now will be discussed in further detail.

To this point, social capital has been discussed as though it is a uniform concept; however, in reality, not all social capital is the same. It was not until Putnam (2000) wrote *Bowling Alone* that this fact was addressed, however (Woolcock, 2001). Putnam (2000) identified two major types of social capital: bonding and bridging.

Bonding social capital is built within communities, organizations, families—people who are physically close and share common traits, beliefs, and culture

(Neck et al., 2018). Putnam (2000) describes this type of social capital as being "exclusive." Macht (2016) observes that it focuses inwardly on the members of the collective. It strengthens the community or organization, itself, but not its connections to the outside. It utilizes what are referred to as "strong ties" in the sociology literature (Granovetter, 1985). These are close or dense connections that are bound by reciprocity, trust, and loyalty. In entrepreneurship, this can be very beneficial to the "brand" of the enterprise and can build comradery, focus, and purpose. Some scholars have argued that building bonding social capital is an essential step on the way to building bridging social capital (Macht, 2016). That is, a community or organization must first strengthen its own bonds before it can effectively reach out to others.

Bridging social capital is built between people within the community or organization and those outside of it. It utilizes "weak ties" to connect people who do not necessarily share a culture or a point of view but who might share common or complementary objectives (Putnam, 2000). Bridging social capital extends an entrepreneur's reach, linking her or him to knowledge and resources that may be unavailable in her or his home community.[1]

All of this suggests that social capital can be important to an entrepreneur's success. Both types of capital have a role to play in this success. Bonding social capital helps the entrepreneur to bring their team together and to build comradery based on shared values and goals. It gives the team, and the enterprise, cohesiveness and a clear "brand" as it prepares to reach out to the larger world. Bridging social capital provides the enterprise with wider access to information, knowledge, financial capital, physical resources, skillsets, and emotional support (Neck et al., 2018). The two types together provide both strong and weak ties, linking social and business networks, something that is particularly important for rural entrepreneurs (Frazier & Niehm, 2004).

Before examining how social capital can be used to address challenges to successful rural entrepreneurship, it is worth noting that some researchers have argued that there is a necessary precondition to social capital building in support of entrepreneurship—*cultural capital* that can make commercial entrepreneurship desirable and acceptable. In their study of a native community in rural Alaska, Light and Dana (2013) observed that despite strong social capital, commercial entrepreneurship was not widely pursued because cultural norms reinforced hunting and fishing as the principal forms of livelihood. Thus, building social capital is not an answer to challenges to business development in rural communities that do not endorse entrepreneurship, in general. Fortunately for those who support entrepreneurship-focused economic development in rural areas, most rural communities in the United States have a culture that does endorse entrepreneurship (Light & Dana, 2013). Nonetheless, the concept of cultural capital remains important because the mere fact that a community values entrepreneurship does not mean that community is capable of collectively and effectively supporting it. Sometimes a complete entrepreneurial culture must be built intentionally, an idea that will be expanded upon later in this chapter.

The Role of Social Capital Building in Addressing Rural Entrepreneurship Challenges

Clearly, there are many significant challenges to pursuing a strategy of entrepreneurship-focused economic development in rural communities. Building social capital is one very promising way to address many of these challenges in a fashion that can be transformational. To better understand the role for social capital building that is most efficacious, it is helpful to review and consolidate what scholars have learned about what works when it comes to fostering rural entrepreneurship/innovation.

Much of the collective wisdom regarding the effective support and encouragement of entrepreneurship in rural communities falls into three major prescriptions (Cole, 2018; Henderson, 2002; Lichtenstein & Lyons, 2001; Markley et al., 2015):

- Take a regional approach;
- Develop a culture of entrepreneurship; and
- Focus on developing entrepreneurs, as opposed to businesses.

Arguably, each of these requires social capital building for its successful implementation.

The lack of economic critical mass discussed earlier in this chapter, and its accompanying limits on resource and market availability and accessibility, is a function of small and declining populations in rural communities and a lack of population density. This can only be overcome by connecting contiguous communities into regions that are large enough to improve economic critical mass (Cole, 2018; Dabson, 2007; Sternberg, 2009). Ideally, these regions include both rural *and* urban areas, providing the former with opportunities to access the larger resource pool and markets of the latter (Lyons, 2002a; Mayer et al., 2016).

Taking a *regional approach* requires building bridging social capital where there were likely few, if any, such connections before. This necessitates reaching out across local jurisdictional boundaries to create weak ties. It is not an easy task because of cultural and political divisions between rural communities and between rural and urban communities. Something as simple as a high school football rivalry between two communities in the same region can damage the ability to work cooperatively. A culture that places a premium on individual freedom also may make it difficult to pursue a more communal approach to problem-solving; however, as Ring et al. (2010) point out, even individualists can successfully build bridging social capital, if they are willing to maintain weak ties.

An example of regional social capital building in support of entrepreneurship-focused rural economic development was the Advantage Valley Entrepreneurial League System® (ELS) project, which spanned a period from roughly 2003 to 2008. While this project was ultimately terminated for lack of funding and sustained political support, it offers a viable starting place for thinking about an effort that linked an entire economic region, including rural and urban areas in support of developing entrepreneurs.

At that time, the Advantage Valley region covered an 11-county area, spanning parts of northwestern West Virginia, eastern Kentucky, and southern Ohio. This region included the cities of Charleston and Huntington, West Virginia and Ashland, Kentucky, as well as considerable rural territory. It was a natural economic region that shared a single economic development organization (EDO) known as "Advantage Valley." In 2003, this EDO was looking for a way to support entrepreneurship in the Valley on a regional scale. They settled upon an approach called the Entrepreneurial League System (ELS)®, which was based on a conceptual model created by Lichtenstein and Lyons (2001). With the support of the Claude Worthington Benedum Foundation, the Advantage Valley ELS® was launched in 2004. The project later received a $2 million grant from the Kellogg Foundation to support its work.

Advantage Valley played the role of champion and convener of this entrepreneurial ecosystem, activating its network of business and government organizations located throughout the region to provide support and participation. The ELS model called for the creation of an entrepreneur coaching system, which was designed to support the development of entrepreneurship skills among the entrepreneurs of the Advantage Valley. It also organized the ESOs of the region into a second system that interfaced with the coaching system.

In the coaching system, the client entrepreneurs were organized by their skill level, as measured by a clinical assessment tool, which at that time was called the Entrepreneurial League System Assessment (ELSA), but later became the Readiness Inventory for Successful Entrepreneurship (RISE).[2] Each entrepreneur was assigned to a coach and a team of peers, based on their skill level. The coach provided personal coaching to the entrepreneur and acted as the facilitator of meetings of the peer coaching group, which was constituted of entrepreneurs at the same skill level. Through personal and peer group coaching, the coach helped her or his coachees to develop their skills to higher levels, climbing a ladder of skill development on the way to mastery (Kutzhanova et al., 2009). Twice per year, the entrepreneurs in the coaching system were brought together for what the ELS termed "community coaching." This was an opportunity for entrepreneurs at all skill levels to engage, yielding role modeling, mentoring, and business partnership relationships. It was a chance for lower-skilled entrepreneurs to learn from their higher-skilled colleagues and for the energy of newcomers to the system to reenergize the more senior entrepreneurs.

The ESO system was created by carrying out a region-wide identification and assessment (mapping) of the entrepreneur-serving organizations. This survey not only catalogued the Advantage Valley's ESOs but also identified the type(s) of service (e.g., business development, technical assistance, financial assistance) offered by each and the predominate skill level of the entrepreneurs with whom they worked. The latter was crucial to aid the coaches in the coaching system in making strategic matches between individual entrepreneurs and ESOs that ensured that entrepreneurs were fully prepared (i.e., had the proper skills) to effectively utilize the service(s) on offer. The ESO system met on a regular basis to share information and coordinate its work, with the help of a professional facilitator.

Through its design, the ELS model built both bonding and bridging social capital. At the most basic level, bonding social capital was built between the entrepreneur and her or his coach. This was both formal and informal. Each incoming entrepreneur was required to enter into a "social contract" with the coaching system, pledging to work diligently with their coach and to share financial information that could be used to measure the system's impact. For its part, the system guaranteed the availability of quality coaching and assistance with accessing sources of support in the region. Informally, a relationship of trust developed between each entrepreneur and her or his coach, which gained strength over time. Entrepreneurs viewed their coaches as trusted colleagues and advisors (Kutzhanova et al., 2009).

Peer coaching groups involved the building of both bonding and bridging social capital. Each peer group (consisting of 8–12 members) was constituted of individual entrepreneurs who did not previously know one another and often hailed from different communities in the region. Thus, the ties were weak. These individuals were a source of information and support to one another. As they gelled as a peer group, trust was created, and they became a team. Many of these entrepreneurs noted that the group had become, in effect, their advisory board (Kutzhanova et al. 2009).

The ESO system was a bridging social capital building mechanism. It brought together ESOs from across the region, many of which were not accustomed to working with each other and may not have been familiar with each other's work. They often saw themselves as in competition with one another to serve the entrepreneurs of the region. The ELS model gave these ESOs a framework within which to think about their relationships to each other. They were a team of entrepreneurship service providers, each of which played a role on that team, based on the service(s) they provided and the skill level of the entrepreneurs they best served. Their third-party facilitated meetings were a vehicle for acting on this mutuality and building the weak ties necessary to providing a regional network of support. Over time, these ties became stronger, as the EDO network helped to familiarize these organizations with each other and provided opportunities to build trust. In this way, the network built bonding social capital.

Through these efforts, entrepreneurs were networked to other entrepreneurs, ESOs were connected to each other, and entrepreneurs were linked to ESOs in an effective way. A form of economic critical mass had been created, intentionally, that helped rural entrepreneurs access resources and other sources of support that may not have been reachable otherwise. Kutzhanova et al. (2009) found that the coaching system of the Advantage Valley ELS® had been quite effective in developing entrepreneurship skills and producing positive business outcomes during its time in existence. Several entrepreneurs advanced in skill level as a result of their coaching, and both average and median revenue of the entrepreneurs' businesses increased by multiples at each progressively higher skill level.

While the ELS model showed considerable promise in building regional social capital for entrepreneurial success in the Advantage Valley, in hindsight, it was only a half-solution. Markley et al. (2015) argue that a complete rural entrepreneurial ecosystem has two major components: one for developing an entrepreneurial community and the other for developing entrepreneurs. The Advantage Valley ELS® successfully created the system for developing entrepreneurs, but it failed to prepare the regional "community" for effectively and sustainably supporting it. This contributed to its demise. Had the leadership adopted the Entrepreneurial Communities Framework (described below), this might potentially have been avoided.

Miles and Morrison (2018) point to leadership as being crucial to the success of any entrepreneurial ecosystem. However, this begs the question, "who should lead?" Advantage Valley attempted to lead that effort, but there was never a full consensus that the EDO should be the leader. As the Advantage Valley ELS® became successful and its profile rose throughout the region, and nationally, other organizations wanted to share in that success and some wanted to control the project, disrupting the overall effort. This might have been avoided if a culture of entrepreneurship (Light & Dana, 2013) and bridging social capital among nonprofit and public entities in the region (other than ESOs), in particular, had been proactively cultivated and maintained.

While there are a variety of prescriptive models for *preparing communities to support entrepreneurship*, Markley et al. (2015) make a compelling case for a model they call the "Entrepreneurial Communities Framework" that has been implemented in several rural communities across the United States by the Center for Rural Entrepreneurship (CRE), which later became Energizing Entrepreneurs (e^2). The framework has four components (Markley et al., 2015):

- **Readiness and Organizing**—This involves educating the community to the value of entrepreneurship as an economic development strategy, building political consensus, creating an organizational structure to lead the effort through social capital building, and ensuring the commitment of the needed financial capital. These scholars and practitioners use the experience of the State of Kansas, which supported entrepreneurship from the top down and facilitated local community capacity building through community coaching, to illustrate this approach.
- **Assessment**—This component prepares the community for developing a strategy for entrepreneur-focused economic development by identifying opportunities, identifying entrepreneurs to serve, cataloging resources, setting goals, and attracting stakeholders.
- **Strategy Development and Implementation**—A plan is created that leverages assets, addresses constraints, and aims to maximize return on investment by supporting the development of entrepreneurs and their businesses.

- **Scaling, Impact, and Transformation**—This is the ultimate goal of the Entrepreneurial Communities Framework, creating communities that think and act entrepreneurially and that strive to transform the prosperity of their rural region.

Putting the Entrepreneurial Communities Framework and the Entrepreneurial League System together might have sustained the Advantage Valley ELS®. It would have finished the bridging social capital work needed to create a complete entrepreneurial ecosystem for that rural region. It also would have reinforced the value of Mitchell's (2015) observation that the institutional and social environments are strong influencers of entrepreneurship development.

The third major prescription for effectively fostering entrepreneurship to help rural regions meet their challenges is *placing the focus of these efforts on the entrepreneur*, as opposed to concentrating on the business. For some time now, scholars have recognized that for many years most of the efforts of communities (urban and rural) and their ESOs were aimed at supporting enterprises—the businesses operated by entrepreneurs (Lichtenstein & Lyons, 2002; Lichtenstein et al., 2004). Support services were often organized by the industry of the business or its stage in the business life cycle. Yet, entrepreneurs run their businesses; the opposite would reflect a serious problem (Gerber, 1990; Lichtenstein & Lyons, 2010).

With this in mind, a shift to an emphasis on entrepreneurship-focused economic development occurred, one which puts human development ahead of business development (Lichtenstein & Lyons, 2001). The tension between these two approaches has its roots in theories of entrepreneurship success. For much of the history of the field of entrepreneurship, so-called "traits" theory was dominant. This theory held that success in entrepreneurship was the function of the possession of innate traits on the part of the entrepreneur (Brockhaus, 1982; Gorman et al., 1997; Greenberg & Sexton, 1988; Huefner & Hunt, 1994; Kassicieh et al., 1997; McClelland et al., 1953; Schumpeter, 1991; Timmons et al., 1985). As a result, economic developers seeking to encourage entrepreneurship believed that they should either try to predict who would be a successful entrepreneur (picking winners) and help them or wait to see who emerged from the "entrepreneurship maze" (Lyons, 2002b), assume this was because they had been born with the right attributes, and assist them. This made the support of individual entrepreneurs difficult and reactive, and caused the business development approach to be more attractive. Economic developers already knew how to work with businesses because of their business attraction and retention activities.

As the field of entrepreneurship has evolved, researchers are pivoting to the realization that the reason that entrepreneurs are successful, and that some are more successful than others, is the possession of a skillset (Lichtenstein & Lyons, 2010; Lyons et al., 2020; Neck et al., 2014). This paved the way to entrepreneurship-focused economic development becoming proactive and developmental. When an entrepreneur's skills are developed, he or she can, in turn, more successfully develop the business. This puts people at the center of entrepreneurship and gives social capital building meaning and viability.

The Advantage Valley ELS®, again, serves as an example. The focus of this project was the entrepreneur and the development of that entrepreneur's skillset through strategic coaching and the creation of a transparent (to the entrepreneur) system of ESOs. By making the entrepreneur the locus of support, the system becomes a human development enterprise that lends itself to the kind of mutual value creation that is the goal of social capital building. Individuals are given the opportunity and support to increase their capability for success through launching and growing their businesses, while the community benefits from the business assets they create, which contribute to community wealth and quality of life.

The takeaway from all of this should be that while social capital has an important role to play in overcoming challenges to rural entrepreneurship, thereby increasing the probability of success for rural entrepreneurs, it cannot be social capital building for its own sake. It must be in support of a sound strategy for fostering entrepreneurship in rural regions. At its essence, social capital building should be a mechanism for creating and sustaining rural entrepreneurial ecosystems. It can build the needed ties, both strong and weak, that enable the community-wide support required to foster entrepreneurship-focused economic development (Lyons, 2002a) and the development of individual entrepreneurs.

Recommendations for Social Capital Building in Support of Rural Entrepreneurship

In light of the extant knowledge presented in this chapter regarding the vicissitudes of engaging in entrepreneurship in rural areas and of social capital and how it is built, the following recommendations for employing social capital building as a means to successfully foster entrepreneurship as a rural economic development strategy are offered:

1 **Acknowledge the need for *both* bonding and bridging social capital.** While the bonding social capital created in smaller rural communities has been found to have some negative impacts on creativity and innovation, it also has an important role to play in both building entrepreneurial ecosystems and developing individual entrepreneurs. As Gomez et al. (2015) note, bonding social capital can be used to create the strength and cohesion necessary to allow communities, organizations, and enterprises to work with others to build bridging social capital. Bridging social capital enables the creation and sustaining of the networks that provide entrepreneurs with access to resources, information, and developmental support that would be otherwise inaccessible. Denser networks afford advantages, as each link provides opportunities to reach new groups (Baker et al., 2010). However, a word of caution is necessary here. Too much network density in the wrong places can be counterproductive. It might be useful to think about

the bonding/bridging social capital interface in terms of a periphery and a core. The periphery is connected by bridging social capital to the core created by bonding social capital. The periphery is the source of information and ideas not necessarily found in the core. Its ties need to be weak, so as not to impede this inward flow. The core permits this information and new ideas to be acted upon and is improved by strong ties. If these are kept in balance, the community can successfully foster entrepreneurship (Burt, 1999; Krebs & Holley, 2002).

2 **Recognize that the rapidly emerging "sharing economy" represents an important form of bridging social capital.** The "sharing economy" is a term employed for digital vehicles that are used to share knowledge and unused capability (known as "crowdsourcing") and available monetary resources ("crowdfunding"). The resources provided by these mechanisms are accessible by anyone, anywhere (Kraus et al., 2018) and are the consummate example of building weak ties for mutual benefit. When broadband is available, they can be easily incorporated into a rural entrepreneurial ecosystem.

3 **Strive to create and sustain a complete entrepreneurial ecosystem.** There are many definitions of "entrepreneurial ecosystem," but Cohen (2006: 3) captures the essence of the concept: "...an interconnected group of factors in a local geographic community committed to sustainable development through the support and facilitation of new sustainable ventures." While there is some disagreement as to what these "factors" are, there seems to be a general consensus that they include government, institutions of higher education, and industry (what some have called the "triple helix"), as well as support service providers (business and technical) and providers of financial capital (debt and equity). All of these factors should be linked via both formal and informal networks—social capital. In addition, it is now widely acknowledged that the "local geographic community" should have a culture of entrepreneurship. With this conception of what constitutes a full, or complete, entrepreneurial ecosystem in mind, the following recommendations for applying this to rural entrepreneurship are offered:

   a **Take a regional approach.** In rural areas, this is essential for reasons discussed earlier in this chapter.
   b **Start by ensuring the region has the capacity and capability to build and sustain an entrepreneurial ecosystem.** The Entrepreneurial Communities Framework (Markley et al., 2015) is both instructive and proven.
   c **Build a system for developing the skills of individual entrepreneurs.** The Advantage Valley ELS provides one model for doing this. E^2 (noted earlier in the chapter) is another. Whatever model is used, the focus should be on entrepreneurs before businesses and on developing their skills. To avoid guesswork relative to which skills need developing, it is useful to have a tool for assessing skills. Markley et al. (2015) provide a description of such a system in rural Australia.

d **Take a "big tent" approach to determining which entrepreneurs to help.** Rather than focusing exclusively on high-growth entrepreneurs, open the ecosystem to all entrepreneurs who are properly motivated to put in the work. Doing so creates a pipeline of entrepreneurs, and their enterprises, that is, more democratic and less likely to exacerbate economic inequalities (Lyons et al., 2018). A healthy rural regional economy is made of a diverse set of businesses, in terms of industry, stage of the business life cycle, skillset of the lead entrepreneur or team, and the gender, socioeconomic status, and ethnicity of entrepreneurs. These entrepreneurs may not start out with HGBs, but field research has shown that as their skills develop, so does their self-efficacy. This, in turn, causes them to "think bigger" about their enterprises (Lyons et al., 2018).

4 **Look for every opportunity to build social capital.** You can never have too much. Seek out more entrepreneurs and ESOs to connect to the ecosystem. Bridging social capital, in particular, is dynamic. The more links one creates, the denser the network becomes and the more quickly participants can find new connections (Baker et al., 2010).

5 **Maintain social capital.** Understand that building a rural entrepreneurial ecosystem **is** not the end, it's just the beginning. Time and resources must be invested in the routine maintenance of all of the networks. These are human networks; therefore, conflict is a given. Put procedures for managing conflict in place at the beginning of the effort (Lyons, 2002a).

Conclusion

Rural communities face daunting challenges to their economic and social well-being. While not a panacea, fostering entrepreneurship can help to address some of these issues by bringing much-needed innovation to these areas. This innovation can create economic wealth for rural individuals, families, and communities.

Fostering entrepreneurship in these areas is not without its challenges, however. A lack of economic critical mass limits resources and markets. Physical isolation limits access to sources of support and larger markets for local goods and services. This becomes a vicious cycle, as these limitations, in turn, limit the ability of rural enterprises to thrive and grow, making them less attractive to financial investment. Arguably, many of these challenges are the result of a lack of access to the networks that connect people, ideas, information, and resources.

This suggests that a viable solution lies in building, and in some cases rebuilding, these crucial networks among rural communities and with urban centers. This is the role of social capital building. It will take the creation and maintenance of both bonding and bridging social capital to make this possible. As demonstrated in this chapter, these forms of capital lie at the core of key best practices in encouraging rural entrepreneurship: take a regional approach, develop a culture of entrepreneurship, and focus on developing entrepreneurs as opposed to businesses.

A promising way to approach this is to create and maintain regional entrepreneurial ecosystems, which epitomize the use of social capital in their construction. A model for accomplishing this in a holistic way involves melding a system for preparing the "community" to understand, lead, and support an entrepreneurial ecosystem[3] and a system for developing the skills of entrepreneurs through coaching and targeted support.[4]

Acknowledgment

The author would like to thank Dustin Holmes, a graduate student at the University of Tennessee at Chattanooga, for his able assistance in carrying out some of the background research for this chapter.

Notes

1 It should be noted that Woolcock later added a third form of social capital, which he calls "linking social capital." He defines this as social capital that, like bridging social capital, builds linkages between the core community and the outside, but also helps to connect the community with other institutions in a hierarchy of authority (e.g.: state and federal government). See Szreter and Woolcock (2004).

2 For more information on the RISE, see Lyons et al. (2020).

3 Two books that provide insights into how to create the cultural capital needed for a successful rural entrepreneurial ecosystem are: Macke et al. (2014) and Markley et al. (2005).

4 For more information on skill-building in rural entrepreneurial ecosystems see Lyons et al. (2020). To learn more about the RISE assessment go to www.taketherise.com. Energizing Entrepreneurs (E^2) offers entrepreneurship coach training (go to www.energizingentrepreneurs.org for contact information).

References

Baker, E., Onyx, J., & Edwards, M. (2010). Emergence, social capital and entrepreneurship: Understanding networks from the inside. *Emergence, Complexity & Organization*, 13 (3): 21–38.

Baldacchino, L. (2009). Entrepreneurial creativity and innovation. Paper presented at First International Conference on Strategic Innovation and Future Creativity, Floriana, Malta, March 23.

Bauer, K. (2010). Training women for success: An evaluation of entrepreneurship training programs in Vermont, USA. *Journal of Entrepreneurship Education*, 14 (1): 1–24.

Besser, T.L., & Miller, N.J. (2013). Community matters: Successful entrepreneurship in remote rural U.S. locations. *International Journal of Entrepreneurship and Innovations*, 14 (1): 15–27.

Bhandari, H., & Yasunobu, K. (2009). What is social capital? A comprehensive review of the concept. *Asian Journal of Social Sciences*, 37 (3): 480–510.

Bourdieu, P. (1983). Forms of capital. In J.C. Richards (Ed.), *Handbook of theory and research for the sociology of education*. New York: Greenwood Press, pp. 241–258.

Brockhaus, R.H. (1982). The psychology of the entrepreneur. In C.L. Kent, D.L. Sexton, & K.N. Vesper (Eds.), *Encyclopedia of entrepreneurship*. Englewood Cliffs, NJ: Prentice-Hall, pp. 39–57.

Burt, R.S. (1999). Entrepreneurs, distrust, and third parties: A strategic look at the dark side of dense networks. In J.M. Levine, L.L. Thompson, & D.M. Messick. (Eds.), *Shared cognition in organizations: The management of knowledge*. Mahwah, NJ: Lawrence Erlbaum Associates, pp. 213–243.

Campopiano, G., Minola, T., & Sainaghi, R. (2016). Students climbing the entrepreneurial ladder: Family social capital and environment-related motives in hospitality and tourism. *International Journal of Contemporary Hospitality Management*, 28 (6): 1115–1136.

Carter, N.M., Gartner, W.B., Shaver, K.G., & Gatewood, E. (2003). The career reasons of nascent entrepreneurs. *Journal of Business Venturing*, 18 (1): 13–39.

Cohen, B. (2006). Sustainable valley entrepreneurial ecosystems. *Business Strategy and the Environment*, 15 (1): 1–14.

Cole, I.M. (2018). Unemployment and entrepreneurship in the mid-Atlantic region of the United States: A spatial panel data analysis. *Review of Regional Studies: Southern Regional Science Association*, 48 (3): 347–375.

Coleman, J.S. (1988). Social capital building in the creation of human capital. *American Journal of Sociology*, 94 (Supplement): S95–S119.

Coleman, J.S. (1994). *Foundations of social theory*. Cambridge, MA: Harvard University Press.

Dabson, B. (2007). Entrepreneurship as rural economic development policy: A changing paradigm. In N. Walzer (Ed.), *Entrepreneurship and local economic development*. Landham, MD: Lexington Books, pp. 21–37.

Deakins, D., Bensemann, J., & Battisti, M. (2016). Entrepreneurial skill and regulation: Evidence from primary sector rural entrepreneurs. *International Journal of Entrepreneurial Behaviour & Research*, 22 (2): 234–259.

Drabenstott, M., Novack, N., & Abraham, B. (2003). Main streets of tomorrow: Growing and financing rural entrepreneurs: A conference summary. *Economic Review, Federal Reserve Bank of Kansas City*, 88 (3): 73–84.

Dweck, C. (2006). *Mindset: The new psychology of success*. New York: Random House.

Flora, J.L., Sharp, J., Newlon, B.L., & Flora, C. (1997). Entrepreneurial social infrastructure and locally initiated economic development in the nonmetropolitan United States. *The Sociological Quarterly*, 38 (4): 623–645.

Florida, R. (2003). *The rise of the creative class*. New York: Basic Books.

Frazier, B., Stoel, L., Niehm, L., & Eckerson, N. (2013). Optimism for new business survival in rural communities: An institutional perspective. *Journal of Small Business & Entrepreneurship*, 26 (5): 443–462.

Frazier, B.J., & Niehm, L.S. (2004). Exploring business information networks of small retailers in rural communities. *Journal of Development Entrepreneurship*, 9 (1): 23–42.

Gerber, M.E. (1990). *The e-myth: Why most businesses don't work and what to do about it*. New York: HarperCollins.

Gomez, C., Perera, B.Y., Weisinger, J.Y., Tobey, D.H., & Zinsmeister-Teeters, T. (2015). The impact of immigrant entrepreneurs' social capital related motivations. *New England Journal of Entrepreneurship*, 18 (2): 19–29.

Gorman, G., Hanlon, D., & King, W. (1997). Some research perspectives on entrepreneurshipeducation, enterprise education and education for small business management: A ten-year literature review. *International Small Business Journal*, 15 (3): 56–77.

Govindarajan, V. (2010). Innovation is not creativity. Harvard Business Review (August 3). hbr.org/2010/08/innovation-is-not-creativity.html. Retrieved May 5, 2020.
Granovetter, M. (1985). Economic action and social structure: The problem of embeddedness. *American Journal of Sociology*, 91 (3): 481–510.
Greenberg, D.B., & Sexton, D.L. (1988). An interactive model of new venture initiation. *Journal of Small Business Management*, 26 (3): 1–7.
Grisham, Jr., V.L. (1999). *Tupelo: The evolution of a community*. Dayton, OH: Kettering Foundation Press.
Hanks, R.R. (2011). *Encyclopedia of geography, themes and concepts*. Santa Barbara, CA: ABC-CLIO.
Henderson, J. (2002). Building the rural economy with high-growth entrepreneurs. *Economic Review, Federal Reserve Bank of Kansas City*, 87 (QIII): 45–70.
Huefner, J.C., & Hunt, H.K. (1994). Broadening the concept of entrepreneurship: Comparing business and consumer entrepreneurs. *Entrepreneurship Theory and Practice*, 18 (3): 61–75.
Jacobs, J. (1961). *The death and life of Great American Cities*. New York: Random House.
Kassicieh, S.K., Radosevich, H.R., & Banbury, C.M. (1997). Using attitudinal, situational, and personal characteristics variables to predict future entrepreneurs from national laboratory inventors. *IEEE Transactions on Engineering Management*, 44 (3): 248–257.
Kraus, S., Palmer, C., Kailer, N., Kallinger, F.L., & Spitzer, J. (2018). Digital entrepreneurship: A research agenda on new business models for the twenty-first century. *International Journal of Entrepreneurial Behavior & Research*, 25 (2): 353–375.
Krebs, V., & Holley, J. (2002). *Rebuilding sustainable communities through network building*. Athens, OH: ACEnet.
Kutzhanova, N., Lyons, T.S., & Lichtenstein, G.A. (2009). Skill-based development of entrepreneurs and the role of personal and peer group coaching in enterprise development. *Economic Development Quarterly*, 23 (3): 193–210.
Lamb, W.B., & Sherman, H.D. (2010). Developing high-growth businesses in rural areas: A study of four U.S. states. *New England Journal of Entrepreneurship*, 13 (2): 9–19.
Leung, A., & Murray, D. (2009). Nurturing high-growth entrepreneurs in rural communities. *American Journal of Entrepreneurship*, 2 (1): 41+.
Levitte, Y. (2004). Bonding social capitalin entrepreneurial developing communities – survival networks or barriers? *Journal of the Community Development Society*, 35 (2): 44–64.
Liang, C., & Dunn, P. (2014). Examining entrepreneurial characteristics, motivations, barriers, and outcomes for small versus large multifunctional farmers in New England. *Journal of Business and Entrepreneurship*, 44–94.
Lichtenstein, G.A., & Lyons, T.S. (1996). *Incubating new enterprises*. Washington, DC: The Aspen Institute.
Lichtenstein, G.A., & Lyons, T.S. (2001). The entrepreneurial development system: Developing business talent and transforming community economies. *Economic Development Quarterly*, 15 (1): 3–20.
Lichtenstein, G.A., & Lyons, T.S. (2010). *Investing in entrepreneurs*. Santa Barbara, CA: Praeger/ABC-CLIO.
Lichtenstein, G.A., Lyons, T.S., & Kutzhanova, N. (2004). Building entrepreneurial communities: The appropriate role of enterprise development activities. *Journal of the Community Development Society*, 35 (1): 5–24.
Light, I., & Dana, L-P. (2013). Boundaries of social capital in entrepreneurship. *Entrepreneurship Theory & Practice*, 37 (3): 603–624.

Lin, N. (1999). Building a network theory of social capital. *Connections*, 22 (1): 28–51.
Loury, G. (1977). A dynamic theory of racial income differences. In P.A. Wallace & A. LaMond (Eds.), *Women, minorities and employment discrimination*. Lexington, MA: Lexington Books, pp. 153–186.
Lyons, T.S. (2002a). Building social capital for rural enterprise development: Three case studies in the United States. *Journal of Developmental Entrepreneurship*, 7 (2): 193–216.
Lyons, T.S. (2002b). *The entrepreneurial league system: Transforming your community's economy through enterprise development*. Washington, DC: The Appalachian Regional Commission.
Lyons, T.S., Alter, T.R., Audretsch, D., & Augustine, D. (2012). Entrepreneurship and community: The next frontier of entrepreneurship inquiry. *Entrepreneurship Research Journal*, 2 (1), Article 1. doi:10.2202/2157–5665.1064.
Lyons, T.S., Hamlin, R.E., & Hamlin, A. (2018). *Using entrepreneurship and social innovation to mitigate wealth inequality*. Boston, MA: DeGruyter.
Lyons, T.S., Lyons, J.S., & Jolley, G.J. (2020). Entrepreneurial skill-building in rural ecosystems: A framework for applying the Readiness Inventory for Successful Entrepreneurship (RISE). *Journal of Entrepreneurship and Public Policy*, 9 (1): 112–136.
Lyons, T.S., Miller, S.R., & Mann, J.T. (2018). A new role for land grant universities in the rural innovation ecosystem. *Journal of Regional Analysis & Policy*, 48 (2): 32–47.
Macht, S.A. (2016). Putting "entrepreneurial finance education on the map: Including social capital in the entrepreneurial finance curriculum. *Education + Training*, 58 (9): 984–1002.
Macke, D., Markley, D., & Fulwider, J. (2014). *Energizing entrepreneurial communities: A pathway to prosperity*. Lincoln, NE: Center for Rural Entrepreneurship.
Markley, D.M., Lyons, T.S., & Macke, D.W. (2015). Creating entrepreneurial communities: Building community capacity for ecosystem development. *Community Development*, 46 (5): 580–598.
Markley, D.M., Macke, D., & Luther. V.B. (2005). *Energizing entrepreneurs: Charting a course for rural communities*. Lincoln, NE: RUPRI Center for Rural Entrepreneurship and Heartland Center for Leadership Development.
Mayer, H., Habersetzer, A., & Meili, R. (2016). Rural-urban linkages and sustainable regional development: The role of entrepreneurs in linking peripheries and centers. *Sustainability*, 8 (8): 1–13.
McClelland, D.C., Atkinson, J.W., Clark, R.A., & Lowell, E.L. (1953). *The achievement motive*. Princeton, NJ: Van Nostrand.
McGranahan, D.A., Wojan, T.R., & Lambert, D.M. (2011). The rural trifecta: Outdoor amenities, creative class and entrepreneurial context. *Journal of Economic Geography*, 11 (3): 529–557.
Mickiewicz, T., Nyakudya, F.W., Theodorakopoulos, N., & Hart, M. (2016). Resource endowment and opportunity cost effects along the stages of entrepreneurship. *Small Business Economics*, 48: 953–976.
Miles, M.P., & Morrison, M. (2018). An effectual leadership perspective for developing rural entrepreneurial ecosystems. *Small Business Economics*, 1–17. doi:10.1007/s11187-018-0128-z.
Mitchell, D.T. (2015). Internal and external factors affecting the perception of entrepreneurial opportunities. *American Journal of Entrepreneurship*, 8 (1): 1–20.
Muller, S., & Korsgaard, S. (2017). Resources and bridging: The role of spatial context in rural entrepreneurship. *Entrepreneurship and Regional Development*, 30 (1–2): 224–255.
Neck, H.M., Greene, P.G., & Brush, C. (2014), *Teaching entrepreneurship: A practice-based approach*. Northampton, MA: Edward Elgar.

Neck, H.M., Neck, C.P., & Murray, E.L. (2018). *Entrepreneurship: The practice and mindset*. Los Angeles, CA: Sage.

Portes. A. (2014). Downsides of social capital. *PNAC*, 111 (52): 18407–18408.

Putnam, R.D. (2000). *Bowling alone: The collapse and revival of American Community*. New York: Simon and Schuster.

Ring, J.K., Peredo, A.M., & Chrisman, J.J. (2010). Business networks and economic development in rural communities in the United States. *Entrepreneurship Theory and Practice*, 34 (1): 171–195.

Robinson, S. (2006). Staying put: Self-employment rates among non-movers. *Academy of Entrepreneurship Journal*, 12 (1): 119–128.

Robinson, S., & Finley, J.T. (2007). Rural women's self-employment: A look at Pennsylvania. *Academy of Entrepreneurship Journal*, 13 (2): 21–30.

Robinson, S., & Shah, S. (2004). Delving into the digital divide: Computer use among the self-employed in metropolitan and nonmetropolitan areas. *Academy of Entrepreneurship Journal*, 10 (1–2): 115–126.

Rupasingha, A., & Contreras, S. (2014). Factors affecting spatial variation of microenterprises in the rural United States. *American Journal of Entrepreneurship*, 7 (2): 17–31.

Schumpeter, J. (1991). Comments on a plan for the study of entrepreneurship. In R. Swedberg (Ed.), *Joseph A. Schumpeter: The economics and sociology of capitalism*. Princeton, NJ: Princeton University Press, pp. 406–428.

Seely, J., Sim, A., & Loosely, E. (1956). *Crestwood heights: A study of the culture of suburban life*. New York: Basic Books.

Servon, L.J. (1998). Credit and social capital: The community development potential of U.S. microenterprise programs. *Housing Policy Debate*, 9 (1): 115–149.

Shields, J.F. (2005). Does rural location matter? The significance of a rural setting for small businesses. *Journal of Developmental Entrepreneurship*, 10 (1): 49–63.

Smith, M.K. (2000–2009). "Social capital," The encyclopedia of pedagogy and informal education. https://infed.org/mobi/social-capital/. Retrieved May 1, 2020.

Sternberg, R. (2009). Regional dimensions of entrepreneurship. *Foundations and Trends in Entrepreneurship*, 5 (4): 211–340.

Szreter, S., & Woolcock, M. (2004). Health by association? Social capital, social theory, and the political economy of public health. *International Journal of Epidemiology*, 33 (4): 650–667.

Timmons, J.A., Smollen, L.E., & Dingee, A.L.M. (1985). *New venture creation*, 2nd ed., Homewood, IL: Irwin Publishing.

Tolbert, C.M., Lyson, T.A., & Irwin, M.D. (1998). Local capitalism, civic engagement, and socioeconomic well being. *Social Forces*, 77 (2): 401–427.

Woolcock, M. (2001). The place of social capital in understanding social and economic outcomes. *Isuma:Canadian Journal of Policy Research* 2: 11–17.

Yu, L., & Artz, G.M. (2019). Does rural entrepreneurship pay? *Small Business Economics*, 53 (3): 647–668.

6

RURAL INNOVATION AT THE COMMUNITY LEVEL

Cornelia Butler Flora

Introduction

Rural people are as innovative as urban people, perhaps more so, as they must resolve issues for which urban dwellers could purchase solutions. Innovation is not just filing a patent, but also includes finding ways to use existing resources more effectively for achieving community well-being. This entails strengthening community capital—natural, cultural, human, social, political, financial, and built—to achieve a healthy ecosystem, economic security for all, and social inclusion (Flora et al., 2016). Innovations can in fact occur at the individual, the firm, or the community level. Our research found that innovation at the community level contributes to innovations at the other two levels in rural communities, despite the challenges of low population density and relative social isolation (Flora and Flora, 1993; Flora et al., 1997). While often innovation is deemed successful when linked to economic development (increasing built capital to increase financial capital), the other capitals are equally important to rural communities. As populations gradually decline in rural communities "shrinking smart" (Peters et al., 2018) becomes part of that innovation.

Entrepreneurial Social Infrastructure (ESI), a whole ecosystem approach, building on the concept of social infrastructure (Swanson, 1992), is a basis of community level innovation (Flora et al., 1997). ESI does not just increase income, although it can mean better distribution of resources within the community. ESI provides the context for innovation by community members individually and collectively. ESI can result in healthy local ecosystems, economic security for all community members, and social inclusion of diverse community members in horizontal and vertical networks, mobilization of resources, and legitimization of alternatives when seeking innovations to enhance the common good. ESI sees

DOI: 10.4324/9781003178552-6

the rural community as a system, based on interactions, rather than simply the sum of the individuals and separate resources in a physical location.

In this chapter, we will use Buena Vista County, Iowa, as an example of ESI in practice. The county's population peaked at 20,622 in 2014. In 2020 its population was estimated to be 19,418. Storm Lake is Buena Vista County's largest community and county seat, with a population of 10,166 in 2020. There are nine other cities in Buena Vista County, which are divided into 20 townships. Buena Vista is an agricultural county, with row crops and animal agriculture. It was hit hard by the 2020 drought and designated as a Primary Natural Disaster Area, with farmers with crop losses eligible for U.S. Department of Agriculture Farm Service Agency emergency loans.

Many indigenous groups passed through the area before colonization by white settlers, who destroyed the buffalo. The first colonists from the eastern United States had small crop and livestock farms and slaughtered their own animals. Gradually, local slaughterhouses were built for the animals not driven to market towns. With the coming of the railroad, hogs and cattle could be shipped live to packers in Chicago and other places. But with the coming of refrigeration, it was more efficient to ship the carcasses of beef and pork. The local plants grew to butcher and cut up the animals for local consumption and shipment to major meat packers. The workers in those plants were unionized. As the power of the highly centralized meat industry increased, local slaughterhouses declined. The unions that supported local workers were broken as local slaughterhouses were bought out by larger meat conglomerates, wages went down, and workers were recruited from around the world (Specht, 2019). The county is now home to a major meat packing plant run by one of the four dominant meat packing companies, Tyson Fresh Meats, the largest employer in the county.

Buena Vista's population is very diverse. The largest ethnic group is Hispanic (38.9% of the population), followed by non-Hispanic white (32.2%), Asian and Pacific Islander (20.5%), Black (3.7%), and the rest of the population of multiple ethnic origins. This results in a wide range of languages and cultures within the community.

That ethnic diversity is echoed in the businesses in town. While Tyson Foods is a multinational corporation, most of the other businesses in town are locally owned, including one of the two local newspapers. *The Storm Lake Times* was started by newspaper professionals with Buena Vista County roots in 1990 (Cullen, 2018), when the previously locally owned newspaper, *The Storm Lake Pilot Tribune*, was bought out by a newspaper company, Northwest Iowa Publishing, which oversees two other newspapers in northwest Iowa and is part of Rust Communications, which publishes more than 40 community newspapers in nine states. Both newspapers continue to publish in the community, although *The Storm Lake Pilot Tribune* has cut back to one print issue a week due to the coronavirus and *The Storm Lake Times* prints twice a week. Both thoroughly cover local sports, in the high school, the college, and the adult sports clubs with copy and photographs. The locally owned *Storm Lake Times* has the largest newspaper readership in the county.

Like other small towns, the local pharmacist/drug stores have been replaced by chains, which have centralized clerical personnel to handle the complexities of various health insurance requirements. Other retailers, especially those that also offered services, like jewelers, barbers, landscapers, and hairdressers, remain as locally owned businesses in Storm Lake, Alta, and other towns in the county. There are small, specialized grocers, as well as regional and national chains. And there are many ethnic restaurants as well as fast food chains.

Buena Vista University is in Storm Lake. Despite national trends of declining enrollments, its enrollment was up in the fall of 2020. It offers online and face-to-face classes for bachelor and master's degrees. The student body is diverse and appreciated in the community. A freshman, Diego Aguilera, came to Storm Lake from Texas to be on the Buena Vista wrestling team. The college helped him find a part-time job at the Storm Lake Walmart (local businesses cooperate with the college to provide jobs for their students). On his first day at work, he saved the life of an older co-worker having a heart attack, noting him clutch his chest and slump over a box of bananas, saying he did not feel well and could not breath. Aguilera checked for the man's pulse and could not find it. He started chest compressions—which he learned through CRP training in high school wrestling. Once the man gained consciousness, Aguilera asked him questions to help him stay awake. He was able to notify the manager, who called the police and an ambulance, which took the man to the Buena Vista Regional Medical Center in Storm Lake and then to a hospital in Sioux City, where he recovered in intensive care (Goodwin, 2020). Diversity and an atmosphere of support for individual initiative for the common good saved a life and integrate even further into the Storm Lake community.

The industrial park, long empty, recently attracted two new tenants: Columbia Gas of Virginia and Indiana-based NIBCO, a valve and flow control device manufacturer, which purchased a former auto parts plant in the county. These businesses build on the human, natural, and built capital of the county.

Symbolic Diversity

Instead of fostering conflict or superficial harmony, symbolic diversity allows communities to engage in constructive controversy to arrive at workable community decisions by focusing on community processes, depersonalization of politics, and broadening of community boundaries. While *The Storm Lake Times* has an editorial stance, letters to the editor and events covered include a wide range of political views. This openness to alternative solutions helps as the community finds ways to act together around shared values, recognizing there is more than one way to move the community forward in an inclusive way.

An ex-Storm Lake resident wrote to *The Storm Lake Times* from Minneapolis, where she was surprised by the deep racial disparities there.

> In conversations on the topic, I told people about Storm Lake, a shining example of how the American dream is still a reality for so many immigrant

> families. I spoke proudly of how my community rose to the transitions in the 30 years I lived there. The churches, schools, healthcare providers and police force all took on the challenges to keep Storm Lake a great place.
>
> *(Douglas, 2020)*

These innovations were built on relationships of trust and mutual respect that sought to include new people and ideas.

There is a great appreciation of diversity and openness to new residents present in the churches, schools, and civic organizations. Many promigrant articles and letters appear in *The Storm Lake Times*. Activities in the community reflect the proposition that diversity is an asset—one that is missed when one leaves the community. A letter to the *Times* from an ex-resident, who had moved to a much larger city, wrote nostalgically of the wonderful choices of restaurants and types of food offered in Storm Lake—and not found in the larger community.

There is general recognition that you can disagree with someone on one issue, agree on another, and find common ground on a third. Controversy arises around means to an end: a healthy community, not the end itself. Controversy and the space to discuss differences without imputing the character or heritage of the person one disagrees with is very different than conflict, where strong barriers are erected, and those "on the other side" are clearly morally and intellectually inferior. And people who strongly disagree about the presidential candidates can work together to figure out the best way to keep children educated during a pandemic.

For example, while Tyson was faulted for not releasing data on COVID-19 among its workers, it was lauded for providing protein to food pantries—and their workers—through undeliverable, but perfectly good pallets of food. There are many service organizations in Buena Vista County organizing the food pantries, which are facing increasing demand as the COVID-19 shutdown continues.

Each issue of *The Storm Lake Times* has a From the Pulpit column from the diversity of pastors serving the 46 churches in the county, all Christian, but with widely different theological stances. Despite the differences, each pastor's columns stress collaboration over conflict and the power of loving God and loving one's neighbor.

Networks

Storm Lake offers many ways for diverse groups to form and for informal gatherings. Besides the school athletic events, adult sports leagues exist, including an adult soccer league. There are six sports bars, so adults can get together after a game. Most important, community institutions and individuals are constantly seeking new ways to interact with different people in different places within the county. These innovations influence the growing arts community, which, in turn, involves new people in creative networks.

Locally owned businesses and many community events, from concerts, sporting events, and fishing and boating activities, provide numerous opportunities for residents to interact with a wide range of fellow community members in non-threatening ways. Local businesses and community organizations are constantly finding new ways of getting the community together, even doing it safely during the pandemic.

Like other police departments around the nation, the Storm Lake Police Department (SLPD) received a military surplus Humvee for off-road use. The SLPD sought more contact with people in the neighborhoods, so they decided to give out ice cream cones, popsicles, and Klondike bars. But the frozen treats often melted before they could be distributed. They repurposed the Humvee into an ice cream truck—a Yumvee—by adding a freezer and magnetic decals, with a community grant from Tyson Foods. The signs are removed for police enforcement matters, but everyone knows the Yumvee is the police. The SLPD got the idea from a police department in Pittsfield, Massachusetts. They were able to use their vertical networks with other police departments to strengthen horizontal networks within the community to innovate to increase trust throughout the community. As Police Chief Chris Cole says, "Who doesn't like free ice cream?" (D. Cullen, 2020a).

The innovative ways of building networks among people who might not ordinarily get together served to build empathy among diverse community members—a key attribute of community building (Beradi et al., 2020).

Mobilization of Resources

Generating Resources within the Community

Local organizations have innovative ways of raising funds, materials, and people for community projects from within the community. The lake provides opportunities for all sorts of civic activities, such as Rotary Club's fundraiser that sells tickets with a preprinted date and time when a car parked on the ice on the lake sinks. Called the "Car Plunge" fundraiser, it awards a cash prize for the person with the right ticket and raises funds for the club's civic activities. Local tow trucks and a dive team pull the car out of the lake, to clean up to be ready for the next year's event.

Relative Equity in Resource Access

There is a fair amount of poverty in Buena Vista County, made worse by COVID-19. In Alta, a small town in Buena Vista County, City Councilman Tom Lane, a resident of Westview Mobile Home Park, has two other jobs, one paid and the other volunteer. Besides his work at Harold Rowley Recycling Center, he runs a food distribution program for the park. The residents, often food insecure, are more so during the COVID-19 outbreak. He delivers vegetables from his organic garden, plus food that did not sell at the local Hy-Vee grocery store the previous week. TeamCAN, the organizing arm of the Teamsters

Union, helps deliver the produce from his garden to other locations. His linkages to his neighbors in the mobile home park helped him save the park when the city council considered condemning it. Now his fellow council members are planning to convene civic organizations to help, as his back problems are worsening (T. Cullen, 2020b). This type of innovative generosity and network building go together to build social inclusion for all and sharing critical resources for community well-being.

Distributed Risk

Buena Vista residents blocked the construction of a paper and packaging company in 2005 out of concern about the increased truck traffic and exhaust fumes would come from the plant and affect the town and its future. The entire county was concerned about the potential damage to the health of those who lived near the plant.

Despite the fact that Iowa does not have a mask mandate, Storm Lake does have a mandate and the police enforce it. There are some people concerned about the schools not having face-to-face instruction, and they voice their concern to the school boards in the county. There are regular discussions about the conflicting needs of children with respect to the social interaction that goes with learning, and the desire to keep children and their families safe.

Schooling by distance requires relatively expensive technology. While there are efforts to provide each child with a laptop, connectivity is not always easy. The schools work hard to keep the children safe and enhance learning in very difficult circumstances. Delivery of lunches and breakfasts by volunteers to those who are studying from home helps ensure that no child will be too hungry to learn. There is a recognition that everyone in the community does well when children learn and individuals and organizations in the community innovate to make sure all children can reach their potential.

Investment of Residents of Their Own Private Capitals Locally

There is a local bank, Security Trust and Savings, that offers a wide number of services. As it is embedded in the community, residents can seek loans to implement their entrepreneurial ideas.

The town's only bait shop closed because the bar and grill in the Marina would not renew their contract with the city. And the bait shop was really missed! Fishing is a 24 hour a day activity in Buena Vista County, and driving an hour to get minnows, chubs, or night crawlers was difficult. Tom Cowell and Mike Keith determined to set up a new bait shop, using Keith's Power Washing (which used to be Oatman's Conoco Station) as the site. Called Big Belly Baits, after the two proprietors, who are large men, they set up a couple of bait tanks and refrigerators. A self-serve station was put up to be able to offer bait 24/7, with a lockbox with a slot for customers outside. There were problems at first. The bait tank with minnows quit functioning, and all the fish died. They put out word they needed another bait tank. Three of them were donated and brought to the shop, with the correct filters rigged up. Business is brisk. Tom and Mike enjoy talking to their fellow anglers and sharing knowledge about the lake, which was dredged and seeded with mussels, which cleaned up the water, which then encouraged water weeds, which nourished the fish, whose size is increasing (D. Cullen, 2020c). The multiple investments, by the Iowa Department of Natural Resources in natural capital in dredging the lake, in cultural capital in terms of linking anglers together around shared values, human capital (the knowledge of the proprietors about the fish and about the machinery), social capital (the networks that led to the tank donations), the political capital (which worked with the state to improve the condition of the lake), financial capital to purchase the inventory, and built capital (the tanks and the existing business space) led to a successful innovative business and enhanced quality of life in Buena Vista County.

When bars were closed by the governor due to COVID-19, Crystal Gronau, the owner of the bar, Brewster's, in Storm Lake, decided it was a good time to remodel. Most supplies and labor were provided by her customers. And the result is creative and impressive—the headline of the story about this innovative process read "From so-so to sensational" (Storm Lake Times, May 13, 2020).

Collective Investment in the Community

In September 2019, Storm Lake voters approved a $15 million school bond issue, 61.16% to 38.84%, to construct a new public elementary school. That meant that property taxes increase $85 per year per $100,000 of valuation.

The town of Storm Lake is on the edge of Storm Lake, from which it gets its name. Storm Lake is the western boundary of the town and the center of Buena Vista County. The lake provides an impetus for tourism and recreation. Ex-residents of Storm Lake continue to contribute to making the lake an attractive place to visit. The Spooner family came to Storm Lake to farm in 1870 and then they opened an insurance business and descents ran a downtown variety store. Jim Spooner and his family, whose mother at 97 is in Methodist Manner, visit often. They have built a 45-foot cobblestone structure with a bench and a sign that says Storm Lake by the edge of the lake. The construction is one of many donated by the public to enhance the area. Such private innovative investments in the common good are common.

Legitimacy of Alternatives

For Latinx in the community, the 15th birthday party is a huge celebration, a tradition difficult to keep with social distancing and the desire to keep everyone healthy. In Storm Lake, the Catarino family organized an amazing drive-by *Quinceañera* for their daughter, Ximena. They had wanted to originally have the celebration in Mexico, but travel was impossible due to COVID-19, so they innovated in a way that included the entire community of Storm Lake. A good time was reported to have been had by all, as many in the county drove by to wish her well and receive a celebratory balloon (D. Cullen, 2020c).

There is much discussion over chicken raising in town. The current regulation allows it only on lots twice the normal size. This is defended to protect town cleanliness. Others see urban chickens as a source of organic chicken eggs and a stewing hen from time to time for the family. The "chicken man," Tim Humes, wears a chicken hat in meetings to make sure the point is made to persuade the City Council to change the regulation. Innovations require changes in political capital that influence rules and regulations as well as good ideas.

Conclusions

Given the volatility in markets and climate, the ability of communities to constantly innovate is imperative. Green (2020) and others write about the danger of rural economies left behind with deindustrialization. Buena Vista County demonstrates the importance of multiple sources of innovation and the social relationships necessary for those innovations to be incorporated into the community.

In Buena Vista County, the innovations that emerge are based on social relationships and utilizing all community capitals, as has occurred in many different places in the world (Altenburg, 2009; Harmon et al., 2020). The diversity within the community, the multiple networks, and the mobilization of multiple resources has led to norms of reciprocity and the ability to disagree without being disagreeable. Security is gained through mutual trust. Thus, Big Belly Baits leaves night crawlers available in the outdoor refrigerator with the paybox 24/7, as mutual trust with those in the community provides security. All community capitals are mobilized for community well-being, so that everyone can give, and everyone can receive. Embeddedness is very important, and the various institutions—including the churches, the businesses, and the schools—are inclusive, respectful of other institutions, and balance the capitals they invest. From the communication that comes from the "exiles" who move to be near children or take new jobs, the embeddedness lasts.

The two newspapers, which are both newsprint and digital, provide a mechanism for awareness in the community not only of common concerns but also of alternative ways of building a better community. Community initiative, responsibility, and adaptability is evident historically and in response to the climate and COVID-19 crises. There is a shared vision for the county as inherently innovative, with a focus on internal resources, collectively seeking alternative ways to respond to constant changes, and little sense of a victim mentality.

While economic security is desired for all, members and groups in the community recognize that it is particularly difficult in these times of crisis. Thus, community efforts to ensure the physical well-being of each person and household are shifted from charity to fellowship. Rural innovation is occurring continuously at the community level.

References

Altenburg, T. 2009. Building inclusive innovation systems in developing countries: challenges for IS research. In B. Lundvall, K. Joseph, C. Chaminade, & J. Vang (Eds.), *Handbook of Innovation Systems in Developing Countries: Building Domestic Capabilities in a Global Setting* (pp. 33–56). Cheltenham: Edward Elgar Publishing.

Berardi, M. K., A. M. White, D. Winters, K. Thorn, M. Brennan, and P. Dolan. 2020. Rebuilding communities with empathy. *Local Development and Society*. 1: 57–67.

Cullen, A. 2018. *Storm Lake: Change, Resilience, and Hope in America's Heartland*. New York, NY: Viking.

Cullen, D. 2020a. Storm Lake police deploy 'Yumvee' to city's neighborhoods. *Storm Lake Times*. September 18.

Cullen, D. 2020b. Turning 15 in a pandemic. *Storm Lake Times*. May 20.

Cullen, D. 2020c. It's tough luring big bellies without some decent chubs. *Storm Lake Times*. July 17.

Cullen, T. 2020. A man with a mission. *Storm Lake Times*. September 18.

Douglas, W. 2020. To my friends back in Iowa, Letter to the Editor, *Storm Lake Times*. October 2.

Flora, C. B., and J. L. Flora. 1993. Entrepreneurial social infrastructure: a necessary ingredient. *Annals of the American Academy of Political and Social Science*. 529: 48–58.

Flora, C. B., J. L. Flora, and S. P. Gasteyer. 2016. *Rural Communities: Legacy and Change*. Boulder, CO: Westview Press.

Flora, J. L., J. Sharp, C. B. Flora, and B. Newlon. 1997. Entrepreneurial social infrastructure and locally initiated economic development in the nonmetropolitan United States. *The Sociological Quarterly*. 38: 623–645.

Goodwin, C. 2020. What a first day on the job: a Buena Vista freshman wrestler, new to Iowa, helps save a co-workers life. *Des Moines Register*. September 30.

Green, G. P. 2020. Deindustrialization of rural America: economic restructuring and the rural ghetto. *Local Development and Society*. 1: 15–25.

Harmon, U., H. Ross, and J. Cavaye. 2020. Using the community capitals framework to understand the potential for inclusive innovation. In P.R. Lachapelle, I. Gutierrez-Montes, and C. B. Flora (Eds.), *Community Capacity and Resilience in Latin America* (pp. 129–152). New York: Routledge.

Peters, D. J., S. Hamideh, K. E. Zarecor, and M. Ghandour. 2018. Using entrepreneurial social infrastructure to understand smart shrinkage in small towns. *Journal of Rural Studies*. 64: 39–49.

Sprecht, J. 2019. *Red Meat Republic: A Hoof-to-Table History of How Beef Changed America*. Princeton, NJ: Princeton University Press.

Swanson, L. 1992. Rural social infrastructure. In T. Rowley, D. Sears, G. Nelson, N. Reid, and M. Yetley (Eds.), *Rural Development Research: Foundations of Policy* (Ch. 7) (pp. 102–122). Westport, CT: Greenwood Press.

7

EMBRACING UNCERTAINTY AND ANTIFRAGILITY IN RURAL INNOVATION AND ENTREPRENEURSHIP

Michael W.P. Fortunato and Theodore R. Alter

Introduction

In this chapter, we highlight the contributions of *antifragility* as a central philosophy for building self-sustaining systems of rural innovation and entrepreneurship that are self-improving and continuously adaptable. That which is *antifragile* is not merely robust to shocks—it is any category of things that loves, seeks out, and embraces volatility the way that oxygen is drawn into a fire. While a person can be (and technically is) antifragile in a biological sense, the term is more often used in the context of complex systems under conditions of uncertainty and volatility, and it is especially useful when thinking about those systems involving human action, decision-making, and the realm of the possible. We argue that the antifragility of systems both creates and is reinforced by *innovation*. We will also make the argument that the special conditions facing rural innovation and the cultivation of entrepreneurial ecosystems requires a rather different approach than the policy and practice recommendations found in much of the current entrepreneurial ecosystem literature—a corpus that primarily draws its practitioner knowledge from larger cities and more developed economies (Roundy, 2017).

The notion that social systems can improve in response to some degree of random disorder and disruption and not just return to a previous state of being is not new and is reflected in theories ranging from entrepreneurship (Schumpeter, 1934) to governance (Ostrom, 1993, 1999), economics to communities (Park, 1925, 1928), ecology, to business. While economic and community development practice seeks to find common ground across diverse actors and development strategies, a lesser focus has been on ways to embrace complexity, randomness, individuality, autonomy, and innovation as drivers of growth and development—while respecting and building a sense of community connectedness from the illusion of disconnected action. Recognizing that many rural ecosystems do not have the complete

DOI: 10.4324/9781003178552-7

set of physical, social, and institutional infrastructure that is often recommended by the literature for ecosystem effectiveness, and that most rural ecosystems will "fly under the radar" of most measures of productive ecosystem outputs due to a low density of high-growth companies—does this mean that rural areas cannot cultivate innovation competitively or build an effective ecosystem? We present Nassim Nicholas Taleb's (2012) concept of *antifragility* as a potential alternative rural ecosystem logic for building a creative, innovative, and enterprising community in low-density areas possessing different cultural values from urban regions.

We begin this chapter with a brief discussion of risk and uncertainty, and why they matter to innovation and entrepreneurship. We then provide a rich description of key ideas from antifragility theory that have specific importance to managing risk, uncertainty, and randomness and can be used in any environment, including in rural places. We then shift our focus to the ecosystem literature to unpack the urban bias in ecosystem development, and to understand how approaches rooted in antifragility and community development can provide alternative pathways to ecosystem building. We conclude the chapter with a brief set of practitioner points grounded in these ideas that any rural ecosystem builder can use to enhance their practice and contribute to building a healthy ecosystem that improves local well-being in places of any size and stage of development.

Innovation, Uncertainty, and Entrepreneurship

Innovation is an enticing topic because of its positive connotations: it is credited as being the wellspring of new ideas, new businesses, and solutions to everyday challenges. The centrality of innovation as the primary driver of entrepreneurship and economic development can be traced to Schumpeter (1934), who saw innovation as giving way to *creative destruction,* or the replacement of old, antiquated models of economic organization with newer business models that improve upon prior approaches and technologies. *Creative destruction* is a glass half-full or half-empty notion. The obsolescence of legacy industries has been a driver of the structural unemployment and economic stagnation seen in regions like America's Rust Belt, particularly in rural areas (Falk and Lobao, 2003). However, it is equally seen as the driver of beneficial innovations necessary for economic growth and the betterment of humanity. Recent studies describe a strong link between innovation, entrepreneurship, and economic development contingent upon the role of institutions and a favorable climate (Acs, Desai and Hessels, 2008; Acs and Szerb, 2007; Galindo and Méndez-Picazo, 2013; Wong, Ho and Autio, 2005), and the link between entrepreneurship, creativity, and economic growth is equally pronounced even in lagging regions of the United States (Stephens, Patridge and Faggian, 2013). While it is no "silver bullet," the role of entrepreneurship and innovation in stimulating economic growth and wealth creation is basic knowledge in economic development circles, even if the nature of innovation (i.e., whether high- or low-tech has a greater sustained impact on human well-being) is less clear (Isenberg, 2010).

Less of a focus, perhaps due to its negative connotations, are *risk* and *uncertainty*. While it is broadly understood that risk is essential to return, there is a great deal of effort given to reducing risk through the institutionalization of economic action, from systematizing innovation processes to creating universal "best practices" for success. *Risk* is a relatively easy concept to understand: it is the assignment of known probabilities to a set of known outcomes, much like one encounters when playing craps in a local casino. *Uncertainty* is more nuanced: this occurs, for example, when the outcomes of a situation are known, but the probabilities attached to each situation are unknown (Knight, 1921). However, most innovation and entrepreneurship situations do not even deal with known sets of outcomes, but rather what Knight (1921) coined as *Knightian uncertainty,* where neither probabilities *nor* the potential outcomes of a situation are known. Put differently, Kay and King (2020) quote Donald Rumsfeld, responding to the events of September 11, 2001, as saying,

> There are known knowns; there are the things we know we know. We also know there are known unknowns; that is to say we know there are some things we do not know. But there are also unknown unknowns—the ones we don't know we don't know.
>
> *(p. 7)*

This is an excellent description of *risk, uncertainty,* and *Knightian uncertainty,* respectively.

Knightian uncertainty is what the average entrepreneur experiences, even though it is called "risk" by most people, and profit is the reward for engaging with this level of uncertainty (Knight, 1921). Auerswald (2015) cites Schumpeterian entrepreneurship as embracing Knightian complexity in this manner, as "an inherently disequilibrium phenomenon that takes place in a world characterized by uncertainty, asymmetric information, indivisibilities, and non-zero transaction costs (p. 9)." Knightian uncertainty and information asymmetries typically do not deter entrepreneurs. Isenberg (2011) argues that entrepreneurs muster the courage to launch innovative businesses because they think they know something that the market does not—even to the point of overestimating their own abilities and capacities (Camerer and Lovallo, 1999). As long as this process of launching a new venture so that failures are relatively small-scale and isolated (i.e., limited downside), the upside growth of even a single success can have an important impact on the overall economy. It is when institutions, scientists, and governments attempt to tame such uncertainty by treating it as *risk* that models are employed that do not fit the complexity of the real world very well, leading sometimes to large-scale undesirable effects (Kay and King, 2020). For example,

> in the run-up to the global financial crisis, as in the preparations for the Abbottabad raid [to eliminate Osama bin Laden], policy advisers not only chose to express uncertainties as probabilities, but were required to do so...

> this expression of uncertainty was at best unhelpful and at worst actively misleading.
>
> *(Kay and King, 2020, p. 9)*

Kay and King (2020) warn of the dangers of attempting to tame uncertainty through probabilistic reasoning, and the hidden (but severe) consequences that are often the result—ideas that have "infected other areas of social science [besides economics], including statistics, sociology and psychology, and even the law (p. 15)." They warn that few world problems can be expressed probabilistically, and unlike economic thought, most real households and businesses (entrepreneurs included) do not optimize. They *cope* by making decisions incrementally and "try to find outcomes that are better and avoid outcomes that are worse (p. 41)." To these economists and others, the global quest to remove uncertainty from everyday economic life is counterproductive, since most innovations are, by definition, born from what is unknown rather than what is known. In this way, complexity is the engine that conserves uncertainty in the system, producing ongoing opportunities for new ideas to emerge and for old ideas to intersect in new ways, all of which create novel and innovative outcomes (Kay and King, 2020).

Antifragility

In a similar fashion, Nassim Nicholas Taleb's 2012 book *Antifragile*[1] catalyzed a vociferous debate about the hidden risks of these institutional attempts to remove risk in everything from medicine to computers, governments to social systems. At the heart of this debate is Taleb's criticism of the human impulse to control human behavior and action using statistical techniques as support, with the unintended (and nearly universal) result of exposing entire human systems—organizations, communities, and nation states—to the effects of black swans. Black swans are rare surprise events with outsized, totally unexpected outcomes. They can be very negative, as in a stock market crash, or very positive, as in the development of new, disruptive technologies and ideas that improve lifestyles. Thus, Taleb asks how organizations, communities, and societies can organize themselves to benefit rather than suffer from uncertainty and disorder, embracing shocks and stressors as the necessary fuel for productive, creative new ideas. This benefit from disorder is called *antifragility*, and it describes perpetual improvement because of noncatastrophic (and sometimes catastrophic) disorder—standing in stark contrast to *resilience*, which is the phenomenon of bouncing back to a previous state of normality.

Taleb notes that many people see *robust* or *resilient* as the opposite of *fragile*. Instead of a coffee mug, we might think of a brick that, upon hitting the floor, remains unharmed and unchanged. For some, this is an ideal and very comfortable state of the world, one that is safe and predictable and relatively unchanging over time. However, Taleb points out that this state tends toward fragility over time in a world where change is inevitable. Besides, this state of 'unchangedness' is not the opposite of fragility, but rather a neutral category of things that ignore volatility and stress. Even fortresses and castles fall eventually, and nearly all empires. What, then, would represent the true *opposite* of fragility? It would be something truly *antifragile,* that which *loves* disorder, volatility, and uncertainty, and that *benefits and improves* through stress. What in the world would constitute such a class of things that benefits from stress? In truth, nearly all complex systems on the planet fall into this category. It represents the class of things that are themselves complex, self-organizing and self-correcting, and nonlinear; versus that class of things that is rigid, predictable, mechanical, explained by cause-and-effect, and linear.

As Taleb states, think of a glass vase (fragile) compared to your hyperactive nephew (antifragile, and smarter for having scuffed his knee at the playground today); a washing machine (linear and fragile) compared to a cat (self-correcting, learning, sensing, nonlinear, and antifragile). Nearly all complex systems on the planet *require* stressors to become stronger and are thus antifragile. The human immune system requires exposure to disease to build immune system antibodies that protect it in the future. Strength training requires breaking down muscle tissue so it can build back stronger. Forest ecosystems require occasional fires to clear underbrush and reduce the local parasite count (an important point for later when we discuss ecosystems). Even democracy itself requires ideological challenge and conflict to build stronger ideas and compromises when it works properly. Taleb endorses the old maxim: that which does not kill you nearly always makes you stronger.

Dealing with risk and uncertainty is basic to any new venture and might seem even more pronounced when building an ecosystem (i.e., risky ventures coming together to support other risky ventures). However, an antifragile approach recognizes that *overcorrection* and *overengineering solutions* instead of dealing with shocks in small doses often create surplus risk that can be avoided by working *with* rather than *against* the current of the local cultural and historical context. While *Antifragile* is a dense book with many important concepts, the central ideas of greatest interest to ecosystem builders and entrepreneurial supporters are, in our estimation, the following:

1 *Risk is good if it is done well.* The main goal of an antifragile system is to not shy away from risk, but rather, recognize that risk can be *internal* or *external.* External risks should be minimized by decreasing exposure, while internal risks can be embraced. The latter are risks that the community controls, such as well-targeted business ventures that leverage local capital and talent, where pivots (changes in strategy) can be locally directed relatively quickly and easily. It is easier to control your product mix based on customer feedback than to control whether you will experience a flood this year by locating your business deep in a river valley.
2 *More options are better in the long run.* There is a difference between investing $5M on one economic development initiative, like a stadium or recruitment

of a branch plant; compared to spending $50,000 on 100 different initiatives with diverse risk profiles. It is helpful to have a solid economic base first prior to taking systemic risks, but this is one of the main challenges faced by many rural communities that find themselves in a strapped economic position (Dabson, 2001; Miles and Morrison, 2020; Roundy, 2017). But smaller, rural communities can take 10% of the money they would spend on economic development and public works and invest it in citizen-driven initiatives aimed at a plurality of entrepreneurial ideas. When mixed with education/mentorship (Lichtenstein and Lyons, 2010), with access to resources (Isenberg, 2011), and with positive business networks (Hoyos-Ruperto, Romaguera, Carlsson and Lyytinen, 2013), the likelihood that at least one entrepreneurial investment will succeed is high. Like a well-diversified investment portfolio, smaller, diverse investments outperform larger, monolithic investments in the long term.

3 *Do less, not more.* It is easier, cheaper, and less risky to remove barriers to entrepreneurial action than to engage in new initiatives with uncertain results. Many state-level efforts at boosting entrepreneurship have historically underperformed in terms of catalyzing entrepreneurial activity (Aziz, 1984; Cornwall, 1998; Lichtenstein and Lyons, 2001). This, in turn, may discredit public efforts to support entrepreneurship through effective policy and public investment in the future. However, by doing *less,* and removing *harmful* policies, policymakers can support entrepreneurs while incurring very little risk by removing unnecessary and outdated policies for situations that are no longer relevant.

4 *Small and incremental change means big long-term change.* A mountain looks impassible from the base, but when a climber begins the climb, little by little, new footholds appear, and new pathways over the mountain seem less steep—if taken one step at a time. In the same way, small, incremental change is akin to climbing a mountain one ledge at a time, rather than leaping the mountain all at once in a catapult (hint: only glorious if it works, and the chance of failure is high). Taking ecosystem development one step at a time enables a process-oriented evaluation of each step along the way, revealing new opportunities that may not have been apparent at the start. Many small changes lead to bigger, less risky changes in the long term.

5 *Embracing failure the right way.* In a healthy and antifragile ecosystem, business failures should occur, and they should be isolated, and information should easily pass to those surviving members still in the ecosystem. Market failures are essential to the overall thriving of the system as talent with market knowledge through their failed ventures are reabsorbed into the ecosystem, passing that knowledge to others so they may avoid the same mistakes or design better business models (Auerswald, 2015; Feld, 2012). Effective ecosystems must have an effective recycling mechanism, as international data demonstrate that most successful businesses are launched during a recession, suggesting that big dead trees (i.e., large, failed companies) often nourish

young saplings (Auerswald, 2015). Recognizing the potential for failure, Taleb (2012) states:

> My dream—the solution—is that we would have a National Entrepreneur Day, with the following message: Most of you will fail, disrespected, impoverished, but we are grateful for the risks you are taking and the sacrifices you are making for the sake of the economic growth of the planet and pulling others out of poverty. *You are the sources of our antifragility* [italics in original]. Our nation thanks you.
>
> *(p. 80)*

In a healthy antifragile system, individuals can and will perish, and this carries a benefit for the survivors. A forest ecosystem cannot survive without the cyclical death of its organisms, which provide nutrients that strengthen the individuals who remain. As weaker and less fortunate businesses perish in an economy, for example, a healthy ecosystem will reabsorb the talent and ideas from those businesses (see also Feld, 2012). The learning of multiple failures and successes, the scars of applied risk-taking and grappling with uncertainty are inherent in these talented individuals. Their experience, including the very valuable experience of failure, nourishes existing businesses and makes their knowledge base stronger. Therefore, the success of others is largely based on the failures of the few, and this is not something to be feared or avoided. This is also where antifragility ties cleanly to the logic of ecosystems. In a functional human ecosystem like an economy, it is not genes that pass along information, but often information passed through networks (see Burt, 2000; Granovetter, 1973) which becomes culturally embedded over time (Berger and Luckmann, 1966; also see Glisby and Holden, 2003, for an innovation-related knowledge management example). This can at least partially account for why some places have persistently higher rates of entrepreneurship, even when the features of the local economy (as in very rural areas) suggest that they should not (Breazeale and Hustedde, 2017; Julien, 2008; Thurik and Dejardin, 2011). It is much the way that a real ecosystem works, which is the subject of the next section.

Ecosystems, Large and Small

What is the Point of an Ecosystem? This book contains several chapters that deal in some way with rural entrepreneurship, and rural entrepreneurial ecosystems. Our goal is not to extensively revisit the literature on ecosystems, but rather to (a) demonstrate that most of the ecosystem building literature focuses on large, urban ecosystems in mature, developed economies and is not always appropriate for the situations facing rural communities and (b) to demonstrate the specific ways that the literature supports an antifragile approach to ecosystem development in rural areas. Ecosystems are a biotic term that exists at the confluence of economics, entrepreneurship, and regional development (Acs, Stam, Audretsch and O'Connor, 2017). Audretsch and Belitski (2017) define an entrepreneurial ecosystem as "institutional and organizational as well as other systemic factors that interact and influence the identification and commercialization of entrepreneurial opportunities... [and] are geographically bounded (p. 1031)." According to Brown and Mason (2017), ecosystems are multiactor, multiperspective systems and are thus necessarily complex. They are different from clusters in that they focus on the entrepreneur and not the firm (O'Connor, Stam, Sussan and Audretsch, 2018), although both clusters and ecosystems are place-based (Acs et al., 2017).

Ecosystems are marked by a heterogeneity of firms and actors and a temporal dimension that evolves over time (Theodoraki and Messeghem, 2017). This mirrors the idea that ecosystems are fundamentally human phenomena that inhere in the relationships between people, and thus the dynamics are like the social dynamics of any community, complete with collaboration, conflict, subdivision into interest groups, and differing values (Schmid, 2004; Wilkinson, 1991). Other definitions have a stronger grounding in the economic role of ecosystems over their social role. Stam (2015) defines an ecosystem very simply as a "set of interdependent actors and factors coordinated in such a way that they enable productive entrepreneurship (p. 5)." The "productive entrepreneurship" in this definition refers to Baumol's conception of "productive entrepreneurship," or "any entrepreneurial activity that contributes directly or indirectly to net output of the economy or to the capacity to produce additional output" (Baumol, 1993, p. 30). To both scholars, entrepreneurial ecosystems are unabashedly about *economic development,* which is a fundamentally place-based activity.

One might even say that an entrepreneurial ecosystem *is* a type of community focused on locality-oriented collective *actions* limited to entrepreneurship and the support of entrepreneurship. Those scholars that view entrepreneurship as a community endeavor (see Flora and Flora, 1993; Johannisson and Nilsson, 1989; Lichtenstein and Lyons, 2010; Lyons, Alter, Audretsch and Augustine, 2012) often find themselves in a silo apart from the broader entrepreneurial ecosystem literature due to their epistemological basis in the somewhat discrete fields of Sociology, Regional Development, and Community Development. The ecosystem term has thus been problematic due to its misuse and differential use across a wide range of fields of study. This was, in turn, the result of many scholars who saw value in the term but began using it empirically before any one field had sufficiently defined and bounded the phenomenon (Stam, 2015). In the shuffle, a preponderance of researchers with business and economics backgrounds who were studying major entrepreneurial ecosystems across the world (think Silicon Valley, Boston, etc.) deeply influenced the conceptualization of entrepreneurial ecosystems, giving this area of the research an urban bias (Miles and Morrison, 2020; Roundy, 2017). One area where scholars consistently agree is that ecosystems put greater emphasis on the entrepreneur and their networks and socioeconomic milieu than other economic development strategies that favor firms, policy, institutions, and other factors.

However, to Stam (2015) and earlier authors writing in a rural and regional context, like Henderson (2002) and Malecki (1994), the ultimate *goal* of entrepreneurship development is tantamount to Baumol's (1993) productive creation of value. In a review of the ecosystem literature, Roundy (2017) argues that "Most theory and findings regarding entrepreneurial ecosystems are based on studies of established ecosystems in large urban and regional hubs, often located in developed countries... focused on either large cities... or on country-level ecosystems" (p. 239). Roundy cites early urban ecosystem studies that focus on Washington, DC (Feldman, 2001), the Silicon Valley (Bahrami and Evans, 1995—and one could easily add Saxenian, 1990, 2002 here), and national-level studies including Estonia and South Korea (Kshetri, 2014) and The Netherlands (Stam, 2014). These authors are not alone: More recent studies continue the tradition of focusing on "high growth" entrepreneurship, which often (although not always) involves an overt focus on the tech sector. For example, O'Connor et al. (2018) focus on the ascendance of tech-oriented growth from the very beginning of their chapter on entrepreneurial ecosystems, although conceding that "every place has an entrepreneurial ecosystem" (p. 2). Acs, Stam, Audretsch and O'Connor (2017) use the number of unicorns in a city (startups valued at over $1 billion) and the prevalence of unicorns per ten million population as measures of ecosystem performance.

Stam (2015) eschews "unicorns" as being too restrictive a measure since few exist in The Netherlands, the focus of his exploration. He instead proxies "productive entrepreneurship with the prevalence of high-growth firms (p. 6)" and notes that, while entrepreneurial *intentions* are a good measure of the entrepreneurial culture of a region or city, they are not equivalent to entrepreneurial *output,* which he measures as "ambitious entrepreneurs, high-growth businesses, and gazelles" (Stam, 2015, p. 6). Similarly, Isenberg (2010), often considered one of the pioneers of the ecosystem literature, places a high value on what he calls the "law of small numbers (p. 7)." According to that law, a small number of very high growth, very successful businesses can inspire would-be entrepreneurs with the intent of starting a business to make the leap and launch the venture. Isenberg (2011) places the ideal number of high-growth firms at about one runaway success for every 50,000–150,000 population (p. 9). Isenberg (2010, 2011) frequently uses the same urban and national-level examples criticized by Roundy (2017) and, of particular importance to rural innovation ecosystems, Isenberg (2010) is not shy about "favoring the high potentials," or an explicit investment in "ambitious, growth-oriented entrepreneurs who address large potential markets (p. 6)" in cases when resources for investment are limited. While Isenberg (2010) is emphatic that such firms are often outside the tech sector, he—along with several of the other scholars listed above—imply that ecosystems are magnificently diverse, but the *point* of the ecosystem is Baumolian productive entrepreneurship. A tree is necessary to grow fruit, but the fruit of the ecosystem tree is the high-growth, export-oriented firm.

One thing that we, as authors, want to make very clear is that the entrepreneurial ecosystem literature has an accelerating focus on smaller entrepreneurial ecosystems, including in developing national contexts—a point that Roundy (2017) clarifies in his own work. However, what constitutes a "small" ecosystem? Isenberg (2010) makes mention of Cali, Columbia, for example with a population of 2.2 million (DANE, 2019). The authors of this chapter have spent their careers working in primarily *rural* areas, those with very small population centers. Even Isenberg's (2011) lower bound of one runaway success per 50,000 population is enough to evoke a chuckle from us. Many of the communities in which we work and practice community and economic development are less than one-tenth that size and lack most of the ecosystem-oriented infrastructure, universities, and venture-oriented finance, for example, credited as being necessary for the successful functioning of an entrepreneurial ecosystem. Rural areas are, however, quite rich in other kinds of capital that are often overlooked by the literature, including natural capital (Miles and Morrison, 2020) and entrepreneurial social capital (Flora and Flora, 1993). What then for smaller communities in both developed and developing economies? Do these places have any chance at building an entrepreneurial or innovation-based ecosystem? Can they possibly sustain the critical momentum necessary to develop and sustain the habitual creation of new and beneficial ideas for society? According to Roundy (2017), the answer is *yes,* but those communities must be as innovative and entrepreneurial in their approach as entrepreneurs themselves, beginning with the nature of value created by smaller ecosystems.

Critically Examining Urban Approaches to the Case of Rural Ecosystems. This is where it is possible to unpack the discussion about rural versus urban ecosystems. The first question that arises from a critical reading of the ecosystem literature has to do with the nature of the "productive value" serving as the goal or purpose of local entrepreneurial efforts. To Stam's (2015) point, there continues to be confusion about the use of ecosystem terminology. While most of the studies cited above in this section focus on a growth orientation for productive economic development, most also appear to make concessions for the ubiquity of entrepreneurial action outside the tech sector and in areas other than the largest ecosystems. The confusion, it seems, stems from Baumol's (1993) definition of productive entrepreneurship as that which creates value in society. We agree, but of course, value is not the same for everyone: it is a subjective and culturally situated term that is differentially experienced by different people and different groups across society (Hofstede and Bond, 1984). Tarantulas are a frightening pest in the Southwestern United States, but a gourmet delicacy in Cambodia. The same resource provides differential opportunities for two very different cultures (culinary versus pest control) due to their culturally situated perceptions about the resource. Wild hogs and boars are similarly considered to be "invasive species" in most developed nations with systematized agriculture systems, which might baffle regions grappling with food insecurity and poor access to meat and high-protein foods more generally.

Different cultures may similarly have different attitudes about entrepreneurship and the value creation process as well. The idea that entrepreneurial ecosystems are fundamentally about economic development, and thus economic growth, is just one lens through which one can examine the potential, possibility, and effectiveness of ecosystems. If a plurality of values is possible, it begs the question: can ecosystems create *multiple* kinds of value, including value to those places that may be smaller and culturally opposed to or indifferent toward historically high-growth industries? More generally, we are asking a question about ecosystems creating value—but value for *whom?* This has considerable importance for the development and cultivation of innovation and entrepreneurship in rural areas, where cultural beliefs about what is valuable may differ considerably from urban value chains and value systems, or where the goals of economic development may differ substantially from efforts in an urban environment (Fortunato, 2014; Flora and Flora, 1993; Wortman, 1990).

According to Shane (2010), the number one factor motivating entrepreneurs to launch a business is not profit, but rather the opportunity *not* to work for a boss. Similarly, different cultures may view the nature of opportunity differently (Dana, 1995), possessing different ways of knowing and identifying that opportunity (Dana and Dana, 2005) and networking and engaging with their markets differently due to their embeddedness in different social milieu with different norms (Klyver and Foley, 2012). Cultural norms shape everything from the acceptance or rejection of entrepreneurship as an honorable vocational choice (Julien, 2008; Spigel, 2013), to the embrace or rejection of innovation and novelty (Breazeale and Hustedde, 2017; Hustedde, 2007), to the nature and distribution of power in the local environment (Gaventa, 1982). Some communities may embrace lifestyle entrepreneurship over high-growth entrepreneurship (Hustedde, 2007), while others are involved in rural-focused industries like agriculture and manufacturing (Henderson, 2002), agri-tourism (Nickerson, Black and McCool, 2001), and export-oriented growth industries that may be quite isolated from the broader community (Sopuck, 2003).

Auerswald states,

> Entrepreneurs and innovators exist in all societies, but not all societies are equally welcoming of the disruptive changes they provoke. Individual entrepreneurs and innovators thus face three options: seek economic rents within the status quo; challenge the status quo through disruptive innovation; or leave the society altogether to seek an environment more welcoming of economic creativity. These three options (taken in reverse order) are analogous to the fundamental political options articulated by Hirschman long ago: exit, voice, and loyalty.
>
> *(2015, p. 9, citing Hirschman, 1970)*

A critical dimension of the ecosystem includes interpersonal relationships, not just relationships among typical organizational players like banks, government, and universities, but culturally situated relationships embedded in local networks and bounded by cultural norms about what is valuable locally. The important dimensions defining any ecosystem are "micro" and fine-grained, and highly differential from place to place. While such a pluralism of culture (apart from the more unified culture of capitalistic growth and productive entrepreneurship expressed by the literature) may seem to pose a challenge to ecosystem builders through its complexity, such complexity is likely to create a multitude of opportunities for developing unique kinds of ecosystems unlikely to be found anywhere else. This uniqueness can pose a special kind of competitive advantage around lifestyle, rural industry, and niche clusters that are unlikely to arise in major ecosystems.

A second critical question that arises from a review of the ecosystem has to do with the *process* of ecosystem development, specifically *who* is the eventual target of ecosystem development efforts? On the one hand, much of the literature follows the example of Isenberg (2010), whose policy recommendation about favoring high-potential firms is expected to provide adequate momentum to the entire ecosystem in the form of positive cues about entrepreneurial opportunity (see Kirzner, 1973; Shane, 2003). Isenberg (2011) focuses on the importance of reaching a "tipping point," where economic spillovers are most evident not in the traditional sense of creating surplus value that can be exploited by other firms, but by trying to get others "hooked" as entrepreneurship "addicts" (p. 5): people who start out as entrepreneurs, but eventually become local leaders, board members, and angel investors, supporting the entire system. This sends signals to other entrepreneurs that the water's fine and heightens those who are most alert to such opportunities (Kirzner, 1973; Shane, 2003). However, Isenberg (2010) himself raises the concern that only supporting those businesses who are already most likely to succeed may seem "elitist and inequitable (p. 6)," but a necessary evil when limited resources are involved.

Shane (2010) similarly warns against investing in entrepreneurs who are less likely to succeed as a matter of public policy—an idea that seems to take direct aim at entrepreneurship emerging from marginalized groups and people of color who have been locked out of networks of entrepreneurial financing and support for generations (Bates, 2011; Carter, Mwaura, Ram, Trehan and Jones, 2015; Fairlie, 2013). In what we find to be a controversial quote exemplifying class biases, Shane states,

> In fact, you already know how to select the companies to bet on. Take, for example, the following two businesses: A personal cleaning business started by an unemployed high school dropout that is pursuing the customers of another personal cleaning business, is capitalized with $10,000 of the founder's savings, and is set up as a sole proprietorship, [or] an Internet company that is started by a former Microsoft employee with fifteen years of experience in the software industry, an MBA and a master's degree in computer science, that is pursuing the next generation of Internet search, is capitalized with $250,000 in money from the founder and the Band of Angels in San Francisco, and is set up as a corporation... It's obvious that the

> second business has a better chance of success than the first one and that, on average, we would be better off putting our resources into such businesses.
> *(2010, p. 164)*

While this is the 12-year-old opinion (as of this writing) of one scholar, do Shane's comments represent a broader bias against businesses that are necessity-driven, launched by people with low education levels, or people below the poverty line—not to mention marginalized populations facing even greater barriers to entry? What is the role of these would-be entrepreneurs in an innovation and entrepreneurship ecosystem? Multigenerational poverty, lower educational levels, and a greater share of the population over age 65 are all disproportionately found in rural areas in the United States (Baernholdt, Yan, Hinton, Rose and Mattos, 2012; Farrigan, 2020; USDA, 2017), and many of these patterns persist worldwide (World Bank, 2020), paired with higher rural rates of rising income inequality in most developing nations (Loewe and Rippin, 2012; United Nations, 2020). According to (the very same) Shane (2010), the average entrepreneur works longer hours but earns less than the average wage employee, most do not create very many jobs, most are in low-tech/low-growth industries, and the majority are launched with the founder's savings or credit cards—*not* venture capital and angel investors. In an age where the average rural citizen experiences a society facing increasing income inequality and an uneven distribution of resources, market/network access and (important to antifragility) *randomness*, is the goal of an entrepreneurial ecosystem to thus (a) encourage more "high-growth" firms, or (b) to open entrepreneurship to more people? Without a sufficient core of high-growth entrepreneurs, the likelihood of creating an effective ecosystem in a rural area is impractical. Isenberg (2011) believes that investment in high-potential firms is about rewarding merit, but how is this manifest in a rural/urban divide with unequal starting points? Shane (2010) himself points out that women and minority entrepreneurs are less likely to start businesses, and more likely to encounter barriers to entry, a point echoed by an older investigation by Blanchflower (2007). In any ecosystem, entrepreneurs do not start from the same place with the same advantages, and this must be taken seriously for the ecosystem not to become elitist and exclusionary.

Investing in Entrepreneurial Capacity and Quality of Life. The inverse of what we will call the "picking winners" approach is an idea that has existed for years in the community development literature: building the *capacity* of individuals and communities, whatever their current situation or status, to solve their own problems, take advantage of opportunities, and to meet the needs of their own communities through self-organization and democratic practice (Boyte, 2004; Wilkinson, 1991). There is already an established link between community development and entrepreneurship. Lyons et al. (2012) review the literature in detail to demonstrate how entrepreneurial action is deeply embedded in community dynamics, from the network structure of a community to its culture to its infrastructure, institutions, and support systems. Similar contributions have been made by Flora and Flora (1993), whose concept of Entrepreneurial Social Infrastructure (ESI) is fully embedded in community dynamics, which can be supportive or a hindrance to entrepreneurship development. Similarly, scholars like Dana (1995) and Johannisson and Nilsson (1989) demonstrate how entrepreneurs commonly work within communities and *as* a community for collective support, networking, and addressing challenging environmental conditions. This is not entirely different from the ecosystem literature, but greater emphasis is placed on what Stam (2015) would call the *process* of entrepreneurial ecosystems rather than the *outcomes* or *outputs*. Both Stam (2015) and Harrington (2017) advance the idea that ecosystem development is fundamentally about the human capital development of the *entrepreneur* as the base unit of the ecosystem, in addition to the entrepreneur's environment. To Harrington (2017), ecosystem development proceeds sequentially, from Discover (hackathons) to Idea (mentoring, pitch events, office hours) to Startup (form a team, proof of concept, IP strategy, fundraising) to finally the Growth phase (once *customer* revenue goes positive). This sequence demonstrates increasing *system* complexity, but Harrington also states that most investors are interested in those entrepreneurs who have made it to the last stage—the *growth* stage. The focus continues to be on traditional means of economic development. Contrasting this idea, Lichtenstein and Lyons (2010) view entrepreneurship development as occurring along a community-supported "pipeline" that has at its core an ethic and process of *investment* in entrepreneurs, primarily by other, more experienced entrepreneurs and supporting institutions. This is echoed in the ecosystem literature by thinkers like Brad Feld (2012), whose exploration of the Boulder ecosystem placed great emphasis on process-level elements like leaders and feeders (i.e., entrepreneurs versus local support organizations), the primacy of networking events, mentorship, a culture of embracing failure, and the primacy of entrepreneurial leadership over institutional leadership.

In Feld (2012), Lyons, Alter, Audretsch and Augustine (2012), Lichtenstein and Lyons (2010) and others, there is a strong sense of *investment* in the entrepreneur and their surrounding social system. The shift in emphasis from those most likely to succeed toward a *collective* increase in entrepreneurial and innovative capacity is particularly important for building rural entrepreneurial and innovation ecosystems. The latter approach is likely to make more sense for rural areas that have a lower density of gazelles and unicorns. An exclusive focus on high growth is like saying that the point of a redwood forest is to grow redwood trees, the tallest and most visible organisms in the forest. Bees, birds, smaller trees, and plants—these are all widely recognized to support redwood growth, and anyone who understands ecosystem logic would thus recognize their importance. But is the purpose of the redwood forest to grow redwoods? Is the purpose of a café owner (a low-growth, low-margin business in a competitive industry) only to serve coffee and danishes to high-growth, "high potential" entrepreneurs? Or is there merit—and a strategic niche—in any venture? In a smaller town, for example, would it be a high-value endeavor to witness the emergence of an innovative café cluster serving a diversity of unusual products that, taken collectively, is sufficient in size to draw customers from across the region looking for a great café scene? Is high-lifestyle (not high-growth) a sufficient motivation for innovation and participation in an ecosystem?

There is some emerging evidence that those communities specializing in quality of life and lifestyle factors, not necessarily economic growth, may indeed stimulate entrepreneurial momentum, which is good news for rural ecosystems with comparatively small economies. Auerswald (2015) found that entrepreneurs at fast-growing firms chose where to live "based on personal connections and quality of life factors years before they start their firms (p. 13)," with access to employee talent, customers, and suppliers immediately following. Entrepreneurs almost never stated that a good policy environment or low taxes were a motivation in their location decision (Auerswald, 2015). While a pool of talented employees may be difficult to find in some rural areas, employees themselves have been found to follow quality of life factors rather than the availability of jobs (Hicks, Faulk and Deveraj, 2016), with job creators often following their employees to high-quality places. This changes the traditional economic development wisdom from people following jobs toward jobs following people (Hicks et al., 2016). In a series of well-known studies, Tolbert, Lyson and Irwin (1998) found that a combination of local capitalism (i.e., a healthy "ecosystem" before such terminology was in common use) and civic engagement had positive effects on local socioeconomic conditions looking across over 3,000 U.S. counties. The potential for a lifestyle orientation to create a virtuous cycle of innovation and entrepreneurship development serves as a starting point for development efforts. While it is unlikely that rural ecosystems will attract every type of entrepreneur, Isenberg's (2010) acknowledgment that growth often occurs outside the vaunted tech sector is a promising indicator for rural areas that may specialize in other types of entrepreneurial activity. And this is, of course, not to turn a blind eye to the potential for rural tech entrepreneurship if the talent is available, but the scope of potential for growth is likely far larger than one industrial sector.

Antifragility and Effectual Logic in Rural Areas. In a recent article, Miles and Morrisson (2020) discuss a different approach for cultivating an entrepreneurial ecosystem in rural areas. Based on Sarasvathy's (2006) concept of *effectuation,* rural areas often do not possess the standard set of social, financial, and infrastructural supports found in urban areas (Flora and Flora, 1993). Effectuation is based on Sarasvathy's (2006) observation that most entrepreneurs do not follow the standard, linear plan-fund-launch model espoused by most of the business planning literature to that point. They do not seek opportunity through the standard pathways of entrepreneurial alertness, with opportunity floating about exogenous to the entrepreneur (Kirzner, 1973; Shane, 2003; Shane and Venkataraman, 2000). Instead, most entrepreneurs look *inward* to find opportunity, cobbling together a business model for a diversity of personal motivations from their talents, networks, and personal resources. Instead of alertness, these entrepreneurs possess excellent awareness of their own capabilities and how they can be leveraged productively.

Similar principles hold true when looking across entrepreneurs and innovators at the total community or ecosystem. For years, community and economic developers have utilized Assets-Based Community development (ABCD) (Kretzmann and McKnight, 1996) to begin conversations about local development efforts by first identifying critical assets in the community across many dimensions: physical, natural, political, infrastructural, and so on (see the Comprehensive Rural Wealth Framework for an application, Johnson and Fannin, 2019). ABCD begins by focusing on what is unique about each community and recognizing how that can be used as an asset to differentiate the community and its economy apart from potential competitors. Similarly, the most efficacious ecosystems are *exclusionary* and focus on what is unique in that place (Auerswald, 2015), and also recognize that complexity and continuous reorganization are the keys to success (Hidalgo and Hausmann, 2009). This continuous reorganization is antifragile in nature, as it represents the collective recognition of changing conditions and randomness, and self-correcting to take advantage of opportunities, often using an effectual logic and using *bricolage* to cobble together new opportunities based on random variation. This is the essence of a thriving ecosystem, and it works more like a cat than a washing machine (Taleb, 2012).

For an effectual logic to work across a social collective like an ecosystem, interpersonal relationships are essential for individual actors to effectively share information, improve collective awareness, and mobilize collective resources in an environment of continuous change. Earlier in the chapter, we discussed how diversity fuels innovation, and this can only be the case if information about what is new and beneficial to society can be shared across relational networks, facilitated by a culture of information sharing (Burt, 2000; Jack and Anderson, 2002). This is true for opportunity as well as pooled resources, as highly diversified networks have better access to nonredundant information (Burt, 2000; Granovetter, 1973). Entrepreneurs commonly use economic resources and social capital to contribute to the vibrancy of their own region (Feldman and Zoller, 2016), but human interdependencies in ecosystems follow *business network dynamics* that are more sociological than economic in nature (O'Connor et al., 2018). Such network dynamics work best when there is high differentiation and coordination of roles, and when leadership is decentralized, encouraging entrepreneurs self-organize into strategic niches to conserve energy and encourage specialization, just like in a biotic ecosystem (Theodoraki and Messeghem, 2017). Flora and Flora (1993) describe the *mosaic fallacy,* that any community (such as an ecosystem), no matter how cohesive it seems on the surface, is comprised of interdependent parts: each part depends on system-level interactions and is highly interdependent on other parts of the system. This means that an effective ecosystem should be structured in such a way that networks form easily, information flows freely, leadership emerges and disappears along with needs, conversations about opportunities occur at the system level, and individuals feel empowered to plug into the ecosystem by doing the work they feel best doing—and getting valuable recognition and support for doing so. Miles and Morrisson (2020) call this system-level leadership *effectual leadership* as it is applied to rural ecosystem development. For ecosystem builders, this involves the following three pillars for regular discussion among ecosystem actors:

- *Creating and/or discovering opportunities.* Who are we and what do we know?
- *Assessing opportunities.* How can the opportunity be exploited in a way to manage risks?
- *Opportunity exploitation.* How can we leverage our means, contingencies, and partnerships to develop a rural entrepreneurial ecosystem? (p. 4).

When ecosystems begin to gain critical mass, they also gain the *capacity* to solve problems collectively in ways that were not possible as a disconnected collection of individuals. This antifragile tendency leverages each other's social and network capital—bounded by a supportive culture—to recognize risks and opportunities quickly, and to support small-scale adjustments to new norms, scaling up quickly when early gains to the overall system become apparent.

Building an Antifragile Ecosystem: Suggestions for Ecosystem Builders

How, then, can ecosystem builders apply antifragility, community development insights, and effectual logic to communities of any size and density? We conclude this chapter with a few suggestions for effective ecosystem building practice. To the extent that ecosystems represent communities with a specific, purposive intent, many of the insights presented here can be combined to address ecosystem building in situations where commonly cited social and infrastructural advantages (i.e., access to capital, market proximity, a research university) are not present. This often means using *bricolage* and an effectual logic to cobble together strategies using any available advantages that can support entrepreneurial flourishing in an area around strategic, locally determined niches. Many of these strategies will inhere in people as much as they do in infrastructure. The goal is to create a virtuous cycle with its own momentum by providing the training, power, mandate, capacity, and resources to build the best ecosystem given local constraints, *and then disband* (Isenberg, 2011). Once catalyzed, the ecosystem has the potential to become habitual and eventually culturally embedded. Such a culture change requires several practices to be present that maximize local antifragility, capitalizing on the upside from uncertainty while limiting exposure to downside uncertainty and accounting for human and business diversity across the entire ecosystem. Whether entrepreneurship is the focus, or simply innovation more broadly (involving companies, governments, or even creative and artistic groups), we make use of these suggestions in our own community and economic development practice in rural areas.

1 *Link systems.* Borrowing from the literature on coopetition, firms in rural regions can become stronger when they compete *together* instead of cannibalizing each other's market share. To the ecosystem builder, this can mean

bringing your entrepreneurs together purposively to discuss a collective strategy for the entire ecosystem, and ways that each member of the ecosystem can contribute to this broader vision with their unique talents. Part of this discussion is a commitment to supporting fellow entrepreneurs, even if friendly rivalries are maintained (which can be positive). Specifically, this strategy reduces risk by ensuring continuity in the economy in the event of a business failure, while encouraging cluster formation, joint promotion, and regional promotional strategies.

2 *Use what is already around.* Community developers have long used asset-based community development to identify key advantages that already exist in the community and that can be leveraged at very little cost (Kretzmann and McKnight, 1996). Similarly, the *bricolage* approach espoused by Sarasvathy's (2006) *effectual logic* and further suggested by Miles and Morrisson (2020) can be used to begin plotting a strategy based on what the community already does well. There is little use in reinventing the wheel when it comes to ecosystem development, as this may require a complete new set of people, talents, and capabilities to get really good at something that has never thrived in that place (i.e., forming a telecommunications cluster *de novo* in a farming community). Just because that community does not contain the necessary inputs to chase current fads, there is great potential in fostering ecosystems around lifestyle and quality of life factors, and industries that are overrepresented in rural areas like agriculture, extraction, and specialty manufacturing (Henderson, 2002). Untested industries have not built up a critical mass of knowledge regarding risk and uncertainty, which could add fragility to the total system.

3 *Build a culture of embracing uncertainty and failure.* Ecosystems need a recycling mechanism (Auerswald, 2015; Feld, 2012). Fear of failure can be a major cultural impediment to innovation and entrepreneurship with very real social consequences for the person failing. Ecosystem builders can change that by fostering an environment where innovators and entrepreneurs see failure as a *natural part of the innovation process,* not a personal shortcoming. This also involves making a commitment to others in the ecosystem that failed businesses, if honest in their intention, are celebrated and applauded, and their talent is absorbed by other businesses. This recycling mechanism ensures that knowledge about risk and uncertainty gets reabsorbed into the total system, increasing its overall antifragility and providing inspiration for new innovations.

4 *Experiment small, fail small, scale up.* An antifragile approach is fundamentally about reducing exposure to downside risk while increasing exposure to upside risk, or a *convex* curve if plotted horizontally as returns to the system over time. That is a highly theoretical idea, but in practical application it is all about taking many very small bets over time instead of investing in one large bet. If, as an economic developer, you had $10 million to invest in a rural town (a sizable sum for such a place), it is the difference between investing all $10 million in one initiative, like a minor league baseball stadium, with the hopes that it would have the intended (and undiversified) economic effects expected by the investment. Or, one could invest $9 million

in something relatively safe, like local business infrastructure improvements, and divide the other $1 million into 100 $10,000 micro-loans for small businesses. The likelihood of microfinance being paid back is quite high to begin with (see Dowla, 2006, for an example), but the chance that at least one or two businesses out of a hundred will become growth-oriented businesses is quite high. For those businesses who default, the economic developer only loses $10,000 per business, maybe less. But even a few successes could create a large amount of jobs and tax revenue in perpetuity. This can be applied in almost any situation. The more diversified the ecosystem, the more options become available through the social and human capital of entrepreneurs, so point 6) on diversification matters here.

5 *Do not attempt to change the culture—too much.* Under antifragility, cultural practices often exist for reasons that are difficult to discern from the outside and may contain hidden wisdom from generations of prior failures and successes. While ecosystem builders should aim their culture change efforts at the level of the ecosystem (often a novel arrangement), changing the existing place-based culture may be both infeasible and insensitive. It also robs many communities of a specific niche in the broader marketplace that may convey important advantages both socially and economically.

6 *Foster interaction and diversity.* Rural areas have a reputation for not being very diverse—after all, how can a town of 5,000 population compare to San Francisco in terms of the variety of small businesses one finds there? But a surprising amount of diversity can be found by forming linkages and partnerships across entire regions. Ecosystem builders may consider partnerships with regional organizations, foundations, nonprofits, and universities who can serve as conveners for conversations that invoke greater economic, cultural, and interpersonal diversity. Another idea is to try a "speed dating" event for entrepreneurs, tried successfully in rural Maine (Fortunato, 2017), where entrepreneurs spend ten minutes with a variety of other entrepreneurs from around the region with diverse interests. This can facilitate unusual combinations of ideas, partnerships, and new joint ventures with high innovative potential in a variety of industries.

7 *Favor newcomers more, incumbents less.* A deliberate action, Auerswald (2015) stresses the idea that government's role in an ecosystem is to reduce barriers to entrepreneurial entry by favoring large, incumbent businesses less. This is often done through tax and policy reform and reducing *defensive complexity* (Chastain, Antia and Bergstrom, 2012), or the tendency of large organizations to be well along the compliance learning curve in ways that small businesses cannot replicate or anticipate.

8 *Build capacity while building community.* Put differently, do not overprescribe outcomes. Invest in *processes.* The ideal ecosystem is one that generates its own momentum and self-corrects and self-actualizes in the moment given the effectual capacities of the diverse individuals involved. Like the adage, ecosystem building is about teaching a person to fish instead of giving them a fish. This capacity to act inheres quite profoundly in social relationships and,

even more importantly, in a *sense of community* and a supportive culture that fosters and promotes working together to address uncertainties, competing as a diverse team with different positions on that team, and embracing and learning from failures collectively, putting failed founders right back in the field again. Effective ecosystem requires more interaction, and fewer incentives and policies. It is the ecosystem builder's job to ensure that conversations remain constructive, synthetic, cognizant of the antifragility of the system, and then—to disappear and let the system continue to evolve on its own.

First Steps Forward

The first steps toward building an antifragile, effectual ecosystems fundamentally begin with *relationships*. Some easy (but important) first steps to catalyzing change in your new or existing ecosystem begins with alignment among people with a shared sense of purpose. In the field of community and economic development, a common first step toward any community goal is the convocation of community: bringing together diverse stakeholders in pursuit of a common purpose. Feld (2012) has chronicled the often scrappy, informal, inchoate beginnings of ecosystem development in his book *Startup Communities,* which commonly begin with a diversity of both entrepreneurs and their supporters—what he calls "leaders" and "feeders"—getting together to simply talk about entrepreneurship, and how to remove barriers and build supports for new enterprises. Ecosystem builders should resist the temptation to overengineer these early steps, trying to copy other successful ecosystems directly or adhering too closely to any one set of best practices (Isenberg, 2010). Doing so prohibits the group from exploring natural synergies across their talent base and following the natural contours of opportunity within their local context.

It has long been observed that rural areas have a greater orientation toward valuing tight-knit relationships and personal reputation over more transactional relationships oriented around professional and economic values (see Becker and Myers, 1942; Redfield, 1947; Weber, 1958). It is a stretch to say that rural areas have a "strategic advantage" in relationship building, but there is a long history of community-oriented, bootstrap gathering to meet needs and solve problems in rural places and agricultural communities dating back centuries (De Tocqueville, 2015). This presents an important cultural advantage to launching a new ecosystem, as more urban ecosystems seek to replicate these very same collaborative relationships grounded in reputation, community spirit, and mutual support for a common cause.

Some first steps for ecosystem-building practitioners could therefore include the following:

- Host a conference or event about entrepreneurial ecosystems in your communities, with speakers and participants from other rural ecosystems. Good speakers and presenters can share success stories while encouraging local participants to explore their own unique strengths and advantages.

- Commit to hosting local entrepreneurship meetups, no matter who shows up. Encourage a diverse range of entrepreneurs and supporting organizations to attend as regularly as possible and host the meeting at a convenient time and neutral location (i.e., at a place where everyone feels comfortable).
- Meet with local (and eventually state) government officials to identify policies and ordinances that present barriers to local entrepreneurs, and if possible, develop a strategy for reducing, removing, or revising policies that pose unnecessary barriers to entrepreneurs.
- Be deliberate in looking around the room to see who *is* and who *is not* represented. Diversity comes in many forms: age, race, gender, ethnicity, religion, income level, educational background—not to mention the types of institutions that are (or *are not*) represented, which could include everything from traditional entrepreneurial supporters like business schools to community groups, activist groups, "hidden" industries like DIY entrepreneurs, and even the faith-based community. To bring such individuals to the table, it takes a personal invitation, which is the first step in building any authentic ecosystem.
- Most of all, use meeting times to identify a common purpose: building a great ecosystem. Recognize that you will not likely know in advance what that ecosystem is going to look like—and that this is part of the excitement of ecosystem-building work.

In summary, we concur with O'Connor et al. (2018) that entrepreneurial ecosystems are purposive and place-based, and likely to exist in any community, even small ones. While the bulk of the ecosystem literature presents a universalist, system-oriented approach in an attempt to normalize ecosystem building and practice (O'Connor et al., 2018), we argue that this relatively abstract approach overlooks the massive plurality of potential advantages found in rural areas that can serve as the basis of ecosystem development efforts. Since there is no standard definition for an ecosystem apart from their focus on entrepreneurs over firms and their ability to create value by creating a virtuous cycle of productive entrepreneurship in a bounded territory (Stam, 2015), such vagueness raises the question of an entrepreneurship and innovation ecosystem raising value for *whom*. If value can be created by any entrepreneur, and value is culturally situated, then it can certainly be created in rural ecosystems that lack some of the high-growth, accelerator-oriented features of some larger places (Roundy, 2017), but grounded in the specific advantages that continue to make rural areas attractive places to live and work even in our massively urbanizing age. Doing so requires creating nothing less than an alternative *culture* of ecosystem development: one that eschews the large, systematized, capital-rich, infrastructure-driven, growth-oriented, and predictable; and replaces it with a culture that is small, highly adaptive, effectual, resourceful, relationship-driven, lifestyle- *and* growth-oriented (perhaps with emphasis on the former), and which loves randomness and uniqueness. Achieving such an ecosystem requires an ecosystem building approach that embraces antifragility and effectual logics in such a way that participants feel capable of doing good works under nearly any circumstances, using those advantages that are already lying about. The result could be a vast network of unique innovation and entrepreneurship ecosystems catered to many types of lifestyle choices, innovative activities, and entrepreneurial actions—and a wealth of supportive home bases for entrepreneurs that are as diverse as the places where they do business.

Note

1 All references to *antifragility* in this section refer to this citation.

References

Acs, Z. J., Desai, S., & Hessels, J. (2008). Entrepreneurship, economic development and institutions. *Small Business Economics, 31*(3), 219–234.

Acs, Z. J., Stam, E., Audretsch, D. B., & O'Connor, A. (2017). The lineages of the entrepreneurial ecosystem approach. *Small Business Economics, 49*(1), 1–10.

Acs, Z. J., & Szerb, L. (2007). Entrepreneurship, economic growth and public policy. *Small Business Economics, 28*(2–3), 109–122.

Audretsch, D. B., & Belitski, M. (2017). Entrepreneurial ecosystems in cities: Establishing the framework conditions. *The Journal of Technology Transfer, 42*(5), 1030–1051.

Auerswald, P. E. (2015). Enabling entrepreneurial ecosystems: Insights from ecology to inform effective entrepreneurship policy. *Kauffman Foundation Research Series on city, metro, and regional entrepreneurship.* Kansas City, MO: The Kauffman Foundation.

Aziz, S. (1984). Rural development – some essential prerequisites. *International Labour Review, 123*(3), 277–285.

Baernholdt, M., Yan, G., Hinton, I., Rose, K., & Mattos, M. (2012). Quality of life in rural and urban adults 65 years and older: Findings from the National Health and Nutrition Examination survey. *The Journal of Rural Health, 28*(4), 339–347.

Bahrami, H., & Evans, S. (1995). Flexible re-cycling and high-technology entrepreneurship. *California Management Review, 37*(3), 62–89.

Bates, T. (2011). Minority entrepreneurship. *Foundations and Trends in Entrepreneurship,* 7(3–4), 151–311.

Baumol, W. J. (1993). *Entrepreneurship, management and the structure of payoffs.* Cambridge: MIT Press.

Becker, H., & Myers, R. C. (1942). Sacred and secular aspects of human sociation. *Sociometry, 5,* 207–229.

Berger, P. L., & Luckmann, T. (1966). *The social construction of reality: A treatise in the sociology of knowledge.* New York: Anchor.

Blanchflower, D. G. (2007). *Entrepreneurship in the United States.* Bonn, Germany: IZA, Discussion Paper No. 3130.

Boyte, H. C. (2004). *Everyday politics: Reconnecting citizens and public life.* Philadelphia: University of Pennsylvania Press.

Breazeale, N. D., & Hustedde, R. J. (2017). Understanding the impact of culture in entrepreneurship. In Fortunato, M. W. P. & Clevenger, M. R. (eds.), *Toward entrepreneurial community development: Leaping cultural and leadership boundaries* (pp. 104–125). New York: Routledge.

Brown, R., & Mason, C. (2017). Looking inside the spiky bits: A critical review and conceptualisation of entrepreneurial ecosystems. *Small Business Economics, 49*(1), 11–30.

Burt, R. S. (2000). The network structure of social capital. *Research in Organizational Behavior, 22*, 345–423.

Camerer, C., & Lovallo, D. (1999). Overconfidence and excess entry: An experimental approach. *American Economic Review, 89*(1), 306–318.

Carter, S., Mwaura, S., Ram, M., Trehan, K., & Jones, T. (2015). Barriers to ethnic minority and women's enterprise: Existing evidence, policy tensions and unsettled questions. *International Small Business Journal, 33*(1), 49–69.

Chastain, E., Antia, R., & Bergstrom, C. T. (2012). Defensive complexity and the phylogenetic conservation of immune control. Working paper. Retrieved from https://arxiv.org/pdf/1211.2878.pdf

Cornwall, J. R. (1998). The entrepreneur as a building block for community. *Journal of Developmental Entrepreneurship, 3*(2), 141.

Dabson, B. (2001). Supporting rural entrepreneurship. *Exploring policy options for a new rural America.* Conference sponsored by the Center for the Study of Rural America, Federal Reserve Bank of Kansas City, pp. 35–48.

Dana, L. P. (1995). Entrepreneurship in a remote sub-Arctic community. *Entrepreneurship Theory and Practice, 20*(1), 57–72.

Dana, L. P., & Dana, T. E. (2005). Expanding the scope of methodologies used in entrepreneurship research. *International Journal of Entrepreneurship and Small Business, 2*(1), 79–88.

DANE (2019). *Información capital.* Retrieved from https://www.dane.gov.co/files/varios/informacion-capital-DANE-2019.pdf

De Tocqueville, A. (2015). *Democracy in America-Vol. I. and II.* New York: Read Books Ltd.

Dowla, A. (2006). In credit we trust: Building social capital by Grameen Bank in Bangladesh. *The Journal of Socio-Economics, 35*(1), 102–122.

Fairlie, R. W. (2013). Entrepreneurship, economic conditions, and the great recession. *Journal of Economics & Management Strategy, 22*(2), 207–231.

Farrigan, T. (2020). Extreme poverty counties found solely in rural areas in 2018. *Amber Waves: The Economics of Food, Farming, Natural Resources, and Rural America.* Retrieved from https://www.ers.usda.gov/amber-waves/2020/may/extreme-poverty-counties-found-solely-in-rural-areas-in-2018/

Falk, W. W., & Lobao, L. M. (2003). Who benefits from economic restructuring? Lessons from the past, challenges for the future. *Challenges for rural America in the twenty-first century*, 2003 Edition, 152–165.

Feld, B. (2012). *Startup communities: Building an entrepreneurial ecosystem in your city.* Hoboken, NJ: John Wiley & Sons.

Feldman, M. P. (2001). The entrepreneurial event revisited: Firm formation in a regional context. *Industrial and Corporate Change, 10*(4), 861–891.

Feldman, M. P., & Zoller, T. D. (2016). Dealmakers in place: Social capital connections in regional entrepreneurial economies. In Westlund, H. & Larsson, J. P. (eds.), *Handbook of social capital and regional development* (pp. 141–165). Cheltenham, England: Edward Elgar Publishing.

Flora, C. B., & Flora, J. L. (1993). Entrepreneurial social infrastructure: A necessary ingredient. *The Annals of the American Academy of Political and Social Science, 529*(1), 48–58.

Fortunato, M. W. P. (2014). Supporting rural entrepreneurship: A review of conceptual developments from research to practice. *Community Development, 45*(4), 387–408.

Fortunato, M. W. P. (2017). High- and low-entrepreneurial communities: A multiple case study. In Fortunato, M. W. P. & Clevenger, M. R. (eds.), *Toward entrepreneurial community development: Leaping cultural and leadership boundaries* (pp. 177–235). New York: Routledge.

Galindo, M., & Méndez-Picazo, M. (2013). Innovation, entrepreneurship and economic growth. *Management Decision, 51*(3), 501–514.

Gaventa, J. (1982). *Power and powerlessness: Quiescence and rebellion in an Appalachian Valley.* Urbana: University of Illinois Press.

Glisby, M., & Holden, N. (2003). Contextual constraints in knowledge management theory: The cultural embeddedness of Nonaka's knowledge-creating company. *Knowledge and Process Management, 10*(1), 29–36.

Granovetter, M. S. (1973). The strength of weak ties. *American Journal of Sociology, 78*(6), 1360–1380.

Harrington, K. (2017). *Entrepreneurial ecosystem momentum and maturity the important role of entrepreneur development organizations and their activities.* SSRN Paper No. 3030886. Retrieved from https://papers.ssrn.com/sol3/papers.cfm?abstract_id=3030886

Henderson, J. (2002). Building the rural economy with high-growth entrepreneurs. *Economic Review-Federal Reserve Bank of Kansas City, 87*(3), 45–75.

Hicks, M. J., Faulk, D., & Devaraj, S. (2016). *What comes first, people or jobs? Evidence and lessons for Indiana.* Muncie, IN: Center for Business and Economic Research, Ball State University.

Hidalgo, C. A., & Hausmann, R. (2009). The building blocks of economic complexity. *Proceedings of the National Academy of Sciences, 106*(26), 10570–10575.

Hirschman, A. O. (1970). *Exit, voice, and loyalty: Responses to decline in firms, organizations, and states.* Cambridge, MA: Harvard University Press.

Hofstede, G., & Bond, M. H. (1984). Hofstede's culture dimensions: An independent validation using Rokeach's value survey. *Journal of Cross-Cultural Psychology, 15*(4), 417–433.

Hoyos-Ruperto, D., Romaguera, J. M., Carlsson, B., & Lyytinen, K. (2013). Networking: A critical success factor for entrepreneurship. *American Journal of Management, 13*(2), 55–72.

Hustedde, R. (2007). What's culture got to do with it? Strategies for strengthening an entrepreneurial culture. In Walzer, N. (ed.), *Entrepreneurship and local economic development* (pp. 39–58). Lanham, MD: Lexington Books.

Isenberg, D. (2010). How to start an entrepreneurial revolution. *Harvard Business Review, 88*(6), 41–49.

Isenberg, D. (2011). *The entrepreneurship ecosystem strategy as a new paradigm for economy policy: Principles for cultivating entrepreneurship.* Babson Park, MA: Babson Global.

Jack, S. L., & Anderson, A. R. (2002). The effects of embeddedness on the entrepreneurial process. *Journal of Business Venturing, 17*(5), 467–487.

Johannisson, B., & Nilsson, A. (1989). Community entrepreneurs: Networking for local development. *Entrepreneurship & Regional Development, 1*(1), 3–19.

Johnson, T. G., & Fannin, J. M. (2019). A new conceptual framework for rural cultural wealth. Occasional Paper No. 2019.2. Iowa City, IA: Rural Policy Research Institute.

Julien, P. A. (2008). *A theory of local entrepreneurship in the knowledge economy.* Cheltenham, England: Edward Elgar Publishing.

Kay, J., & King, M. (2020). *Radical uncertainty.* New York: W.W. Norton.

Kirzner, I. M. (1973). *Entrepreneurship and competition.* Chicago, IL: University of Chicago Press.

Klyver, K., & Foley, D. (2012). Networking and culture in entrepreneurship. *Entrepreneurship & Regional Development, 24*(7–8), 561–588.

Knight, F. H. (1921). *Risk, uncertainty and profit* (Vol. 31). Boston, MA: Houghton Mifflin.
Kretzmann, J., & McKnight, J. P. (1996). Assets-based community development. *National Civic Review, 85*(4), 23–29.
Kshetri, N. (2014). Developing successful entrepreneurial ecosystems: Lessons from a comparison of an Asian tiger and a Baltic tiger. *Baltic Journal of Management, 9*(3), 330–356.
Lichtenstein, G. A., & Lyons, T. S. (2001). The entrepreneurial development system: Transforming business talent and community economies. *Economic Development Quarterly, 15*(1), 3–20.
Lichtenstein, G. A., & Lyons, T. S. (2010). *Investing in entrepreneurs: A strategic approach for strengthening your regional and community economy.* Santa Barbara, CA: ABC-CLIO.
Loewe, M., & Rippin, N. (2012). *Changing global patterns of poverty.* Briefing Paper No. 3/2012. Bonn, Germany: German Development Institute.
Lyons, T. S., Alter, T. R., Audretsch, D., & Augustine, D. (2012). Entrepreneurship and community: The next frontier of entrepreneurship inquiry. *Entrepreneurship Research Journal, 2*(1), 1–26.
Malecki, E. J. (1993). Entrepreneurship in regional and local development. *International Regional Science Review, 16*(1–2), 119–153.
Miles, M. P., & Morrison, M. (2020). An effectual leadership perspective for developing rural entrepreneurial ecosystems. *Small Business Economics, 54*(4), 933–949.
Nickerson, N. P., Black, R. J., & McCool, S. F. (2001). Agritourism: Motivations behind farm/ranch business diversification. *Journal of Travel Research, 40*(1), 19–26.
O'Connor, A., Stam, E., Sussan, F., & Audretsch, D. B. (2018). Entrepreneurial ecosystems: The foundations of place-based renewal. In O'Connor, A., Stam, E., Sussan, F., & Audretsch, D. B. (eds.), *Entrepreneurial ecosystems: Place-based transformations and transitions* (pp. 1–21). Cham, Switzerland: Springer International Publishing.
Ostrom, E. (1993). A communitarian approach to local governance. *National Civic Review, 82*(3), 226–233.
Ostrom, E. (1999). *Self-governance and forest resources.* Occasional Paper #20. Bogor, Indonesia: Center for International Forestry Research.
Park, R. E. (1925). *The city.* Chicago, IL: University of Chicago Press.
Park, R. E. (1928). Human migration and the marginal man. *American Journal of Sociology, 5*(1), 881–893.
Redfield, R. (1947). The folk society. *American Journal of Sociology, 52*(4), 293–308.
Roundy, P. T. (2017). "Small town" entrepreneurial ecosystems: Implications for developed and emerging economies. *Journal of Entrepreneurship in Emerging Economies, 9*(3), 238–262.
Sarasvathy, S. (2006). *Effectuation.* Cheltenham, England: Edward Elgar Publishing.
Saxenian, A. (1990). Regional networks and the resurgence of Silicon Valley. *California Management Review, 33*(1), 89–112.
Saxenian, A. (2002). Silicon Valley's new immigrant high-growth entrepreneurs. *Economic Development Quarterly, 16*(1), 20–31.
Schmid, A. A. (2004). *Conflict and cooperation: Institutional and behavioral economics.* Hoboken, NJ: John Wiley & Sons.
Schumpeter, J. (1934). *The theory of economic development.* Cambridge, MA: Harvard University Press.
Shane, S. A. (2003). *A general theory of entrepreneurship: The individual-opportunity nexus.* Cheltenham, England: Edward Elgar Publishing.
Shane, S. A. (2010). *Illusions of entrepreneurship: The costly myths that entrepreneurs, investors, and policy makers live by.* New Haven, CT: Yale University Press.

Shane, S., & Venkataraman, S. (2000). The promise of entrepreneurship as a field of research. *Academy of Management Review, 25*(1), 217–226.

Sopuck, R. D. (2003). *The lone eagles: Information professionals and rural economic development.* Policy Series Paper #19. Winnipeg, Manitoba: Frontier Centre for Public Policy.

Spigel, B. (2013). Bourdieuian approaches to the geography of entrepreneurial cultures. *Entrepreneurship & Regional Development, 25*(9–10), 804–818.

Stam, E. (2014). *The Dutch entrepreneurial ecosystem.* SSRN Working Paper #2473475. Retrieved from http://ssrn.com/abstract=2473475

Stam, E. (2015). Entrepreneurial ecosystems and regional policy: A sympathetic critique. *European Planning Studies, 23*(9), 1759–1769.

Stephens, H. M., Partridge, M. D., & Faggian, A. (2013). Innovation, entrepreneurship and economic growth in lagging regions. *Journal of Regional Science, 53*(5), 778–812.

Taleb, N. N. (2012). *Antifragile: Things that gain from disorder.* New York: Random House.

Theodoraki, C., & Messeghem, K. (2017). Exploring the entrepreneurial ecosystem in the field of entrepreneurial support: A multi-level approach. *International Journal of Entrepreneurship and Small Business, 31*(1), 47–66.

Thurik, R., & Dejardin, M. A. F. G. (2011). The impact of culture on entrepreneurship. *The European Business Review, 1*(2), 57–59.

Tolbert, C. M., Lyson, T. A., & Irwin, M. D. (1998). Local capitalism, civic engagement, and socioeconomic well-being. *Social Forces,* 77(2), 401–427.

United Nations. (2020). *World social report 2020: Inequality in a rapidly changing world.* New York: United Nations Department of Economic and Social Affairs.

USDA (2017). *Rural education at a glance, 2017 edition.* Washington, DC: United States Department of Agriculture, Economic Research Service.

Weber, M. (1958). *The protestant ethic and the spirit of capitalism (1905).* New York: Charles Scribner's Sons.

Wilkinson, K. P. (1991). *The community in rural America.* Westport, CT: Greenwood Publishing.

Wong, P. K., Ho, Y. P., & Autio, E. (2005). Entrepreneurship, innovation and economic growth: Evidence from GEM data. *Small Business Economics, 24*(3), 335–350.

World Bank. (2020). LAC equity lab: Income inequality—rural/urban inequality. Retrieved from https://www.worldbank.org/en/topic/poverty/lac-equity-lab1/income-inequality/urban-rural-inequality

Wortman Jr., M. S. (1990). Rural entrepreneurship research: An integration into the entrepreneurship field. *Agribusiness, 6*(4), 329–344.

8

DIGITAL INCLUSION AND ITS ROLE IN FOSTERING INNOVATION AND ENTREPRENEURSHIP

Roberto Gallardo

Introduction

The 21st century is starting its third decade. Urbanization, globalization, and industrialization were trademarks of the 20th century, affecting communities in different ways. As a result, innovation and entrepreneurship have benefitted urban more than rural communities. According to the United Nations, urbanization took off in the 20th century. In 1950, 30% of the world's population lived in urban areas. By the year 2050, it is estimated that 68% of the world population—a more than twofold increase—will live in urban areas. In other words, the 21st century is poised to follow a similar trajectory as the 20th century, benefitting more urban communities. However, two recent events—both interrelated and still unfolding—have the potential to alter this trajectory: the global COVID-19 pandemic and the digital age.

COVID-19 has had a tremendous impact on urban and rural communities alike. Entire sectors of the U.S. economy were shut down in the spring of 2020 to contain the spread of the virus. The economic consequences were devastating. Millions of workers lost their jobs and the U.S. economy shrank by 31% in the second quarter of 2020. On the other hand, because of the pandemic entrepreneurship in the country is booming after decades of decline. At the same time, millions of students were asked to engage in e-learning while millions of workers were forced to remote work.

These rather sudden changes became one of the largest natural experiments ever conducted with significant implications for innovation, entrepreneurship, and the industrialization-related legacy trends of the 20th century. These mitigation strategies to contain the virus also shined a very bright light on an issue first identified in the 1990s: the digital divide.

DOI: 10.4324/9781003178552-8

As communities and businesses scrambled to slow the spread of the virus by engaging in e-learning and remote work, a painful realization of the critical importance of adequate broadband connectivity became clearer. Thousands of children missed out on e-learning; workers, whose jobs were remote work friendly, could not benefit from this work strategy; and in many cases entire communities struggled simply because they happened to be on the wrong side of the divide. Small businesses and entrepreneurs who suddenly needed an online presence did not fare well when they realized they did not have the digital knowledge or skills and/or adequate internet connectivity. Government services were shut down and because there were no online options, citizens suffered the consequences.

Roughly during the same time and parallel to the growth of digital applications, the economy in the United States is undergoing a transformation from a service economy to a knowledge economy. This knowledge economy—highly reliant on human capital, innovation, and increasingly in digital connectivity—has come to dominate the economic landscape. Consider that in the year 2001, three high-tech companies (Microsoft, Intel, and IBM) worth $151 billion were in the top 10 brands. By the year 2019, high-tech companies had secured five of the top ten spots (Microsoft, Google, Amazon, Samsung, and Apple) and were worth $700 billion. However, this rising tide has not lifted all boats because the knowledge economy also tends to geographical agglomeration, similar to the traditional goods-producing industries of the 20th century.

As a result, the United States has two economies that are diverging fast.

Despite all this struggling and inequality, COVID-19 and the digital age have opened a window of opportunity for innovation and entrepreneurship to be unleashed in rural areas. Although the knowledge economy is also susceptible to geographic agglomeration, COVID-19 and adequate connectivity can change this trend. However, rural communities need to be aware of this opportunity and take the steps necessary to ensure this opportunity is maximized. While the roadmap involved is not a relatively simple straight shot, it does require a level of awareness and mindset change that is not readily available. Therefore, rural community leaders, economic development practitioners, and extension educators among others need to understand this opportunity and benefit from it.

This chapter is structured in the following way so that readers better understand this changing landscape and opportunity. First, a series of key concepts are reviewed to set the stage for the discussion to come. Second, innovation and entrepreneurship trends are showcased as well as levels of digital connectivity and inclusion to provide a richer context. Third, the implications of these concepts on community and economic development are reviewed to make the case of the opportunity to unleash innovation and entrepreneurship in rural areas.

Key Concepts

In this knowledge economy multiple factors are critical including but not limited to innovation, entrepreneurship, and digital inclusiveness. While an in-depth discussion to define innovation and entrepreneurship is beyond the scope of this chapter, basic definitions are discussed while also providing a more in-depth discussion around digital inclusion for conceptual purposes.

Perhaps the best-known definition of innovation comes from Schumpeter and his "creative destruction" concept, which is the engine of capitalism due to a constant creation and destruction of businesses, products, services, and processes. This "creative destruction" results in economic growth and is driven by innovation. A key player throughout this turnover are entrepreneurs who transform knowledge into innovation, taking new products or services to the market through the creation of businesses. In other words, innovation, entrepreneurship, and knowledge or IEK play a significant role not only in the creation of new businesses but also in improving competitiveness of existing businesses and economic growth.

Another wrinkle to this dynamic is the fact that not all entrepreneurs are the same and tend to agglomerate differently (e.g., urban versus rural). Researchers have identified different types of entrepreneurs based on their innovative capabilities ranging from innovative, common, or reactive to innovative or replicative. This means that the IEK process is better leveraged by specific types of entrepreneurs and in specific geographic areas.

While rural areas tend to have lower entrepreneurship levels—measured by business start-ups—they also have a higher share of older residents that through entrepreneurship of preretirement and retirees may offset the migration of younger more educated residents and its economic impact. After all, recent studies have shown that up to 25% of entrepreneurs were ages 55–64 in 2019 and that individuals ages 55 or older owned 43% of small businesses as of 2020. Regarding innovation, traditional metrics (e.g., patents, and research and development investments) show urban areas benefit more though recent studies using broader measures of innovation have found that significant spillovers, affecting rural areas, exist.

Related to innovation, the emergence of new businesses, and the need to remain competitive is the concept of digital transformation. Digital transformation refers to the transformation of business products, processes, and organizational aspects leveraging digital technology and strategies that go beyond known information technology strategies (e.g., process automation and optimization) and crosses into end-user products, value creation, and new ways to interact with customers.

In addition, as the workforce continues to digitize, this digital transformation affects not only innovation and entrepreneurs but also the economy, organizations, and social relationships. Thus, the emphasis becomes community-wide, making digital inclusive strategies especially important to ensure IEK, digital transformation, and community development thrive.

A digital inclusive mindset and community can augment or undermine IEK as well as businesses and workers as they continue to digitize. A study of more than 180 nations found that social norms and societal culture were the strongest predictors of entrepreneurship, even more so than patents, research and development expenditures, and quality of science, technology, engineering and math education among other entrepreneurship-related metrics. Therefore, if a community's culture and norms are digital exclusive, IEK will struggle to flourish.

Before we define digital inclusion, it is worth discussing first a similar more popular term: the digital divide. The digital divide refers to those with access to digital technology and the knowledge to utilize it versus those that do not. This concept, however, has evolved over time from a first-level binary yes/no internet access to a second-level looking at different skills and uses to a third-level identifying different social and economic outcomes. In other words, the divide becomes more of a continuum requiring a more encompassing concept that can integrate these different levels while also accounting for different social and economic contexts. This brings us to the concept of digital inclusion.

The National Digital Inclusion Alliance identifies five dimensions of digital inclusion: (1) affordable and robust broadband; (2) internet-enabled devices that meet needs of users; (3) digital literacy training; (4) quality technical support; and (5) relevant online content that encourage self-sufficiency, participation, and collaboration. To put it more succinctly, digital inclusion refers to the adoption and meaningful use of digital applications for social and economic benefits revolving around three digital pillars: connectivity, devices, and skills. In fact, research points to adoption having a larger impact on businesses and number of employees in rural areas compared to only availability. Likewise, more robust digital inclusion metrics compared to simply access or availability had more explanatory power when it came to job productivity.

Rural areas and low-income neighborhoods in urban areas struggle with connectivity and more likely than not end up on the wrong side of the digital divide. On the other hand, and although device ownership is close to 70% among U.S. adults, those with mobile only devices engage in fewer online activities. For example, some college students had lower grades and more stress because of their difficulty accessing technology. Lastly, digital literacy and skills are not equally distributed among the population. These interrelated layers lead to multiple degrees of digital exclusion between different groups and geographies resulting in an uneven playing field for IEK to blossom in the digital age.

Therefore, communities and regions need to work on making digital equity a reality. This can be accomplished by focusing first on digital parity—similar levels of digital connectivity, devices, and skills between groups—that, in turn, leads to a more digital inclusive community and ultimately fulfilling the digital equity goal. Digital equity, in turn, allows for residents, organizations, and businesses to participate fully and in a meaningful way in this increasingly digitized economy and society. It can also level the playing field with respect to IEK, potentially unleashing existing rural capacity.

Innovation, Entrepreneurship, and Digital Inclusion Trends

As discussed previously, the association between innovation, entrepreneurs, and knowledge is strong. However, macro trends have not been favorable in the United States over the past decades. The share of companies one year or younger declined by almost half between 1980 and 2015, resulting in the economy becoming "old and fat." New firms are essential for a healthy and dynamic economy. Moreover and because of the increasingly accelerating digital age, digital inclusion needs to be included in the mix to ensure innovation and entrepreneurship strengthen. But what is the state of innovation, entrepreneurship, and digital inclusion among urban and rural?

In the following figures and tables, urban refers to large and small metro counties as well as any adjacent counties. Rural refers to all other counties as defined by the United States Department of Agriculture Economic Research Service urban influence codes.[1] Several innovation, entrepreneurship, and digital inclusion proxies are reviewed. These proxies are not meant to be comprehensive but rather, provide a glimpse of IEK and digital inclusion differences between urban and rural.

Table 8.1 shows multiple metrics related to innovation and entrepreneurship for the nation, urban, and rural counties. Note that the latest year available are not the same due to data availability. Regarding utility patents—those that protect the functionality and use of an invention, and anyone who invents a unique process, device, machine, method, chemical compound, or manufactured product—granted per 100,000 residents, urban counties had a share almost five times higher compared to rural (48.3 versus 9.7).

The percent of nonfarm proprietors of total employed—a widely used entrepreneurship metric—was slightly higher in urban counties compared to rural counties (22.2% versus 21.9%). However, and in an effort to account for different entrepreneur types, the innovative entrepreneurs per 100,000 residents—self-employed and extended proprietors[2] of 35 industries considered innovative—was higher in urban counties compared to rural counties.

Finally, Table 8.1 also shows the average innovation index by county type. This index considers multiple indicators around human capital and knowledge creation, business dynamics, and business profiles as well as output metrics including employment and productivity and economic well-being. A higher number denotes a higher innovation capacity. In this metric too, we see rural counties lagging behind urban counties.

In conclusion, the story is clear and consistent: rural indeed lags behind urban across multiple innovation and entrepreneur metrics. In other words, rural

TABLE 8.1 Innovation and Entrepreneur Metrics by County Type

Innovation and Entrepreneurship Metrics	*United States*	*Urban*	*Rural*
Utility patents per 100,000 residents (2015)[a]	44.0	48.3	9.7
Percent nonfarm proprietors of total employed (2018)[b]	22.2	22.2	21.9
Innovative entrepreneurs per 100,000 residents (2018)[c]	1,566	1,640	964
Average innovation index score (2016)[d]	85.5	91.6	80.4

Source: [a] U.S. Patent and Trademark Office; [b] Bureau of Economic Analysis; [c] Economic Modeling Specialists Incorporated & Low and Isserman (2015); [d] Indiana University Business Research Center.

counties were already behind urban at the time when the economy began to digitize, affecting IEK, at a significant pace. So, how does the digital inclusion landscape look like for urban and rural?

Next, Table 8.2 includes multiple metrics associated with the other key element identified in the previous section playing an increasingly important role in IEK—digital inclusion. The share of homes in the United States with access to fiber-optic broadband was slightly more than one-third (37.9%) compared to 40.5% in urban counties and 20.3% in rural counties. Or put another way, the rural share was half of the urban share. While there are multiple broadband technologies available, fiber-optic has an advantage when it comes to providing symmetrical speeds or identical download and upload speeds.

A metric related to digital inclusion is digital distress. Homes in digital distress include those that rely only on cellular data plans—and their data limits—to access the internet or have no internet access at all. Likewise, homes in digital distress also include those that rely only on mobile devices—no laptop or desktop—to access the internet or have no computing devices at all. These factors place any home in digital distress leading to digital exclusion. In the United States, around 10.8% of homes relied on a mobile device only to access the internet compared to an additional 11.2% with no computing devices at all. In other words, one-fifth of homes in the United States relied on mobile devices only or had no computing devices at all. On the other hand, close to one-quarter of homes in rural counties did not have internet access compared to 14.7% in urban counties, a difference of almost ten percentage points.

Regarding digital equity, Table 8.2 shows the percent of homes without internet access by income type. In the United States, close to 40% of homes making

TABLE 8.2 Digital Inclusion Metrics by County Type

Innovation and Entrepreneurship Metrics	*United States*	*Urban*	*Rural*
Percent Housing Units with access to Fiber-optic (2018)[a]	37.9	40.5	20.3
Percent Households using cellular data only for internet access (2018)[b]	8.8	8.5	11.3
Percent Households with no internet access (2018)[b]	15.8	14.7	24.1
Percent Households with mobile devices only (2018)[b]	10.8	10.5	13.4
Percent Households with no computing devices (2018)[b]	11.2	10.4	17.8
Percent Households with no internet access making less than $35,000 (2018)[b]	39.0	37.7	46.4
Percent Households with no internet access making $75,000 or more (2018)[b]	6.0	5.7	10.1
Average Venture Density per 100 residents (2018)[c]	2.7	3.5	2.0
Average Highly Active Venture Density per 100 residents (2018)[c]	0.6	0.8	0.5

Source: [a] Federal Communication Commission Form 477; [b] 2014–2018 Census Bureau American Community Survey; [c] GoDaddy.

less than \$35,000 had no internet access compared to only 6% of homes making \$75,000 or more. Similar patterns play out in urban and rural, where the share of homes without internet access making less than \$35,000 is significantly higher compared to homes making \$75,000 or more. Note that almost half of homes in rural counties (46.4%) making less than \$35,000 had no internet access compared to 37.7% in urban counties. In other words, in addition to spatial inequity, there is also an income inequity playing out.

Thus far, the digital inclusion metrics have focused on internet and device access. However, the average venture density metrics gauge internet use in an indirect way. The metrics measure ventures—websites and its redirects including email, payments, and social media—per 100 residents obtained from the hosting company GoDaddy. These ventures include businesses and nonprofits and identify a subset of highly active ventures—looking at age, traffic, associated links, and how built-out is the site. Research has found that venture density has a positive impact on local economic outcomes. As shown, rural counties have a lower venture density (2.0) compared to urban counties (3.5). However, the difference between urban and rural regarding highly active ventures was only 0.3 compared to 1.5 for ventures in general.

In summary, the digital inclusion story is not unlike the innovation and entrepreneurs' story. Rural counties are not only lagging in the innovation and entrepreneurship metrics but also playing in an uneven digital field. To ensure rural resiliency and augment IEK, digital inclusion is a must. Next, we discuss the community and economic development implications as rural counties work toward augmenting IEK, in part, by focusing on digital inclusion.

Community and Economic Development Implications

As shown in the previous section, innovation—measured by utility patents—tend to cluster in urban areas. Entrepreneurship, on the other hand, is visible in urban and rural areas, though innovative entrepreneurs also aggregate more in urban areas. Multiple digital inclusion metrics discussed also show urban areas with an advantage. In other words, the playing field is not leveled. Given the digitization of IEK, innovation and entrepreneurship could increase in rural areas if digital parity were a reality.

Prior to COVID-19, research found that remote work had a positive impact on local income and still was not considered a feasible economic development strategy, particularly for rural. However, during the pandemic roughly two-thirds of the country's gross domestic product was generated by workers from home and surveys indicate that anywhere from 14 to 23 million Americans are planning to move as a result of remote work of which, 20.6% were located in a major city. These remote work trends can augment IEK in rural communities, considering that most remote workers are educated higher-income employees.

But not only are remote work trends poised to augment rural IEK. Innovation and small business potential—who also innovate—are affected as well. Consider that the average distance between inventors listed on the same patent tripled between 1970 and 2015. In fact, additional research shows that geographically dispersed establishments are more likely to have joint inventors listed on patents and cite the other establishment's patents. Moreover, related research shows that the internet helps slow the geographic agglomeration of innovative activity. Lastly, technology itself—artificial intelligence—may change how innovation takes place potentially not requiring physical proximity like in the past.

Regarding the potential of small businesses, who also engage in innovation as discussed previously, a study commissioned by Amazon and conducted by the United States Chamber of Commerce Technology Engagement Center concluded that if the digital potential of rural businesses were unleashed, it would result in more than 360,000 jobs over three years, growing small rural businesses' revenue by 21%, equivalent to $84.5 billion per year. However, this potential can only be unleashed by increasing connectivity in rural areas, increasing the talent pipeline with digital skills, and adoption of digital strategies and tools by rural small businesses.

How would these urban-rural differences play out if we looked only at a group of counties with similar internet access at home? To answer this, counties were grouped into four equal groups based on the percent of households without internet access. Table 8.3 includes the recalculated innovation and entrepreneurship metrics using the lowest group where the percent of homes without internet access was 16.9% or less (United States n = 776, Urban n = 597; Rural n = 179).

As expected, innovation and entrepreneurship metrics are higher in the lowest group. However, and although urban exceeded rural (except for the percent of nonfarm proprietors where rural counties outperformed urban counties), the ratio of utility patents per 100,000 residents was roughly three times higher (60.9/20.7) in the lowest group compared to five times higher in the overall group (48.3/9.7).

TABLE 8.3 Innovation and Entrepreneurship Metrics by County Type, Overall and Lowest Group

Innovation and Entrepreneurship Metrics	*United States*		*Urban*		*Rural*	
	Overall	*Lowest*	*Overall*	*Lowest*	*Overall*	*Lowest*
Utility patents per 100,000 residents (2015)[a]	44.0	60.0	48.3	60.9	9.7	20.7
Percent nonfarm proprietors of total employed (2018)[b]	22.2	22.6	22.2	22.6	21.9	23.8
Innovative entrepreneurs per 100,000 residents (2018)[c]	1,566	2,825	1,640	2,840	964	2,237
Average innovation index score (2016)[d]	85.5	99.4	91.6	102.2	80.4	90.0

Source: [a] U.S. Patent and Trademark Office; [b] Bureau of Economic Analysis; [c] Economic Modeling Specialists Incorporated & Low & Isserman (2015); [d] Indiana University Business Research Center.

In addition, notice how the innovative entrepreneurs per 100,000 residents increased significantly in rural counties among the lowest group versus the overall group from 964 to 2,237. Likewise, the average innovation index in rural counties increased from 80.4 to 90, a similar level to the average innovation index score among urban counties in the overall group. Interestingly, the percent of nonfarm proprietors in the lowest group did not change for the country and urban counties but did increase slightly in rural counties from 21.9% to 23.8%.

Granted, homes without internet access are far from a robust digital parity scenario, the causality assumption can be inverted, and other variables need to be controlled for to draw solid conclusions. However, this exercise does highlight trends that seem to support the argument where a more leveled digital playing field can lead to more IEK in rural counties.

As shown with the simple digital parity exercise, digital inclusion is critical to ensure rural counties can augment their IEK and improve their quality of life. Digital inclusion alone will not resolve all the issues faced by rural communities today nor place rural IEK at the level of urban overnight. What is clear, however, is that digital exclusion will most certainly undermine efforts to augment IEK, improve quality of life, and make rural communities more resilient. Rural community leaders and policymakers can take several steps toward digital inclusion.

First, awareness is key. Rural policymakers and community leaders need to be made aware that digital exclusion is a serious threat to the quality of life and community and economic development in their communities. A reason for this lack of awareness may be that rural communities face other issues—poverty, outmigration, overdoses—that further limit rural leader's attention and resources toward digital inclusion. To resolve this, a local and diverse digital inclusion taskforce should focus on making this issue a community priority. More importantly, it will build community capacity so that the community can plan accordingly, especially dovetailing off broadband infrastructure projects.

Second, broadband infrastructure only is not digital inclusion. Digital inclusion is more robust that goes beyond infrastructure and is, unfortunately, many times overlooked. Local leaders should take advantage that broadband infrastructure is high on the priority list, especially during COVID-19, and make efforts to also plan for digital inclusion. Perhaps the best way to link these two related but lopsided efforts is to tie rural broadband infrastructure project with broader, digital inclusion efforts. This digital inclusion piece can make a stronger sustainability argument of the broadband infrastructure investments since successful digital inclusion efforts can leverage the infrastructure for community and economic development.

Third, digital inclusion strategies should be designed such that they can be "stand-alone" efforts or folded into larger, more comprehensive community and economic development strategies. While digital inclusion can focus on social justice issues ensuring disadvantaged and minority groups can participate fully in this digital society, it should also focus on making sure local businesses, organizations, and workers remain productive, competitive, and employable. This is critical as changing shopping trends toward e-commerce will benefit businesses with an effective online presence. Similarly, a comprehensive digital inclusion strategy should help with the digital transformation of industries, businesses, and governments that is now beginning to gain more momentum as a result of the COVID-19 pandemic. Lastly, digital inclusive communities can help local governments be more responsive and transparent.

Consider that inadequate digital inclusion planning will impact workforce development since it may hinder the one-third of workers that are expected to switch occupations by the end of this decade or make it harder for workers to secure middle-skill jobs (do not require a bachelor's degree yet pay above the national living wage) of which 82% require digital skills. Workers will also be least productive as research has shown that broader digital inclusion metrics, compared to simple broadband availability, have a larger impact on job productivity after controlling for other factors.

These steps can be taken by rural local and regional leaders to begin the process to make their communities digitally inclusive, improving their quality of life, and strengthening IEK. However, there are municipal, state, and federal policy issues, which local and regional leaders need to discuss and keep in mind, to ensure digital inclusion efforts are not undermined.

Federal and state governments need to allocate funding specifically for digital inclusion planning and implementation in addition to broadband infrastructure. State broadband policies do matter when it comes to broadband deployment so there is no reason to believe they would not work for digital inclusion. The best digital inclusion solutions tend to be local and therefore communities and regions must be incentivized to address digital exclusion. Lastly, the federal government must come up with a new national broadband agenda tackling mapping issues, competition, and affordability while rural specific broadband programs and resources should move away from their current "good enough" policy.

Fortunately, there are programs and resources available to assist rural leaders and stakeholders as they work to improve innovation, knowledge, and entrepreneurship in their communities through digital inclusion. The Center on Rural Innovation helps communities build a digital economy ecosystem while the cooperative extension system deploys an asset-mapping program based on the intelligent community concept and the Purdue Center for Regional Development assists regions in developing a comprehensive regional digital inclusion plan.

Of course, digital inclusion efforts should be paired with additional efforts to make rural communities more resilient. Dedicated efforts to improve placemaking, entrepreneurial ecosystems, leadership, housing, and civic engagement among others are needed. An all hands-on deck is needed, which implies extensive collaboration and similar levels of awareness. Rural communities can and should take advantage of the opportunities the digital age presents. The COVID-19 pandemic has heightened the need for digital equity across communities. Let us work together to ensure all communities are digital inclusive, innovative, and entrepreneurial.

Notes

1 Urban includes codes 1-4 while rural includes codes 5-12. This typology is not perfect. Rural communities that are included in urban influence areas may not be eligible for rural-designated broadband funds and programs.
2 Covers the same types of jobs as the "Self-Employed" dataset, but these jobs represent miscellaneous labor income for persons who do not consider it a primary job.

Bibliography

Ali, C. (2020). The Politics of Good Enough: Rural Broadband and Policy Failure in the United States. *International Journal of Communication, 14*, 5982–6004.

Assenova, V. (2019a). What Is the Relationship between Entrepreneurship and Innovation Output? Evidence from 219 Economies over 1960–2018. *SSRN*. doi:10.2139/ssrn.3449757

Assenova, V. (2019b). Why Are Some Societies more Entrepreneurial than Others? Evidence from 192 Countries over 2001–2018. *SSRN*. doi:10.2139/ssrn.3449762.

Bairoch, P., & Kozul-Wright, R. (1998). Globalization Myths: Some Historical Reflections on Integration, Industrialization and Growth in the World Economy. In Kozul-Wright, R. & Rowthorn (Eds), *Transnational Corporations and the Global Economy* (pp. 37–68). London: Palgrave Macmillan.

Baumol, W. J. (2010). *The Microtheory of Innovative Entrepreneurship*. Princeton, NJ: Princeton University Press.

Bergson-Shilcock, A. (2020). *The New Landscape of Digital Literacy*. National Skills Coalition. Retrieved from https://nationalskillscoalition.org/resources/publications/file/New-Digital-Landscape-web.pdf

Bloom, N. (2020). *How Working from Home Works Out*. Stanford Institute for Economic Policy Research. Retrieved from https://siepr.stanford.edu/research/publications/how-working-home-works-out

Brady, D., & Denniston, R. (2006, September). Economic Globalization, Industrialization and Deindustrialization in Affluent Democracies. *Social Forces, 85*(1), 297–329. doi:10.1353/sof.2006.0117

Burning Glass Technologies. (2017). *The Digital Age: Middle-Skill Workers and Careers*. Retrieved from https://www.burning-glass.com/wp-content/uploads/Digital_Edge_report_2017_final.pdf

Casselman, B. (2017, September). *A Start-Up Slump Is a Drag on the Economy. Big Business May Be to Blame*. Retrieved from The New York Times: https://www.nytimes.com/2017/09/20/business/economy/startup-business.html

Center on Rural Innovation. (2019). *Our Digital Economy Ecosystem Model*. Retrieved from Center on Rural Innovation: https://ruralinnovation.us/rural-innovation-initiative/our-model/

Clancy, M. (2020). *The Case for Remote Work*. The Entrepreneurs Network. Retrieved from https://static1.squarespace.com/static/58ed40453a04116f46e8d99b/t/5f7603279993bf06c4e1ea93/1601569577104/The+Case+for+Remote+Work.pdf

Crawford, S. (2019). *Fiber: The Coming Tech Revolution—and Why America Might Miss It*. New Haven, CT: Yale University Press.

Crawford, S., & Goldsmith, S. (2014). *The Responsive City: Engaging Communities Through Data-Smart Governance*. Jossey-Bass.

Deller, S., & Conroy, T. (2016). Survival Rates of Rural Businesses: What the Evidence Tells Us. *Choices, Quarter 4*. Retrieved from https://www.choicesmagazine.org/choices-magazine/submitted-articles/survival-rates-of-rural-businesses-what-the-evidence-tells-us

Deller, S., Kures, M., & Conroy, T. (2019). Rural Entrepreneurship and Migration. *Journal of Rural Studies, 66*, 30–42. doi:10.1016/j.jrurstud.2019.01.026

Forman, C., Goldfarb, A., & Greenstein, S. (2014a). Information Technology and the Distribution of Inventive Activity. *National Bureau of Economic Research*. Retrieved from https://www.nber.org/system/files/working_papers/w20036/w20036.pdf

Forman, C., Goldfarb, A., & Greenstein, S. (2014b). Information Technology and the Distribution of Inventive Activity. *National Bureau of Economic Research*. doi:10.3386/w20036

Forman, C., & van Zeebroeck, N. (2019, October). Digital Technology Adoption and Knowledge Flows within Firms: Can the Internet Overcome Geographic and Technological Distance? *Research Policy, 48*(8). doi:10.1016/j.respol.2018.10.021

Gallardo, R., Beaulieu, L. J., & Geideman, C. (2020). Digital Inclusion and Parity: Implications for Community Development. *Community Development*. doi:10.1080/15575330.2020.1830815

Gallardo, R., Collins, A., & North, E. G. (2018, August). Community Development in the Digital Age: Role of Extension. *Journal of Extension, 56*(4). Retrieved from https://www.joe.org/joe/2018august/a2.php

Gallardo, R., & Whitacre, B. (2018). 21st century Economic Development: Telework and Its Impact on Local Income. *Regional Science Policy and Practice, 10*(2), 1–21.

Gallardo, R., Whitacre, B., Kumar, I., & Upendram, S. (2020). Broadband Metrics and Job Productivity: A Look at County-level Data. *The Annals of Regional Science*. doi:10.1007/s00168-020-01015-0

Goetz, S. J., & Han, Y. (2020). Latent Innovation in Local Economies. *Research Policy, 49*(2). doi:10.1016/j.respol.2019.103909

Gonzales, A. L., Calarco, J. M., & Lynch, T. (2018). Technology Problems and Student Achievement Gaps: A Validation and Extension of the Technology Maintenance Construct. *Communication Research*, 1–21. Retrieved from https://journals.sagepub.com/doi/abs/10.1177/0093650218796366?journalCode=crxa&

Hathaway, I., & Litan, R. (2014). *The Other Aging of America: The Increasing Dominance of Older Firms*. Brookings Institute. Retrieved from https://www.brookings.edu/wp-content/uploads/2016/06/other_aging_america_dominance_older_firms_hathaway_litan.pdf

Hegle, J. (2018, May). *Why Digital Inclusion Matters*. Retrieved from Federal Reserve Bank of Kansas City: https://www.kansascityfed.org/en/publications/community/connections/articles/2018/q22018/digitalinclusion

Henderson, J., & Weiler, S. (2010). Entrepreneurs and Job Growth: Probing the Boundaries of Time and Space. *Economic Development Quarterly, 1*, 23–32.

Horrigan, J. B. (2016). *Digital Readiness Gaps*. Pew Research Center. Retrieved from http://www.pewinternet.org/2016/09/20/digital-readiness-gaps/

Jones, K. (2019, November). *Animation: How Tech Is Eating the Brand World*. Retrieved from Visual Capitalist: https://www.visualcapitalist.com/technology-companies-eating-brand/

Low, S., & Isserman, A. A. (2015). Where Are the Innovative Entrepreneurs? Identifying Innovative Industries and Measuring Innovative Entrepreneurship. *International Regional Science Review, 38*(2), 171–201.

Manyika, J., Lund, S., Chui, M., Bughin, J., Woetzel, J., Batra, P., … Sanghvi, S. (2017). *What the Future of Work Will Mean for Jobs, Skills, and Wages*. McKinsey Global Institute. Retrieved from https://www.mckinsey.com/global-themes/future-of-organizations-and-work/what-the-future-of-work-will-mean-for-jobs-skills-and-wages

Matt, C., Hess, T., & Benlian, A. (2015). Digital Transformation Strategies. *Business & Information Systems Engineering, 57*(5), 339–343. doi:10.1007/s12599-015-0401-5

Meyers, K. (2020, August). *Entrepreneurs of a Certain Age, in this Uncertain Time.* Retrieved from Ewing Marion Kauffman Foundation: https://www.kauffman.org/currents/entrepreneurs-of-a-certain-age-uncertain-time/

Moretti, E. (2013). *The New Geography of Jobs.* Mariner Books.

Mossberger, K., Tolbert, C., & LaCombe, S. (2020). *A New Measure of Digital Participation and Its Impact on Economic Opportunity.* Retrieved from https://img1.wsimg.com/cdn/Other/All/FOS-Intl/1/en-US/db5fd8b8-1e0f-4eaf-9ba2-da0dd19a5ea9/White_Paper_VF-final-website.pdf

Muro, M., Liu, S., Whiton, J., & Kulkarni, S. (2017). *Digitilization and the American Workforce.* Brookings Institute. Retrieved from https://www.brookings.edu/research/digitalization-and-the-american-workforce/

Muro, M., & Whiton, J. (2019). *America Has Two Economies--and They're Diverging Fast.* Brookings Institute. Retrieved from https://www.brookings.edu/blog/the-avenue/2019/09/10/america-has-two-economies-and-theyre-diverging-fast/

Nambisan, S., Wright, M., & Feldman, M. (2019, October). The Digital Transformation of Innovation and Entrepreneurship: Progress, Challenges and Key Themes. *Research Policy, 48*(8). doi:10.1016/j.respol.2019.03.018

National Digital Inclusion Alliance. (2019). *Definitions.* Retrieved from National Digital Inclusion Alliance: https://www.digitalinclusion.org/definitions/

OECD. (2016). *Skills Matter: Further Results from the Survey of Adult Skills.* Paris: OECD Publishing. doi:10.1787/9789264258051-en

Pearce, K. E., & Rice, R. E. (2013). Digital Divides from Access to Activities: Comparing Mobile and Personal Computer Internet Users. *Journal of Communication, 63*(4), 721–744. Retrieved from https://academic.oup.com/joc/article-abstract/63/4/721/4086094

Perrin, A. (2019). *Digital Gap between Rural and Nonrural America Persists.* Retrieved from Pew Research Center: https://www.pewresearch.org/fact-tank/2019/05/31/digital-gap-between-rural-and-nonrural-america-persists/

Pew Research Center. (2018). *Mobile Fact Sheet.* Retrieved from Pew Research Center: https://www.pewinternet.org/fact-sheet/mobile/

Piñeiro-Chousa, J., Lopez-Cabarcos, M., Romero-Castro, N., & Perez-Pico, A. (2020, July). Innovation, Entrepreneurship and Knowledge in the Business Scientific Field: Mapping the Research Front. *Journal of Business Research, 115*, 475–485. doi:10.1016/j.jbusres.2019.11.045

Rotman, D. (2019, February 15). *AI Is Reinventing the Way We Invent.* Retrieved from MIT Technology Review: https://www.technologyreview.com/2019/02/15/137023/ai-is-reinventing-the-way-we-invent/

Rupasingha, A., & Goetz, S. J. (2013, March). Self-employment and Local Economic Performance: Evidence from US Counties. *Papers in Regional Science, 92*(1), 141–161. doi:10.1111/j.1435-5957.2011.00396.x

Sallet, J. (2019). *Broadband for America's Future: A Vision for the 2020s.* Retrieved from Benton Institute for Broadband and Society: https://www.benton.org/sites/default/files/BBA_full_F5_10.30.pdf

Schumpeter, J. A. (1942). *Capitalism, Socialism and Democracy.* London: Routledge.

Spurgeon, A. (2018, November). Closing the Digital Divide: How Banks Can Help Rural Communities with Broadband. *Community Development Investments*, 6–9. Retrieved from https://www.dallasfed.org/~/media/documents/cd/pubs/digitaldivide.pdf

The Economist. (2020, October). *The Number of New Businesses in America is Booming.* Retrieved from The Economist: https://www.economist.com/united-states/2020/10/10/the-number-of-new-businesses-in-america-is-booming

Torry, H. (2020, November). *Pandemic Speeds Americans' Embrace of Digital Commerce.* Retrieved from Wall Street Journal: https://www.wsj.com/articles/pandemic-speeds-americans-embrace-of-digital-commerce-11605436200

United Nations. (2018). *World Urbanization Prospects.* United Nations.

Upwork. (2020). *Economist Report: Remote Workers on the Move.* Retrieved from https://www.upwork.com/press/releases/economist-report-remote-workers-on-the-move

U.S. Chamber Technology Engagement Center. (2019). *Unlocking the Digital Potential of Rural America.* Retrieved from www.empoweringruralbusinesses.com

Wamuyu, P. K. (2017, December). Bridging the Digital Divide among Low Income Urban Communities. Leveraging Use of Community Technology Centers. *Telematics and Informatics, 34*(8), 1709–1720. Retrieved from https://www.sciencedirect.com/science/article/abs/pii/S0736585317303210

Wei, K.-K., Teo, H.-H., Chan, H. C., & Tan, B. C. (2011). Conceptualizing and Testing a Social Cognitive Model of the Digital Divide. *Information Systems Research, 22*(1), 170–187. Retrieved from https://pubsonline.informs.org/doi/abs/10.1287/isre.1090.0273

Whitacre, B., & Gallardo, R. (2020, October). State Broadband Policy: Impacts on Availability. *Telecommunications Policy, 44*(9). doi:10.1016/j.telpol.2020.102025

Whitacre, B., Gallardo, R., & Strover, S. (2014, November). Does Rural Broadband Impact Jobs and Income? Evidence from Spatial and First-differenced Regressions. *The Annals of Regional Science, 53*(3), 649–670.

Whitacre, B. E., Meadowcraft, D., & Gallardo, R. (2019). Firm and Regional Economic Outcomes Associated with a New, Broad Measure of Business Innovation. *Entrepreneurship & Regional Development, 31*(9–10), 930–952. doi:10.1080/08985626.2019.1630486

9

RURAL FLOURISHING THROUGH ARTISTIC IMAGINATION

Unleashing the Advantages of Nonmetropolitan America

Timothy R. Wojan

Introduction

The perceived inability of rural areas to contribute fully to the innovation economy is reinforced by the rational explanation of innovation defined as scientism. In this view, scientific and engineering discoveries enlarge the realm of possibility that are exploited by entrepreneurs and commercialized as innovations that consumers value. The concentration of scientific and engineering resources makes large cities the privileged location for innovative activities, relegating lower order places with less capability for producing new knowledge to routine manufacturing, logistics, footloose service provision, and the production of food and fiber (World Bank 2009). Monopoly rents flow to the centers of innovation while the flattening of the world of production through globalization ensures increasingly thin margins. The stories of places left behind can be understood as the erosion of the ability to capture value given the transition from agrarian and industrial economies to the innovation economy.

An alternative view espoused by John Dewey (1929) is that innovation is dependent on two essential inputs: science and imagination. Science is required for a firm grounding in what is, while imagination is required to envision the full realm of possibilities. Early 19th-century America provides a strong challenge to scientism as a robust explanation of innovation as New World productivity growth outpaced that of the Old World by 1830, despite U.S. status as a scientific backwater at the time (Phelps 2013). The innovation advantage of the United States came instead from unfettered "imaginariums" for deriving novel technological solutions and accelerating the rate of exaptation—co-opting technologies and products for use in seemingly unrelated domains. Imagination—the creative spark—emerges from the nonrational combination of disparate ideas that is at the

DOI: 10.4324/9781003178552-9

core of the innovation process. It is only after the potential utility of these combinations are demonstrated that innovations are deemed rational, *ex post*.

This chapter will investigate the possible role that imagination plays in rural innovation, examine the empirical evidence supporting this alternative view of the phenomenon, and discuss the implications for how rural innovation is conceived, assessed, and fostered. A critical assumption throughout is that artistic imagination is a primary enabler of technological or commercial imagination, which provides an empirical toehold for the nebulous and ephemeral character of creative imagination more generally.

The Elephant in the Room: Innovation without Origination

The argument that economics as it has developed tells us very little about the process of innovation has thankfully been broached by such august thinkers as James March, Edmund Phelps, and William Baumol. In a conference on creativity marking the centennial of the Harvard Business School, James March deemed all current theories of innovative entrepreneurship incomplete by the simple fact that none of them address the generation of novelty (Amabile and Khaire 2008). It is as if innovation as the central source of economic growth is treated like the punchline to the joke about an economist stranded on a desert island with a can of tuna: assume a can opener. The novelty of ideas—most of which are bad and all of which are nonrational *ex ante*—that is the essential seminal spark of all innovation is seemingly of no concern. The ideas that make it through to be deemed rational *ex post* arrive fully formed, ready for inserting into some rational process for creating value. The innovation economist is like an agricultural economist studying farming at the supermarket.

The Schumpeterian gales of creative destruction are often invoked as evidence that economists are in fact concerned with the process of origination, and the imagination and creativity that undergird it. While "gales of creative destruction" is an evocative metaphor that effectively captures the process by which new, successful innovation makes current technological solutions obsolete, creativity here too pertains to value creation. The process of discovery in Schumpeterian theory is scientific discovery consistent with scientism—phenomena that are "out there" that scientists discover. Entrepreneurs then explore how these discoveries might add value and bring the various factors together required to introduce an innovation to the market. Imagination plays no part in a process of scientific discovery founded in scientism as both Baumol (2010) and Phelps (2013) convincingly argue.

The great appeal of Schumpeter is in making the processes of innovation and entrepreneurship safe for economists (Baumol 2010; Phelps 2013). Baumol lays out exactly why innovation is so foreign to economic analysis: "Innovation is an entirely heterogeneous output" (Baumol 2010, p. 14). Production of yesterday's invention is merely replication, which is homogenous and lends itself well to the tools of an economist. If the task of the entrepreneur is to identify how new discoveries—external to economic phenomena being studied—can be brought into production to create value, then the intractable nature of innovation can be sidestepped completely. Baumol's strategy for bringing innovative entrepreneurship back within the fold of economic analysis is to segment the innovation market from the product market. The resulting division of innovative labor regards small start-ups as the source of radical innovation, driven by a thirst for breakthrough discoveries, unfettered by the need to produce quarterly revenue to sustain a large organization, along with the rational expectation of zero profits. If innovative entrepreneurs are rationally assessing their probability of a huge initial public offering (IPO) payday, what keeps them going? The thirst for discovery. In contrast, the division of innovative labor on the production side is located in the large R&D department of incumbents, making substantial investments in incremental innovation required by oligopolistic competition. Schumpeter's prediction that corporate R&D would become the primary source of discoveries fueling creative destruction (Schumpeter 1942) is seemingly at odds with the comparative advantage of start-ups in pursuing radical innovation (Baumol 2010).

Baumol makes the case that innovation as a subject for economic study can be accomplished by separating the innovation market, the market for ideas, from the product market. Phelps (2013) takes the nonpecuniary motive driving Baumol's innovative entrepreneurs and applies it to multitudes of actors in the economy. He argues that only a "mass flourishing" of creativity and ingenuity to envision new ways of doing things can explain the explosion in productivity growth that characterized the 19th and much of the 20th century. And this explosion was not set off by scientific discoveries or invention of transformative general-purpose technologies but rather by the grassroots innovation in countless "imaginariums." These imaginariums were found on shop floors, in industrial districts, in farming communities, and in corporate headquarters. Fueled by a seemingly insatiable demand for novelty and the personal achievement associated with inventing a successful—or at least interesting—approach to a problem, imaginariums served as the economic dimension of "the good life" (Phelps 2013, p. 301). Phelps equates the productivity slowdown in Western economies in the latter part of the 20th century with a devaluation of imagination in the search for novelty, as pecuniary rewards came to dominate political and economic discourse. In direct contradiction to the Schumpeterian model of the profit-motivated entrepreneur, the productivity malaise can be explained by the observation that "[w]ealth seeking competes with innovation seeking" (Phelps 2013, p. 247).

Baumol's argument that innovation is an entirely heterogenous output establishes a strong parallel between the creative processes in the technological or commercial imagination, and that of artistic imagination. In both innovation markets and art markets, replication or imitation is not only devalued but may also warrant sanction in the form of patent or copyright infringement. The huge difference between the two is that value in the innovation market is ultimately connected to the transformation of the original ideas into identical goods sold in product markets. In contrast, the arts provide the opportunity for a nearly limitless search for novelty in personal expression, in which the aesthetic value from creation is intrinsic, not reliant on replication in a product market. The search for artistic novelty in this case is largely inconsequential. This provides significant advantages over the search for technological novelty that can impinge on the solvency of a business or the physical safety of a prototype. Pursuing the arts as an avocation would appear to be an ideal cognitive exercise for tapping into the nonrational mental processes required for both artistic and technological imagination.

Before moving onto a discussion of the evolution of thinking on the arts-innovation nexus in economic geography, readers are encouraged to investigate the claim here that the economics of innovation has been devoid of a serious consideration of the nonrational processes inherent in imagination, required for generation of novelty that lead ultimately to groundbreaking innovations. Google Scholar makes a casual investigation quite easy. Using the very low bar of the existence of the word in an article, a search for articles containing "innovation," "imagination," and "nonrational" produces 16,800 hits. If we limit the source to *Research Policy*—the top-ranked journal in the field of innovation—we get three hits but only one substantively addressing the issue of interest here (Loasby 2002). The *Journal of Economic Geography* has published no articles containing these three words. The topic would appear to be wide open so well worth a deeper dive.

The Arts-Innovation Nexus: From Rational to Cognitive Science Explanations

The *Journal of Economic Geography* published Richard Florida's article entitled "The Economic Geography of Bohemia" in 2002 that identified and discussed the strong association between the concentration of artists in metropolitan labor markets and concentrations of highly skilled workers and high technology industry. The central hypotheses tested were that

> the presence and concentration of bohemians in an area signals an environment or milieux (sic) that attracts other types of talented or high human capital individuals. The presence of such human capital concentrations in a region in turn attracts and generates innovative technology-based industries.
>
> *(Florida 2002, p. 56)*

The article provided a test of Florida's broader Creative Class thesis that attracting workers in creative occupations was the key to economic development, and that the most compelling attractions were amenities that supported creative activities outside of work. For the purposes of this chapter, it is important to recognize that the role of the arts was to signal a highly creative milieu. There was no suggestion or conjecture that arts activities of themselves would contribute to the success of innovative technology-based industries.

A summary of the critiques of "The Economic Geography of Bohemia" is provided in Wojan et al. (2007a), who conclude that the unobserved milieu posited in the article could just as likely be attributable to omitted variables such as the presence of research universities, or merely the rank of a metro area in the central place hierarchy. Wojan et al. (2007a) developed a hard test of the creative/artistic milieu hypothesis drawing from the indicator species literature in conservation biology, which demonstrates that counts of animal or plant species that are more easily observed can provide information on the presence of difficult to observe environmental conditions. Modeling the sources of variation in the arts employment share across areas produced a residual of the arts employment share, indicating whether an area had more or fewer artists than would otherwise be expected. This artist residual—equivalent to the surplus of an indicator species—provided a better conceptual measure of a conjectured creative/artistic milieu than the observed arts employment share. The residual was strongly associated with growth in the creative class in both metro and nonmetro counties, confirming the findings in Florida (2002). In addition, the residual was also strongly associated with faster rates of employment growth and new firm formation in nonmetro counties. The connection between the arts and economic dynamism was still presumed to be attributable to attraction to a common unobserved creative milieu that was not premised on any direct influence of the arts on other sectors. However, the association with employment growth and firm births was suggestive of a possible arts spillover to other sectors, at least in nonmetro counties.

The possible implications of arts employment on innovation in a metropolitan area was investigated by Rodriguez-Pose and Lee (2020) in a *Cities* article entitled "Hipsters vs Geeks? Creative Workers, STEM and Innovation in US Cities." Examining the association between STEM (geeks) and creative worker (hipsters) employment shares on patents per capita, Rodriguez-Pose and Lee conclude that creative workers (who approximate the Bohemian definition that Florida uses) enable higher rates of patenting when combined with STEM workers but have no independent effect on patent productivity. The use of patents per capita is problematic as the measure confounds a rate measure (patents produced by workers plausibly participating in patenting) with a composition measure (the share of the population that might plausibly participate in patenting) (Wojan et al. 2015) that the authors note will bias the analysis toward detecting a geek effect. This limitation will be relaxed in the analysis below. Conjectures regarding the enabling effects of creatives on invention in technology-based industries is still firmly grounded in a rational process of observable interactions between these occupational groups (Siepel et al. 2016). An artistic spillover to the technological imagination is not raised as a possible explanation, but this conjecture is also consistent with the data.

The Rodriguez-Pose and Lee (2020) analysis presents two problems for assessing the impact of "creatives" on innovation: (1) the aforementioned bias of the patents per capita measure that will be higher in regions specialized in patent-intensive industries even when no patent productivity advantage is present, and (2) the very limited range of technological innovation captured by patents that dismisses technological innovation that is unpatentable, and all nontechnological innovation. Wojan and Nichols (2018) address both weaknesses by examining how the design and innovation orientation of individual establishments is associated with the artistic milieu of a nonmetro county. They drew on the 2014 USDA Economic Research Service (ERS) Rural Establishment Innovation Survey (REIS), which describes the degree to which rural businesses engage in innovative activities.

For example, 80% of businesses with a strong orientation toward design (called "Design-Integrated" businesses) were found to be "Substantial Innovators." Artistic milieu was proxied by the presence of performing arts organizations with paid employees, which limited the analysis to nonmetro areas given the ubiquity of these organizations in metro counties. Rural Design-Integrated establishments tended to locate in counties with more highly educated workforces and containing at least one performing arts organization. To preempt criticism that the association between design orientation and the presence of arts organizations may merely be coincidental—i.e., that the design and innovation orientation was due to unobserved or omitted characteristics that tend to co-locate with arts organizations—a reestimation using a proxy strongly correlated with the presence of arts organization and not correlated with business strategy confirmed the initial findings. In contrast to other work examining an arts-innovation nexus, Wojan and Nichols (2018) do not rely on arts employment but on the presence of local institutions likely to have some influence on the artistic imagination of local residents. This conjecture of the artistic milieu affecting business strategy has one missing link—the actual mechanism by which interest or participation in the arts might influence technological, scientific, or commercial imagination in other fields.

A series of papers by Robert Root-Bernstein with various co-authors have examined the association of polymathy—specifically the pursuit of interests in both the arts and sciences—with success in one's core professional field (LaMore et al. 2013; Root-Bernstein 2003; Root-Bernstein et al. 2008). Among stellar achievers, Root-Bernstein et al. (2008) find that Nobel Laureates are roughly 30 times more likely to engage in an arts avocation than the general public, and three times more likely than members of the National Academies of Sciences, Engineering, and Medicine. A study of a somewhat less august population found that science and technology graduates of the Honors College at Michigan State University with lifelong participation and exposure in the arts yielded the most significant impacts for innovators and entrepreneurs (LaMore et al. 2013). The importance of imagination for scientific discovery was best expressed by John Dewey (1929) who wrote that "[e]very great advance in science has issued from a new audacity of imagination." For skeptics, the most recent publication by Root-Bernstein and Root-Bernstein (2020) may help explain why the idea of the artistic imagination influencing innovation in other domains has not had much purchase in economics or economic geography: Nobel Laureates in economics are less than half as likely as those in the sciences to pursue an arts avocation.

Cognitive science and the development of functional magnetic resonance imaging (fMRI) provide greater insight into how imaginative artistic activity might enable imaginative activity more generally. Charles Limb's (2010) popular TED Talk "Your Brain on Improv" summarizes findings from his National Institutes of Health (NIH) study of brain activity in improvising jazz musicians (Limb and Braun 2008). The brain function associated with jazz improvisation critical for understanding a much more fecund generation of novelty is the suppression of activity in those parts of the brain that regulate self-censoring. All truly innovative ideas are nonrational *ex ante* because they would otherwise be available to our rational thinking. But if these *ex ante* nonrational thoughts are censored, then we have been denied the opportunity to investigate their possible utility. By suppressing self-censoring while improvising, the musician can assess the "interestingness" of musical ideas that may have neither been planned nor intended (Stanley and Lehman 2015). These "mistakes" that can form the truly inspired aspects of a solo are recognized by jazz greats like Thelonious Monk, who characterized an unsatisfying performance by saying "I made the wrong mistakes" (Feurzeig 2011).

James March (2011), in his discussion of the generation of novelty, frames the innovation problem as a balance between reliable exploitation (routine intelligence) and potentially disastrous, but with the rare breakthrough, exploration (utopian intelligence). Utopian intelligence hitchhikes on routine intelligence to minimize the probability of repeated errors but maintain availability for a potential discovery. The jazz musician's routine intelligence is knowledge of the chord changes, key centers, and form of the tune with the utopian intelligence open to musical ideas that may be outside safe, high-probability choices. Innovation and improvisation both require this willingness to make mistakes, which in the jazz case has been shown to be associated with the suppression of self-censoring. This would appear to be at the core of human creativity that Sir Ken Robinson (2006) described in the most viewed TED Talk ever as of this writing ("Do Schools Kill Creativity"):

> If you're not prepared to be wrong, you'll never come up with anything original… We stigmatize mistakes in school, mistakes are the worst thing you can make. We are educating our kids out of their creative capacities.

The arts are clearly not the only path to original thought as the Nobel Laureates with no arts avocations prove. But in a world of increasing specialization it is easy to commit all of one's cognitive resources to mastering March's characterization of routine intelligence. Making room for the imagination by stellar scientists and inventors may rely on a large variety of idiosyncratic devices that are likely unobservable. Participation in the arts provides a known device for making room for imagination leading to original creations (National Academies of Sciences, Engineering, and Medicine 2018) and should be observable.

Conceptually, it is straightforward to extend the analysis by Root-Bernstein of polymathy among Nobel Laureates to the effect of polymathy on everyday STEM workers. The challenge is how to implement it. The next section will outline such a test as a proof of concept. A definitive test of the effect of arts avocations on individual STEM workers requiring access to confidential microdata is planned future research.

An Empirical Test: Does the Artistic Imagination Enable the Technological Imagination?

The hypothesis that the arts produce a spillover that benefits the technological imagination is consistent with the "Hipsters vs Geeks?" study that found that per capita patenting rates were positively associated with higher employment shares of both creative workers (hipsters) and STEM worker (geeks) (Rodriguez-Pose and Lee 2020). However, support for the conjecture is weak given the poor construct validity of patents per capita as an indicator of patent productivity (Wojan et al. 2015) and the failure to posit just how the presence of artists might influence that productivity. A much harder test of the hypothesis is possible by isolating that subset of the population who might plausibly participate in a patent application, and by deriving a measure of the likelihood of participation in the arts by the local population. If the subpopulation in an area active in arts avocations produces more patents than the subpopulation in areas with little interest in arts avocations controlling for confounds and endogeneity, then the conclusion that the arts-innovation nexus derives from the interaction of the artistic and technological imagination will be strongly supported by empirical evidence. This section describes in detail an analysis aimed at providing this evidence. For a concise summary of the key takeaways of this analysis, see the sidebar on page 13.

A patenting rate analogous to the fertility rate from demography corrects the compositional bias that plagues patents per capita (Wojan et al. 2015). This is done by identifying those occupations that might plausibly participate in a patent application which is analogous to women of childbearing age who might plausibly give birth. This 'inventive class' was constructed by combining the Science, Engineering and Technical (SET) occupations tracked by the National Science Foundation with 11 detailed occupations consistently associated with patenting at the local level using an iterative regression protocol (Dotzel 2017). A validation exercise confirmed that the inventive class did a better job explaining patenting in nonmetro areas than other collections of knowledge workers made up of college graduates, Richard Florida's Creative Class, or SET occupations alone. The number of patents produced at the local level by the local contingent of the inventive class provides an unbiased estimate of patenting productivity.

The National Endowment for the Arts has collected data on arts avocations of Americans since 1992 in the Survey of Public Participation in the Arts (SPPA) and more recently in the Annual Arts Basic Survey (AABS). As a supplement to the Current Population Survey (CPS), these surveys have the added advantage of making the rich information on the economic and demographic characteristics of respondents available for analyzing arts activity. These data will be used below to identify local characteristics associated with active participation in the arts. However, the sample size is much too small to provide reliable estimates of arts activity at the local level, and geographic identifiers are not even provided for rural respondents below state level. Questions on arts avocations are not likely to be included in the American Community Survey so any hope for producing precise local estimates of arts participation from conventional sources is nil.

This analysis relies instead on unconventional Big Data derived from billions of website visits from geolocated devices. An Arts Avocation index was produced by DStillery, a marketing firm that applies data science techniques to identify customers or "crafted audiences" for a diverse client base. DStillery entered into an agreement with the Indiana University Regional Economic Development (IU RED) project, applying their data science expertise to the study of economic activity. The main objective of the collaboration was examining the value of web browsing activity applied to nowcasting on economic development dashboards (Wojan and Slaper 2020). Crafted audiences related to entrepreneurship, design, and arts avocations were created by DStillery using lists of websites provided by IU-RED and ERS. The websites selected were both popular and viewed as valued sources of information for people interested in: (1) starting or growing a business; (2) all forms of industrial, graphic and web design; and (3) amateur pursuit of fine, performing, or applied arts. The compiled hits to these websites from geolocated devices were then modeled to produce an index by ZIP code that indicates the relative propensity of area residents to click on those websites.

Arts Avocation hotspots are mapped in Figure 9.1, identifying ZIP codes in the 95th percentile of the index. The SSPA/AABA provide strong priors on where we expect arts avocation activity to be highest, at least at the state level. Colorado and northern New England have traditionally had the highest rate of residents actively involved in creating or performing art and these patterns are evident in the map. However, Utah emerges as the state with the largest number of contiguous hot spots. Hot spots are generally not clustered around the largest metro areas, suggesting that the creative class magnets are more likely to be characterized by spectating and arts consumption rather than arts participation. Metro/nonmetro trends evident in SSPA/AABA also confirm this finding, which will be examined further below.

An association between the Arts Avocation index and patenting, controlling for the size of the inventive class in a locale, would provide suggestive evidence of valuable spillovers from the artistic imagination to the technological imagination. However, such an association could be easily dismissed as the result of unobserved heterogeneity—that is, the possibility that the association is due to other factors that happen to be correlated with the Arts Avocation index. If people pursuing arts avocations tend to be more prevalent in university town and cities, in areas with abundant natural or built amenities, or in wealthier communities, the true source of increased patenting productivity may not be reliant on

FIGURE 9.1 Arts avocation hotspots (Index > 1.3209) Mapped at ZIP code level.

the artistic imagination at all. The most parsimonious way to control for possible endogeneity is to find valid instruments for the Arts Avocation index. These would be place characteristics that are strongly associated with the Arts Avocation index but not associated with patenting productivity. The AABA data are used for the metro/nonmetro portions of states to identify possible instruments associated with the prevalence of amateur artists controlling for the full complement of personal characteristics available in the CPS. The added benefit of this analysis is to provide a better estimate of any nonmetro arts avocation advantage.

The candidate variables selected include the level of natural amenities, the share of population over age 25 with a bachelor's degree in an arts major, the share of the workforce that bikes or walks to work, and ERS County Typology categories related to Retirement Destination counties, Recreation counties, and State/Federal Government dependent counties. The level of natural amenities has been strongly associated with the location of the creative class (McGranahan and Wojan 2007), bohemians or the artistic subset of the creative class (Wojan et al. 2007a, 2007b), and the location of arts organizations with paid employees in rural areas (Wojan and Nichols 2018). The decision to major in the arts in college represents a strong interest in the arts that is likely to be pursued after graduation. And since some arts majors will go on to work in the field there is the possibility that the variable will be picking up arts activity in the AABS that is in fact professional. To control for this potentially confounding factor, coefficients will be estimated excluding respondents that report being employed in an artistic occupation. The strong association between active commuting (biking or walking to work) and the artistic or creative milieu of an area was uncovered in research examining the association between active commuting and body mass index (Wojan and Hamrick 2015). In the course of the research, it was found that the surplus or deficit of artists in an area (Wojan, Lambert and McGranahan 2007a) was strongly associated with the share of the population walking or biking to work.

Findings from an analysis of the likelihood of pursuing any of the 11 arts that are asked about in the 2018 AABA (singing, playing a musical instrument, photography as artistic activity, leatherwork, metalwork, woodwork, dance, ceramics, fine arts, and creative writing) are presented in Table 9.1.

The personal characteristic control variables are generally consistent with predictions and earlier research. The most important finding regarding the control

TABLE 9.1 Odds Ratios Associated with a 1 Unit Change in Place and Personal Characteristics

Variable	*Estimate*	*Odds Ratio*
Place Characteristics		
Metro (1 or 0)	−0.1155	0.891
Share of Commuters Walk or Bike (0.005–0.092 max)	3.4306	30.896
Share of College Grads w/BA Arts Degree (0.0189–0.068 max)	5.7994	330.112
Government Dependent County (1 or 0)	0.2761	1.318
(Coefficient Estimates Not Statistically Significant)		
Natural Amenities Scale	0.0128	
Retirement Destination County	0.1273	
Recreation County	−0.2715	
Personal Characteristics		
Education Some College (1 or 0)	0.5257	1.692
Education BA (1 or 0)	0.5287	1.697
Education Graduate Degree (1 or 0)	0.6945	2.003
Household Income $50K to $100 (1 or 0)k	−0.0962	0.908
Household Income Greater than $100k (1 or 0)	−0.328	0.72
Number of People in Household (1 or greater)	−0.157	0.855
Occupation Computer/Mathematical Science (1 or 0)	0.3352	1.398
Occupation Arts Design Entertainment Media (1 or 0)	0.8279	2.289
Owns a Business (1 or 0)	0.2325	1.262
Employee of Nonprofit (1 or 0)	0.3289	1.389
Race Multiracial (1 or 0)	0.2843	1.329
Race Black (1 or 0)	−0.3473	0.707
Ethnicity Hispanic (1 or 0)	−0.3348	0.715
Foreign Born (1 or 0)	−0.2956	0.744
62 Years or Older (1 or 0)	−0.1609	0.851

Source: 2018 AABS and 2012–2016 ACS, ERS Natural Amenities Scale.
Coefficient Estimates Significant at 0.05 Level Reported, N = 18,116.
Odds ratio < 1 indicates characteristic reduces arts participation, > 1 increases participation. Odds ratio magnitude comparable for all (1 or 0) variables.

variables for the current analysis is the large number of significant coefficient estimates suggesting that differences in socioeconomic and demographic characteristics explain a lot of the variation in the pursuit of arts avocations. These controls applied at the individual level provide much more confidence that the effects of place characteristics on the phenomenon estimated in these regressions are robust to differences in aggregate personal characteristics across places.

Regarding place characteristics, the Natural Amenities Scale estimate was not statistically significant but both the Share of Active Commuters and the Share of College Graduates with a degree in the Arts displayed a strong positive association with arts activity by respondents. Regarding magnitude, since the variation in share is only about 0.05, the observed increase in odds in the sample would be about 1/20 of the estimated odds (which is based on a unit increase in the independent variable). These are still very large effects, suggesting that both variables would be prime candidates as instruments for the Arts Avocation Index for assessing the impact of arts avocations on the inventiveness of STEM workers. The place characteristic of particular interest is the Metro indicator, suggesting that a metro resident is generally 11% less likely to pursue an arts avocation than their similarly situated nonmetro peer.

Before examining the association between the Arts Avocation index and patenting, verifying that the inventive class provides a powerful gauge of patent production in an area is instructive. Table 9.2 demonstrates a close correspondence between the size of the Inventive Class and the number of patents produced in a county, controlling for the overall size of the local economy (via total employment). The intercept in both metro and nonmetro regressions is not statistically different from zero and the estimated coefficient on Inventive Class employment suggests a precise increment that such workers can be expected to increase patenting. Unexplained variation due to differences in the patenting productivity of Inventive Class workers is examined next.

The geography used in this final stage of the analysis is dictated by the patent productivity dependent variable that is defined simply as average number of

TABLE 9.2 Regression of Average Number of Patents (2013–2015) on Inventive Class Employment Indicates Average Contribution of Each Additional Worker to Patent Production

Variable	*Metro Estimate*	*Metro t-value*	*Nonmetro Estimate*	*Nonmetro t-value*
Intercept	−1.67093	−0.18	0.08664	0.39
Inventive Class Employment	0.04479[a]	42.06	0.01559[a]	26.46
Total Employment	−0.00247[a]	−26.62	−0.000389[a]	−11.49
Adj. R2	0.7147		0.4657	
N	1142		1804	

Source: USPTO; Pooled American Community Survey 2013–2017.
Note: a indicates statistically significant at the 0.01 level.

patents from 2013 to 2015 divided by inventive class employment in each county. This differs from the geography used in the analysis based on metro/nonmetro portions of states (AABS analysis) and ZIP Codes (Arts Avocation index). Resolving the inconsistency with the first analysis is easy enough as the potential instruments identified at the state portion level are available in ACS at the county level. Translating the ZIP Code index from the second analysis to a county level is possible with a ZIP Code/County crosswalk provided by the Housing and Urban Development. However, because ZIP codes can cross county lines it not possible to simply aggregate up to the county level using a population weighted average of ZIP Code index values. Instead we select the index value from the ZIP Code that makes up the largest portion of county residents and apply it to the whole county. Anticipated future analysis with microdata will provide firm data at the ZIP code level.

The first empirical question is whether the place characteristics identified in the AABS analysis have any explanatory power with respect to the Arts Avocation Index. Table 9.3 provides mixed metro/nonmetro results for the College Graduates with a BA in the Arts variable but very strong support for the Active Commuting variable. A county specialization in Government Services that was significant in the AABS analysis was not significantly related to the Arts Avocation Index, replaced by Retirement Destination Counties. However, partial correlations confirm a strong association between the Arts Avocation Index and Arts Degree variable in both metro and nonmetro counties. In contrast, Retirement Destination is not associated with the Arts Avocation Index in metro counties but there is a strong association in nonmetro counties. All three place characteristic variables remain strong candidates as instruments for the Arts Avocation Index.

The final step in selecting valid instruments for the Arts Avocation index is to examine their association with patent productivity, defined as patents per inventive class worker. Valid instruments should have no association, or only be

TABLE 9.3 Regression of the Arts Avocation Index on Place Characteristics Identified in AABS Analysis

Variable	*Metro Estimate*	*Metro t-value*	*Nonmetro Estimate*	*Nonmetro t-value*
Intercept	0.91549[a]	75.36	0.79606[a]	109.63
ActiveCommute	3.22228[a]	8.27	5.53033[a]	19.26
BA Arts	0.16088	0.5	1.70192[a]	7.57
Retirement Destination	0.02718[b]	2.06	0.07352[a]	6.86
Adj R2	0.0888		0.2613	
N	1128		1821	

Source: DStillery Arts Avocation Index; Pooled American Community Survey 2013–2017; 2015 ERS County Typology Codes.

Note: a and b indicate statistically significant at the 0.05 and 0.01 level, respectively.

weakly associated, with patent productivity. Our priors are that BA Arts and Retirement Destination are not likely to be associated with Patent Productivity but ActiveCommute might be, as it is a reasonable proxy for settlement density that has shown an association with innovation. It was found that ActiveCommuting is strongly associated with patent productivity in both metro and nonmetro counties and will thus be included as an exogenous independent variable. BA Arts was not associated with patent productivity in either metro or nonmetro areas and will thus be used to instrument the Arts Avocation index for both. The biggest surprise was Retirement Destination which was positively associated with patent productivity in metro areas but not in nonmetro areas. It will thus be included as an exogenous independent variable in the metro equation but be used as a second instrument for the Arts Avocation index in the nonmetro equation.

Table 9.4 provides results from the instrumental variable regression of patent productivity in a county between 2013 and 2015, the latest years available at the county level from the US Patent and Trademark Office.

The instrumented Arts Avocation Index coefficient estimate is positive and significant in both metro and nonmetro equations. Since this variable is predicted by the BA Arts (metro and nonmetro) and Retirement Destination (nonmetro only) variables, arguments to dismiss this result due to unobservable factors influencing both patenting productivity and amateur arts pursuits are preempted. The magnitudes of these coefficient estimates warrant additional discussion below. In terms of control variables, the Patent Stock in a county is strongly associated with current patent productivity, suggesting that earlier patenting success engenders current

TABLE 9.4 Instrumental Variable Regression of 2013–2015 Patent Productivity on Arts Avocation Index, Patent Stock Control, and Included Exogenous Regressors

Variable	*Metro Estimate*	*Metro t-value*	*Nonmetro Estimate*	*Nonmetro t-value*
Intercept	−0.00833[a]	−5.29	0.000101	0.1
Instrumented Arts Avocation Index	0.016088[a]	9.64	0.003808[a]	3.28
Patent Stock	1.21E-06[a]	21.34	0.000045[a]	17.56
ActiveCommute	0.011382	0.62	0.05348[a]	3.46
Retirement Destination	0.002264[a]	3.08		
Adj R2	0.37027		0.18549	
N	1107		1684	
Dependent Mean	0.01088		0.00594	
Excluded Exogenous Regressors	BA Arts		BA Arts Retirement Destination	

Source: USPTO Patent Count, DStillery Arts Avocation Index; Pooled American Community Survey 2013–2017; 2015 ERS County Typology Codes.

Note: a indicates statistically significant at the 0.01 level.

patenting success. The ActiveCommute coefficient estimate was positive and significant in the nonmetro equation but was not significant in the metro equation. This suggests that rural areas with more compact settlement patterns required for active commuting also tend to be more inventive. The initially perplexing association between Retirement Destination and metropolitan patenting productivity may be explained by ex-urban counties of global cities attractive to both wealthy retirees and prolific inventors with significant royalty income. Ex-urban counties surrounding Seattle, Portland, Austin, Atlanta, Minneapolis-St, Paul, Chicago, and Los Angeles support this explanation (USDA-ERS 2019).

Examining the magnitudes of the instrumented Arts Avocation Index coefficient estimates is critical to assessing the claim that promoting amateur participation in the arts could plausibly influence innovative flourishing of urban and rural areas. The mean of the patent productivity dependent variable provides a natural gauge for assessing magnitude. In metro counties, a patent is produced by 92 (1/0.01088) inventive class workers on average while it takes nearly twice that many in rural counties (182 or 1/0.00549). A one-unit increase in the Arts Avocation Index is associated with only 37 metro inventive class workers required to produce a patent, or 107 in rural areas. In terms of patenting productivity, that is a 147% increase in metro areas and a 69% increase in nonmetro areas. These effects are considerably larger than for the other independent variables included in the analysis. A doubling of the patent stock from mean is associated with a 27% increase in patenting productivity in metro areas and a 24% increase in nonmetro areas. Retirement Destination counties are associated with a 20% increase in metro counties. Doubling the share of workers biking or walking to work from the mean is associated with a 13.7% increase in patenting productivity in nonmetro counties.

The disregard of imagination in the economic formulation of the innovation process that was discussed earlier is not likely to be swayed by the large magnitudes of the effects estimated here. However, it is instructive to compare these magnitudes to the estimated magnitudes of variables that do fit within the rational formulation of innovation based on scientism. For example, expenditure on R&D is regarded as a determinant of national innovative capacity as examined by Furman et al. (2002). And yet when patent stock is included in a regression examining new-to-the-world patents, the R&D variable is not statistically significant. An analysis much closer to the explanation of substate variation in patent productivity examined here was able to detect an association between university R&D and patents in nonmetro areas, suggesting that an addition million dollars was associated with 0.498 patents (Dotzel 2017). The coefficient estimate in metro areas was not statistically significant. The Science and Engineering workforce and patent stock are the two "determinants of innovative capacity" consistently associated with higher patent production, but the supposed theoretical slam dunk of R&D increasing patent productivity has been empirically elusive.

The empirical support for an arts-innovation nexus presented here is encouraging, but there are a few weaknesses that keep it from being definitive. The most obvious is the time inconsistency of the 2018 Arts Avocation index explaining patenting from 2015 and before. A proposed study using the 2018 Annual Business Survey (ABS) will address this. The other weakness the 2018 ABS analysis will address is the reliance on county-level aggregates for the inventive class and patents produced. As microdata, the 2018 ABS analysis will allow examining the patenting productivity of STEM workers within individual firms, providing a much tighter connection between the specialized human capital inputs and inventive outputs. Finally, the 2018 ABS will allow identifying the innovative entrepreneurial firms that Baumol described, operating in innovation markets rather than product markets as that segment of the innovative division of labor more likely to produce radical innovation. Lower value patents linked either to the incremental innovation that characterizes the majority of corporate R&D, or to the strategic production of patent thickets to ward off would-be competitors, will not dilute the patent measure as an indicator of innovative entrepreneurship.

Even with more definitive evidence, the huge advantage that R&D expenditures have over STEM workers pursuing arts avocations is that we know how to increase the former: write a check. Promoting the latter, which seemingly has strong empirical support, will require more imagination. The final section discusses some possible approaches and identifies the rural characteristics likely to reinforce the arts-innovation nexus.

Promoting an Environment for Rural Innovative Entrepreneurship

The premise of this chapter—that a way to increase innovative entrepreneurship is for entrepreneurs to pursue the arts in their free time—is likely to generate lots of scoffs, particularly from the entrepreneurship research community. This group is likely to find the connection between playing an instrument or performing in community theater far removed from value creation in new businesses. However, just as someone who has never studied blood circulation will scoff at the idea that the best remedy for cold feet is a wool cap, those who have never struggled with what underlies the generation of novelty will likely fail to see the connection between nonrational thought and discovery.

Baumol (2010) argues that entrepreneurship taught in business schools and promoted by economic development agencies should really be classified as replicative entrepreneurship. It is concerned with value creation that motivates the Schumpeterian theory of entrepreneurship but is silent on the process of origination and ideation required of innovative entrepreneurship. James March's claim that all theories of innovative entrepreneurship are incomplete because they do not address the generation of novelty need not apply to theories of replicative entrepreneurship because they do not explicitly concern themselves with the process of innovation. The concern regarding the conflating of innovation with entrepreneurship can be partly resolved by recognizing that some entrepreneurship is innovative, but that most entrepreneurship is replicative. Promoting an environment conducive to innovative entrepreneurship is the focus of this discussion. The reader is encouraged to contrast the discussion here with the corresponding sections in other chapters of this book that should reveal some of the differences in promoting replicative versus innovative entrepreneurship.

March (2011) identifies some of the salient features that a theory of the generation of novelty would include but recognizes his efforts are more of a hand wave than a scientific explanation. However, since the practice of innovative entrepreneurship greatly outstrips any attempts at explanation, these features are a good place to start. March identifies three conditions that appear to be necessary for the generation of novelty: slack, hubris, and optimism. These characteristics would seem to have more in common with descriptions of play than with invention or entrepreneurship and that seems to be the point. In other work, March has written about a technology of foolishness as a method of ensuring that organizations devote some resources to exploration, often foreclosed by the preoccupation with exploiting sure bets (March 2006). Exploiting sure bets may be the short-term path to efficiency, but at the cost of long-term resiliency and adapting to scenarios that bring a business or community far from its status quo ante.

The empirical test above (Table 9.4) demonstrated that STEM workers in metro areas are likely to get a bigger boost to patent productivity from an arts avocation than their nonmetro peers. This may reflect the richer interaction of seemingly unrelated expertise available in urban environments (Berkes & Gaetani 2021). However, the empirical evidence in Table 9.1 suggests that the nonmetro STEM workers may have an advantage in following March's prescription of slack. Rural residents are 11% more likely to pursue an arts avocation than their urban peers, after controlling for a full complement of socioeconomic and demographic factors. Figure 9.1 reinforces the findings in Table 9.1 by identifying arts avocation hotspots in many rural areas. The rural dividend of lower cost of living that translates to a less hectic lifestyle may have a real payoff in finding nonobvious solutions if some of that slack is used to exercise the artistic imagination.

Imagination in the arts or in high-tech industry may be necessary for expressive or market disruptive breakthroughs, respectively, but it is not sufficient. Hubris comes from technical competence—the command of a discipline or art form—that allows one to step outside commonly accepted parameters. The willingness to make mistakes—to suppress self-censoring—is reinforced when one is confident that diversions are not unforced known errors that rookies commonly make (see Box 9.1). Innovation as the exploration of the adjacent possible requires a firm grasp of the possible (Johnson 2010). Rural innovative entrepreneurship from the scientism perspective would appear to be disadvantaged on this dimension of hubris. However, the history of such innovative breakthroughs as the steam engine or the computer industry in Silicon Valley locate the hubris not in scientific discovery but in the deep tacit knowledge created through artisanal tinkering (Lécuyer 2006; Mokyr 2018). Deep particular knowledge of a local ecosystem, an abandoned production method, or an adventure sport is now much more easily combined with generalizable scientific knowledge or with spatially distributed artisanal tinkerers in emerging open source communities of interest (Wojan 2017). Studies examining the winners of innovation competitions have demonstrated that "expertise" is much more randomly distributed than that imposed by our mental maps of industry specialization (Lakhani 2015).

Box 9.1 Artistic Imagination Enabling Innovation

The focus of the analysis is patents produced by the Inventive Class—occupations most likely to participate in a patent application.

Patents require nonobviousness—a discovery not available through the mere application of skill.

The number of Inventive Class in a county is a powerful predictor of the number of patents produced.

Web behavior (clicking on websites catering to amateur artists) at the local level is used as a proxy for arts participation by the local Inventive Class.

The Inventive Class is 69% more likely to patent in those nonmetro counties where residents are twice as likely as average to click on arts avocation websites.

Advanced econometric techniques are used to preempt criticism that the findings are nothing more than a suggestive association.

The main takeaway: Attracting engineers will increase the patent production of a county. Attracting engineers who play blues guitar, perform in community theater, or write poetry are likely to have an even larger effect.

Optimism as a requirement for novelty generation is best expressed by a quote attributed to Thomas Edison: "I have not failed. I've just found 10,000 ways that won't work." There is much more than the doggedness of blind optimism or a random walk of trial and error in this statement. This type of optimism as a motivating force for inventors or entrepreneurs comes from a vague vision of a promising future state and the capability to discern the difference between potentially instructive failures and total wastes of time. The successful exploration of the adjacent possible will often require unearthing numerous steppingstones, where the path from the status quo to the new discovery will only be revealed in hindsight. The hypothesis that "interestingness" provides a faster path to complex solutions than incremental improvement in an objective function has been affirmed in computer simulations (Stanley and Lehman 2015). "Interestingness" in the case of invention or innovative entrepreneurship is something to be assessed by the artisanal *savoir faire* contributing to hubris. And it is here where the arts-innovation nexus comes full circle: a great innovation is not something that presents itself first as being highly profitable but, rather, as something beautiful. The innovation has aesthetic quality.

Fine art and technological art share this essential aesthetic quality. John Dewey (1934, p. 49) describes aesthetic as "refer[ing]...to experience as appreciative, perceiving, and enjoying...Craftsmanship to be artistic in the final sense must be 'loving'; it must care deeply for the subject matter upon which skill is exercised." Which provides the simplest guidepost for thinking about and assessing initiatives that have the purpose of promoting innovative entrepreneurship: Does this initiative enrich the aesthetic experience of local residents? Stimulating the artistic imagination may provide the innovative payback identified above. But even if it is ineffective in improving prospects for innovative entrepreneurship, the initiatives are still likely to provide benefits in the form of greater self-efficacy and community solidarity. Given the newness of the hypothesis that there is an arts spillover to technological innovation, the possibilities for rural development programming directed to this objective are wide open. The bullets below scratch the surface of possible initiatives:

- The importance of "third spaces" such as coffee shops or bookstores that promote interaction that is different than what occurs at work or home have been identified as an important element of an innovation ecosystem. Third spaces that promote even richer aesthetic experience are those that have introduced open mic nights, or find other ways to introduce art, music, or poetry programming. The Des Moines Social Club provides an excellent example of how these third spaces can contribute to creative placemaking.
- A discussion at the OECD Rural Development conference in 2018 investigated fuller utilization of local high schools as a rural strategy to promote lifelong exploration among the adult population related to the arts and entrepreneurship. Daytime facilities for teaching home economics or industrial arts can easily be repurposed as evening kitchen incubators and makerspaces. Rural art and music teachers that may currently be hired as circuit riders shared among schools might instead split their time between secondary and continuing exploration in a single school.
- Salaries and facilities that will require funds and tests of the arts spillover to innovation and entrepreneurship could be compelling to local or regional foundations. More generally, grant writing for rural arts nonprofits might benefit from strategies that demonstrate the innovation benefits of an arts spillover.
- Cooperative extension has supported robust arts extension programs in the past, most notably the Community Arts Development office of the Wisconsin Extension Service. The rediscovery of arts extension has sparked initiatives in Idaho, Kentucky, Massachusetts, Missouri, and Wisconsin. Sharing examples of arts innovation spillovers through the extension network could help catalyze adoption in other states.

A consequence of the much greater emphasis on pecuniary rewards that Edmund Phelps connects to the productivity slowdown of the past 50 years has also contributed to the devaluation of aesthetic experience. Clearly, if money is the one true measure of value, then the enjoyment and appreciation received from an aesthetic arts experience would be that priced in markets.

> Stimulating the artistic imagination may provide the innovative payback identified above. But even if it is ineffective in improving prospects for innovative entrepreneurship, the initiatives are still likely to provide benefits in the form of greater self-efficacy and community solidarity.

From the economic perspective of pecuniary rewards, the approach suggested here would have to rely on some extra-economic justification of "art for art's sake." The demonstration that it is nonpecuniary rewards that underlie the generation of novelty that is the foundation of all innovation recasts the argument as "art for exploration's sake." From this perspective, the summary justification for the Community Arts Development office in Wisconsin to "accept the goodness of art where we are and expand its worth in the places where people live" (Gard 1968, p. 4) takes on new power. The arts as the most concentrated distillation of aesthetic experience do apparently spillover into the aesthetic experience of ideation and invention—the creative sparks that are the provenance of innovative entrepreneurship.

References

Amabile, T., & Khaire, M. (2008). Creativity and the role of the leader. *Harvard Business Review*, October, 86(10): 100–109.

Baumol, W. (2010). *The microtheory of innovative entrepreneurship*. Princeton, NJ: Princeton University Press.

Berkes, E., & Gaetani, R. (2021). The geography of unconventional innovation. *The Economic Journal*, 131(636): 1466–1514. doi:10.1093/ej/ueaa111.

Dewey, J. (1929). *The quest for certainty: A study of the relation of knowledge and action*. New York: Minton, Balch.

Dewey, J. (1934). *Art as experience*. New York: Penguin.

Dotzel, K.R. (2017). Three essays on human capital and innovation in the United States. PhD Dissertation, The Ohio State University. Available from http://rave.ohiolink.edu/etdc/view?acc_num=osu1499284768818425

Feurzeig, D. (2011). The right mistakes: Confronting the "old question" of Thelonious Monk's chops. *Jazz Perspectives*, 5(1): 29–59. doi:10.1080/17494060.2011.590679

Florida, R. (2002). Bohemia and economic geography. *Journal of Economic Geography*, 2(1): 55–71. doi:10.1093/jeg/2.1.55.

Furman, J.L., Porter, M.E., & Stern. (2002). The determinants of national innovative capacity. *Research Policy*, 31(6): 899–933.

Gard, R.E. (1968). *The arts in the small community—A national plan*. Madison, WI: Office of Community Arts Development, University of Wisconsin-Extension.

Johnson, S. (2010) *Where good ideas come from: The natural history of innovation*. New York: Riverhead Books.

Lakhani, K.R. (2015). Innovation field experiments: Empirical insights and policy implications from organizing innovation contests, NBER Innovation and Policy Conference, April 14, Washington, DC.

LaMore, R., Root-Bernstein, R., Root-Bernstein, M., Schweitzer, J.H., Lawton, J.L., Roraback, E., Peruski, A., VanDyke, M., & Fernandez, L. (2013). Arts and crafts: Critical to economic innovation. *Economic Development Quarterly*, 27(3): 221–229.
Lécuyer, C. (2006). *Making Silicon Valley: Innovation and the growth of high tech, 1930–1970.* Cambridge: MIT Press.
Limb, C.J. (2010 November) *Your brain on improv.* [Video] TED Conferences. Available from https://www.ted.com/talks/charles_limb_your_brain_on_improv?language=en#t-29562
Limb, C.J., & Braun, A.R. (2008). Neural substrates of spontaneous musical performance: An fMRI study of jazz improvisation. *PLoS One*. doi:10.1371/journal.pone.0001679.
Loasby, B.J. (2002). The evolution of knowledge: Beyond the biological model. *Research Policy*, 31(8–9): 1227–1239.
March, J.G. (2006). Rationality, foolishness, and adaptive intelligence. *Strategic Management Journal*, 27(3): 201–214. doi:10.1002/smj.515.
March, J.G. (2011). *The ambiguities of experience.* Ithaca, NY: Cornell University Press.
McGranahan, D.A., & Wojan, T.R. (2007). Recasting the creative class to examine growth processes in rural and urban counties. *Regional Studies*, 41(2): 197–216. doi:10.1080/00343400600928285.
Mokyr, J. (2018). Bottom-up or top-down? The origins of the Industrial Revolution. *Journal of Institutional Economics*, 14(6): 1003–1024.
National Academies of Sciences, Engineering, and Medicine. (2018). *The integration of the humanities and arts with sciences, engineering, and medicine in higher education: Branches from the same tree.* Washington, DC: The National Academies Press. doi:10.17226/24988.
Phelps, E.S. (2013). *Mass flourishing: How grassroots innovation created jobs, challenge, and change*. Princeton, NJ: Princeton University Press.
Robinson, K. (2006, February). *Do schools kill creativity?* [Video] TED Conferences. Available from https://www.ted.com/talks/sir_ken_robinson_do_schools_kill_creativity?language=en#t-21083
Rodriguez-Pose, A., & Lee, N. (2020). Hipsters vs geeks? Creative workers, STEM and innovation in US cities. *Cities*, 100(May): 102653.
Root-Bernstein, R. (2003). The art of innovation: Polymaths and universality of the creative process. In L.V. Shavinina (ed.), *International handbook on innovation* (pp. 267–278). Amsterdam: Elsevier Science Ltd.
Root-Berstein, R., Allen, L., Beach, L., Bhadula, R., Fast, J., Hosey, C., Kremkow, B., Lapp, J., Lone, K., Pawelec, K., Podufaly, A., Russ, C., Tennant, L., Vrtis, E., & Weinlander, S. (2008). Arts foster scientific success: Avocations of Nobel, National Academy, Royal Society, and Sigma Xi members. *Journal of Psychology of Science and Technology*, 1(2): 51–63.
Root-Bernstein, R., & Root-Bernstein, M. (2020). A statistical study of intra-domain and trans-domain polymathy among Nobel Laureates, *Creativity Research Journal*, 32(2): 93–112. doi:10.1080/10400419.2020.1751545.
Schumpeter, J. (1942). *Capitalism, socialism, and democracy.* New York: Harper and Row.
Siepel, J., Camerani, R., Pellegrino, G., & Masucci, M. (2016). *The fusion effect: The economic returns to combining arts and science skills. A report for Nesta*. London: Nesta.
Stanley, K., & Lehman, J. (2015). *Why greatness cannot be planned: The myth of the objective.* Cham, CH: Springer International Publishing.
U.S. Department of Agriculture/Economic Research Service. (2019). 2015 county typology codes. Available from https://www.ers.usda.gov/webdocs/charts/62758/retirementdestination.png?v=6272. Accessed September 7, 2020.
Wojan, T.R. (2017). Opportunities and challenges of spatially distributed innovation imaginariums. In R. Jackson & P. Schaeffer (eds.), *Regional research frontiers* (Vol. 1, pp. 3–20). Cham, CH: Springer.

Wojan, T.R., Dotzel, K.R., & Low, S.A. (2015). Decomposing regional patenting rates: How the composition factor confounds the rate factor. *Regional Studies, Regional Science*, 2(1): 535–551. doi:10.1080/21681376.2015.1095112.
Wojan, T.R., & Hamrick, K.S. (2015) Can walking or biking to work really make a difference? Compact development, observed commuter choice and body mass index. *PLoS One*, 10(7): e0130903. doi:10.1371/journal.pone.0130903.
Wojan, T.R., Lambert, D.M., & McGranahan, D.A. (2007a). Emoting with their feet: Bohemian attraction to creative milieu. *Journal of Economic Geography*, 7(6): 711–736. doi:10.1093/jeg/lbm029.
Wojan, T.R., Lambert, D.M., & McGranahan, D.A. (2007b). The emergence of rural artistic havens: A first look. *Agricultural and Resource Economics Review*, 36(1): 53–70.
Wojan, T.R., & Nichols, B. (2018). Design, innovation, and rural creative places: Are the arts the cherry on top, or the secret sauce? *PLoS One*, 13(2): e0192962. doi:10.1371/journal.pone.0192962.
Wojan, T.R., & Slaper, T.F. (2020). Are the problem spaces of economic actors increasingly virtual? What geolocated web activity might tell us about economic dynamism. *PLoS One*, 15(9): e0239256. doi:10.1371/journal.pone.0239256.
World Bank (2009). World development report 2009: Reshaping economic geography. Washington, DC: World Bank. Available from https://openknowledge.worldbank.org/handle/10986/5991

10

INNOVATING WITH PEOPLE POWER

Bolstering Regional Food Economies through Value Chain Coordination Networks

Sarah Rocker and Jodee Smith

Introduction

This book describes innovation ecosystems as resources and support structures that help get ideas off the ground and grow businesses. This chapter falls into the support structure category of innovation wherein we suggest that the framework of value chain coordination (VCC) is an innovative mechanism for guiding the organization and strategy of small and mid-scale regional agri-food development. This chapter examines a case study in the state of Indiana in which a community engagement specialist at a public university is taking the leading role to develop a more coordinated local and regional food system across the state. The framework of VCC has gained traction in research, policy, and public funding initiatives in the past decade; however, most previous initiatives have focused on individual coordinators and less so on the interaction among many individuals who perform VCC roles. This case study examines the pathway from vision to funding, and ultimately implementing the beginnings of a coordinated state-wide network of value chain professionals in the state of Indiana. The innovation not only fills a gap in agri-food development literature but also exemplifies the need for collaborative organizing strategies of technical assistance support called for in entrepreneurial development literature (Lichtenstein & Lyons, 2001).

This chapter introduces the novel contribution of developing a *regional network of food systems practitioners*, also called VCC professionals, who share the common goal of increasing local growers' capacity and creating demand for local farm products, especially among large, local institutional buyers. While this chapter focuses on the benefits of establishing a formalized network or association of coordination professionals to strengthen outcomes of success for local food and agriculture businesses, this model could be meaningfully extrapolated into other entrepreneurial sectors beyond food and agriculture.

DOI: 10.4324/9781003178552-10

Background

This chapter describes the concept of VCC as a strategy for developing local and regional food systems with a particular goal of supporting small and mid-scale businesses from input suppliers to end consumers along the value chain. While a discussion of this strategy could extend to international contexts and cases, this chapter focuses on the history and potential future of the VCC strategy in a domestic context within the United States. VCC is defined as a set of roles or activities that foster linkages to knowledge, skills, resources, and relationships, which create added value to individuals, firms, product chains, and the broader regional economies in which these activities take place (Rocker, 2019). Table 10.1 outlines the list of roles that coordination professionals perform. Dunning (2016) suggests that there are three main types of outcomes of VCC work building capacity, fostering relationships, and creating enabling market environments. Primary roles are ones that they focus on most, which build capacity and markets for the value chain, enabling roles help support broader environments for markets and chains to develop and thrive.

In 2009, the Ford Foundation's Wealth Creation in Rural Communities Project[1] helped to propel the concept of wealth building value chains (WBVCs) as a development strategy for rural Appalachian communities (Ratner & Allen, 2013). WBVCs are defined as "a business model based on shared economic, social and environmental values in which buyers, processors, producers and others work together for mutual benefit to create value in response to market demand" (Ratner & Markley, 2014: 346). In WBVCs, Ratner and colleagues describe a coordinated network of people, businesses, organizations, and agencies that address market opportunities and meet demand for products and services, while being rooted in a commitment to building local and regional wealth.

Around the same time, the concept of value chains was also gaining traction within the United States Department of Agriculture, seen as a promising business model for small and mid-scale niche food and agricultural businesses to establish viable pathways outside of commodity markets through forming strategic alliances (Diamond et al., 2014). From 2016 to 2018, the USDA Rural Development and Wallace Center at Winrock International funded a program called Food LINC, an acronym for Levering Investment through Network

TABLE 10.1 Roles of Value Chain Coordination for Developing Local Food Systems (Rocker, 2019)

Primary Roles	*Enabling Roles*
Market matchmaking	Resource prospecting
Providing technical assistance	Policy advocacy
	Developing and maintaining relationships
Convening stakeholders	Research, assessment, and education
Innovating and catalyzing new ideas	Facilitating accountability and negotiation

Coordination (USDA, 2016).[2] Food LINC borrowed language from the earlier Ford Foundation development work and applied the strategy of training and supporting value chain coordinators in specific regions to develop wealth building in the context of local food and agriculture. Its goal was to bolster local and regional food development in 13 communities across the United States to increase production, jobs, and access from local food production, processing, and sales. It did so by elevating the framework of VCC and the role of value chain coordinators to connect businesses and stakeholders in developing their local and regional food systems.

Food LINC was successful at bringing together a pilot national community of practice of coordination professionals through phone calls, webinars, email LISTSERV, in-person site visits, workshops, and trainings, while also funding coordinator salaries with a 1-1 match for a grant period of two years. The project elevated the importance of the value chain strategy within the USDA programming and future grant development,[3] and influenced the language of value chains and VCC into policy discussions, including the 2018 Farm Bill.[4] Evaluation of the Food LINC program showed that the program was successful at increasing producer's sales, 2.25 million increase reported in two years across 13 communities and leveraging 4.04 million in additional funding through new grants for the VCC organizations (Dunning, 2017). In addition, research was conducted on the Food LINC pilot to understand the more social impacts of VCC work. Using social network analysis to map advice and business exchange connections established from coordinator-organized convening events, Rocker (2019) demonstrated the development of 'soft' social infrastructure in the form of business relationships and knowledge and new opportunities, resulting from the efforts of value chain coordinators.

In literature on local and regional food systems developments, the concept of networks is far from novel. Scholars have discussed the development of hybrid chains (Cohen & Derryck, 2011), value webs and agri-food webs (Block et al., 2008; Marsden, 2010). Some scholars have challenged the notion of thinking in linear agricultural chains, instead giving rose to notions of relational and situated agri-food networks (Whatmore & Thorne, 1997) or value networks (Meter, 2011). Cohen and Derryck (2011) link value chains to the community-oriented concept of civic agriculture defined as networks of small-scale producers, bounded in local communities, working together towards a more decentralized, socially, and environmentally just food production system (Lyson, 2004). Broader applied economics literature has described the notion of support activities as a "support ecosystem" in the context of regional food networks or RFNs (Lyons & Lee, 2018: 33), while geography scholarship has given rise to the idea of considering RFNs as a unit of analysis to help reveal the embeddedness of the chains within communities (Jarosz, 2000). Networks bring "industrial and organic, large scale and small-scale producers, brokers, retailers, and consumers together spatially and socially through their relations and interactions within regional agri-food networks" (Jarosz, 2000: 281).

Attention has been given to the importance of coordination of agri-food networks, including facilitating disparate and diverse actors (Stevenson & Pirog, 2008) including having an entity to "drive" the network and maintain values such as trust, transparency, and equity (Clancy & Ruhf, 2010). Others have referred more generally to the important actors outside of the chain itself (Lerman, 2012) such as nonprofits to help to facilitate, offer outreach and education (Diamond & Barham, 2011; Zajfen, 2008), and provide access to grants and funding to support food chain activity (Schmidt et al., 2011), as well as community partners who act as liaisons between different value chain actors and help to institutionalize processes (Conner et al., 2011).

What the food systems development literature does not address is the manner in which VCC professionals and the organizations they work for, do or do not work with each other, particularly in a shared region. Again, from research on the pilot Food LINC program, Rocker (2019) discovered in case studies of Food LINC communities, that though a single coordinator was selected to be funded by this national project, the roles of VCC were being performed by many different types of actors in a similar region. Sometimes several people within a single organization would divide or share certain roles, for example one colleague may focus on policy advocacy while another worked on grant writing and relationship building. In other instances, a coordination professional working in a university of nonprofit who is skilled in providing education and technical assistance may partner with a local aggregation and distribution business for helping with market matchmaking. In more challenging scenarios, there could be a lack of awareness of who is performing these roles, for example an Extension educator who coordinates local producers would not be aware of a city nonprofit who has relationships with local restaurants who are looking for supply. Perhaps the most problematic of all is the conflict that arises when territory, such as geography, scope of work, product focus, or stakeholder focus overlaps and tensions can arise over competing for resources to do the same work.

All these challenges point to several important points of consideration for the future of the VCC strategy. The first, is that regional VCC is not performed by a single person, or even hardly ever a single organization or business entity. The roles are complex and it is highly unlikely that any one person or organization would have the capacity to be successful at all of them. It is also undesirable from a resilience perspective to "put all of the coordination eggs in one basket." If all coordination takes place with one individual or one organization, and that individual changes jobs, moves, or the organization folds, the coordination efforts would come to a halt and be very slow to rebound. The second point is that it is critical to refocus the strategy of VCC as a set of shared roles among diverse individuals, rather than training and skilling up a single coordinator. To expand further, the roles of VCC are useful at the level of a specific geography than of an individual. A community, region, or local economy will be well served if it has each of these roles being performed by the most skilled and adept individuals, businesses, and organizations to best do the job. What has been the missing link is developing the strategy for identifying and convening partners who have these skills and a willingness to work together to build a robust network of strategically coordinated and interconnected local and regional food system development initiatives. What follows in this chapter is the case of a state which is blazing the trail, writing the playbook while living it, by developing the first ever state-wide network of VCC professionals.

This chapter builds upon the various streams of literature on coordination of value chains and agri-food networks, which have laid the groundwork for the roles and activities that individual coordinators can play, but say little to nothing about how professionals should work together. Motivated by the belief that VCC professionals are most successful when they work regionally and collaboratively, we detail the process of establishing a network of food and agricultural professionals within a specific region or territory. We describe the origin story from conceptualization through the first two years of establishing a network of food systems coordinating professionals in the state of Indiana. While this book focuses on innovations that are either born out of or are particularly applicable to rural places, we engage in a conversation about how agri-food development is a particularly poignant lens to understand the fundamental interdependence of rural-urban communities in the growth and development of local food economies.

Origins of the Indiana Value Chain Coordination Network

In winter 2018 Indiana had several local food aggregation efforts occurring, in different regions with different models and a number of public, private, and nonprofit organizations interested in building "food hubs." Based on research conducted at the Center for Regional Food Systems, it was clear that the lack of strong markets would remain a barrier for the brick-and-mortar model of food hubs being explored in Indiana. Most of the technical assistance coming from Purdue Extension focused on farm production, and none of the business support agencies were versed in small and mid-sized food businesses in a local supply chain. At the same time, the USDA and the Wallace Center had begun conducting research on "value chain coordination" through the Food LINC project and the concept of utilizing human capital to build social capital and a value chain seemed a good fit for Indiana where businesses and markets were struggling to become profitable in communities and regions with low demand for local food. Working statewide, the Purdue Extension Local Food Coordinator regularly communicated with these diverse organizations seeking to rebuild local value chains by aggregating and distributing from local farms to local buyers such as home consumers and food services. The concept for the statewide value chain network was borne out of a strong need for region-to-region connectivity within the state, tireless efforts by individuals and organizations working to build markets, and recognition that the creative local talent needed support and technical assistance that was not currently available from Extension.

A draft concept of a statewide network that could be launched with funding and supported and coordinated was created, and then shared with Jim Barham from USDA Rural Development, who founded the pilot national project for value chain coordination, Food LINC, and Rich Pirog from Michigan State University, who laid the foundation for these concepts in Iowa with the regional local food coordinators. Both were generous with time and ideas, including the opportunity to apply for federal funding through the USDA Local Food Promotion Program. A second version of the idea as well as the potential funding opportunity was then shared with numerous stakeholders, including nonprofits, agencies, public institutions, and farm businesses across Indiana via phone, email, and meetings over several months. Those who were interested were from a range of sectors: (1) nonprofit farmer-focused organization; (2) nonprofit food council organization; (3) for-profit farm business; and (4) municipal government.

Recruiting Participants to the Network Idea

The network and value chain concepts were assembled and initial outreach to entities in Indiana included: (1) transactional partners selling to wholesale buyers; (2) transactional partners who wanted to start or expand efforts in this market channel; (3) support partners from the public and nonprofit sectors who were working to build capacity in their region. The draft concept included information on how a network of VCPs in transactional and supporting roles would build capacity in Indiana to increase sales in wholesale market channels, how the VCPs would raise awareness of value chain concepts by acting in their various roles and drive home the idea that we are stronger together, even when selling/buying in same arenas.

Jodee Smith had been working with the well-established Food and Growers Association in Batesville, Indiana, since 2012, when they were chosen as a pilot community for a new Purdue Extension program, Rebuilding Your Local Food System. She worked with the FGA on community meetings, asset mapping, learning workshops, travel tours, and visioning. By the end of the pilot, the FGA had created a new strategic plan for their organization, with one of their goals to become a supporting partner and assist growers with more wholesale market sales. They applied for and were awarded a grant from Interact for Health, a health foundation in Ohio, to pursue their concept of the Southern Indiana Farmer Training Initiative (SIFTI). When the concept of a value chain network was presented to the FGA, their nonprofit board was in favor.

Fischer Farms, LLC, was a well-known name in beef sales for both the home consumer and restaurateur in several Indiana towns where their product was sold including Bloomington and Indianapolis. Jodee met Dave Fischer at a Dubois County Economic Development event, hosted by Purdue Extension. Over pulled pork and mashed potatoes, she learned much more about the deep commitment to local and sustainable on the part of Fischer Farms, and the fact that he was adding products from other farms in his distribution and sales channels to restaurants, including maple and sorghum syrup, honey, produce and pork. To hone the idea of a value chain network, Jodee and Dave exchanged several phone calls and he was fully supportive of the concept and grant application as a transactional partner for the network.

The NWI Food Council envisioned themselves as a supporting partner and connector for an 11-county regional food system that borders Chicago. They had a number of organizations at the table discussing how to build the capacity of the region to feed itself with local food, and how partner organizations such as the food bank could have a key role in the physical movement of foodstuffs. They were immediately on board with the idea of a value chain network as a food council, realizing the benefits of working with others and developing a network of peers.

The City of Bloomington had a history of exploring the idea of a food hub, but growers had been resistant to the idea of selling into wholesale market channels due to their consistent direct to consumer sales opportunity at the Bloomington Community Farmers Market. More than eight years after the initial feasibility study for a food hub, undertaken by the Local Growers Guild, the Bloomington Food Policy Council initiated a feasibility study to explore three concepts: (1) food hub; (2) food innovation district; (3) VCC development and support. An Indiana University student scholar led the data collection and generated a report that supported the value chain concepts for the City and was presented to the mayor and supported by the BFPC. That report was shared with Smith at Purdue at the time the concept for the network was being developed. The City and food council agreed on the supporting partner role, rather than a transactional role that a food hub would have in their region.

Other entities were also consulted in the formation of the value chain network concept including: (1) mid-sized produce farmer already selling and self-distributing to restaurants; (2) virtual food market for home consumers; (3) regional network group organizing economic development initiatives including a food hub; (4) county extension office interested in launching a kitchen incubator. All these entities exited the conversation for two main reasons: lack of understanding or interest or a lack of strength or agreement among local community partnerships.

From Grant to Implementation, Formation of the Network

In summer of 2018, the Indiana Farm Connect grant moved into technical review in the granting process at the same time Smith was transitioning to the Indiana University Sustainable Food Systems Science group. Between Dr. Rhonda Phillips at Purdue University, Jodee Smith and Dr. James Farmer at Indiana University and the USDA, it was decided that coordination of the grant and leadership of the network would remain with Smith, at Indiana University, while Purdue University would manage the grant.

Assembling project partners across a geographical region is difficult and regular virtual meetings were established to tackle the first objective: to hire and onboard four value chain professionals. This process took six months, longer than estimated, but a fortunate outcome in terms of preparing the organizations for the work of value chain coordination. Once the CPs were hired by partner organizations, they immediately onboarded the VCPs as a network, beginning with weekly phone calls. This simultaneous launch of VCC within and between organizations was key for trust building and the type of peer-to-peer support necessary for working outside of established networks and knowledge. Working simultaneously in their regions, the VCPs took a needs assessment and asset identification approach to their regional conversations to objectively understand farmers' and buyers' interest, level of commitment and motivations for participating in a local value chain effort. In the weekly meetings the VCPs discuss the nuts and bolts of their work, and engage in topics as peers, learning from each other and finding commonalities among their work. They have engaged in a number of conferences and events together, as outreach to farmers and buyers, and sharing the concept of VCC with local and regional food stakeholders.

As a network, they have invited attendees from state agencies, and others doing VCP work, but have found that the focused efforts on trust building as part of the regular communication and grant activities have helped lay the groundwork for a high level of sharing and collaboration between the VCPs. Moving forward, the group would like to extend these conversations with other VCPs in the state and will work together to figure out what that looks like to ensure the value proposition is a match for them.

Structure and Partner Composition in the Network

Since its formation, the network structure has been maintained over the past two years mainly through coordinated outreach to farmer and food network meetings and weekly phone calls. These calls involve announcements, sharing of updates, upcoming opportunities, and the ability to share resources, insights, and brainstorm solutions to challenges that group members may be having. The group has an articulated common goal of increasing local growers' capacity and resiliency and creating demand for local farm products, especially among large, local institutional buyers, which is articulated in the grant that brought them together to fund their positions fully or partially within their organizations. How they achieve this is largely dependent on their unique contexts, including where they work geographically, the type of organization or business they work for, and other foci of their work including market channel, product, and which types of stakeholders they most interact with. Table 10.2 shows the diversity of the group is primarily along the dimensions of geography, market channel focus, primarily stakeholder connections and the organizational structures in which they work.

Geographic Considerations of Value Chain Coordination

TABLE 10.2 Characteristics of Four Coordination Professionals in the Indiana Network

	Entity	*Geography*	*Market Channel Focus*	*Stakeholder Focus*	*Product Focus*
A	Non-profit	Rural production to rural and urban markets, Southeast Indiana	Online food aggregation and marketplace hub	Small producers	Mixed, produce focus
B	Non-profit	Rural production to urban markets and future rural markets, Northwest Indiana	Direct markets, potential planning future online sales	Small producers, support organizations	Mixed
C	City Government	Urban market focus and surrounding rural counties, South Central Indiana	Planning future online sales, farmer-owned cooperative retail structure	Policymakers and planners	Mixed
D	Farm/ aggregation business	Rural production and aggregation to mainly urban markets, Indiana and adjacent states	Wholesale, restaurants, institutional some direct online sales	Small producers, processors, end buyers	Primarily meat, some other mixed products

This next section brings into focus the geographic dimensions of the coordination efforts represented by the four members of the Indiana network. Figure 10.1 includes a map for each coordination professional, with a blue triangle designating where their organization or business is located and a gold circle to designate the area in which they consider the boundary for their coordination work, which includes where the food was produced, processed, aggregated, distributed, and sold.

In the case of coordinators C and D, they each used a single circle to represent their regions. Coordinator C, a farm which produces, aggregates, and distributes their products as well as products from other Indiana farms and processors, distributes food all over the state to market channels including restaurants, colleges, and end consumers through a series of pick-up locations around the state and even surrounding states, including the Chicago market. Coordinator D, who works within city government mainly with the goal to bring more local food into the city markets including developing a new cooperative retail outlet and promoting local foods in hospitals and public schools. Coordinators A and B chose to use overlapping and concentric circles when describing their work to help articulate their strategy. Coordinator A describes the inner circle (1) a predominantly rural area which is also the location of his organization, as the main production area, whereas the larger circle (2) encompasses the markets. Coordinator B also

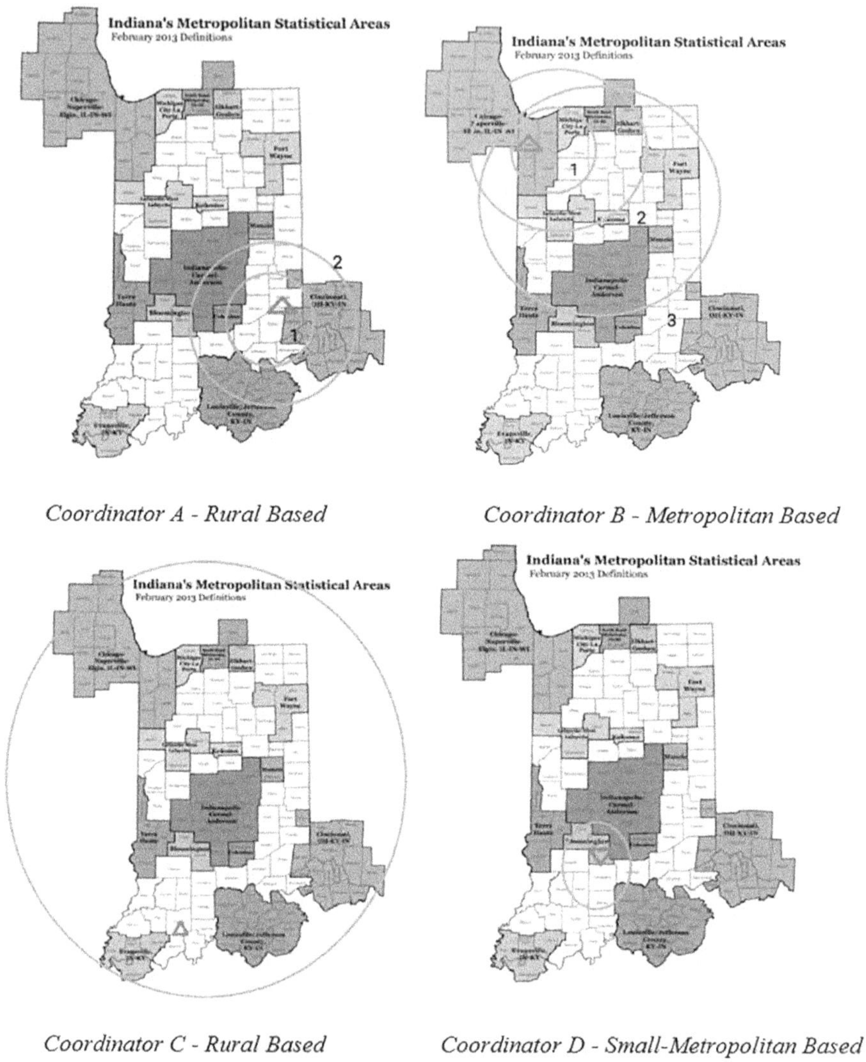

FIGURE 10.1 Locations of four Indiana-based value chain coordinators and their reported regions of work (Original Map Source: Indiana Business Research Center).

works in concentric circles outward from her organization's home in the smallest circle (1) represents a seven-county region which is the core area of her focus as determined by her home organization's primary geographic scope. The slightly larger circle (2) is her personal goal for growing the food system coordination work, in which she believes that working just outside her primary focus area, for example by connecting more producers to markets, or building up capacity to fill the need of larger institutional buyers will help to further strengthen the success of markets and food access in the seven-county core. She includes a final, even larger circle (3) as she describes the importance for transparency and collaboration with other parts of the state, and overall thinking and planning in a higher systems level when doing coordination work. In one example, a project of a future online produce marketplace, there would be the possibility to collaborate with other neighboring regions who may also be aggregating from small farms, and possibly create new distribution routes and an aggregation point to connect those efforts under a single online market platform.

Mapping out the boundaries of coordination professional's work is critical for understanding the reach of the statewide network. It identifies coverage and gaps in terms of areas of production and markets and can be used to show dimensions of prioritization and future aspirations of the work. Each of the coordinators in the network has come to understand these geographic and other dimensions of scope in their colleagues' work. This allows them to make referrals when they learn of new opportunities and reduce redundancy in their efforts.

Rural-Urban Interdependence

Though geography is a critical factor to help identify boundaries of local and regional value chains, they are not self-sufficient or develop in isolation. Rather they could be described as "proximally self-reliant," depending on neighboring regions for social and natural resources (Kloppenburg et al., 1996). The history of public investment in food VCC shows that coordination professionals are located primarily in urban or peri-urban areas and tend to coordinate producers from surrounding rural areas to move products to urban market centers (Wallace, 2017). As seen in the four maps of the Indiana network coordination boundaries, the development of the value chains tends to occur in the regions where the organizations and businesses that are playing the roles of VCC are based. In the case where public or government agencies such as a city government are supporting the work, a coordinator may focus their efforts on developing the foodshed of that city, by coordinating producers to grow and sell to urban markets, restaurants, and schools.

Additionally, there is growing attention about the need for a VCC strategy to *work in rural places for rural people* (Federal Reserve, 2018). Broader national examples of rural-focused initiatives include developing a network of aggregation and distribution networks to serve small-scale rural producers in Appalachia[5] and fostering institutional sales and local food education programming in rural K-5 school districts in the state of Texas, buying food which is produced, aggregated, and distributed within the same rural county.[6] These efforts challenge the paradigm that food systems coordination is not just about developing pathways for local food to serve more wealthy urban markets and consumer preferences (Donald & Blay-Palmer, 2006). However, what may sound simple in intention is nuanced with complexity in practice.

One Indiana coordination professional, whose home base is a rural town with a population less than 7,000 residents,[7] describes the focus and strategy for his work.

> The goal is to increase the livelihood and increase the capacity of the rural production area, with the recognition that if we only focus on that small market area, it could limit the potential for that growth. With the goal of both, growing the market area and productive capacity, exploring this larger market area as a catalyst for both of those.

This coordination professional's strategy highlights the interdependence of rural and urban areas when it comes to new opportunities in food chains. To develop the rural production before developing demand would be an incredible risk for producers. This coordination professional started out his work in the region by making maps of the counties he focused in, using ArcGIS to look at the density of existing market outlets in his region, which he chose to examine K-12 schools, hospitals, colleges, and universities. He found that the density of these potential wholesale outlets was incredibly sparse in the rural region which he is focusing on. Thus, he determined that he needed to leverage the adjacent metropolitan markets to help provide market scale to build up the scale and capacity of the rural producers, while he simultaneously worked to grow rural markets.

Figure 10.2 shows circle 1 as the rural production area, circle 2 as the rural market area which the coordinator is hoping to grow, and circle 3 as the nearby urban market areas which is a strategic part of the growth, providing stable markets to support new and developing rural efforts. The dynamics of interdependence are that the rural can provide the access to products which urban consumers are not, and perhaps could not, produce in their population dense areas, while the wealth of the urban consumers is supporting rural producers' ability to grow their production while rural markets are underway being developed.

Another example of rural production serving rural demand (within the same county) is developing a retail food cooperative with 1,700 members in a county with 19,000 residents. This retail cooperative has concertedly worked to invest in market coordination activities and establishing rapport with two local Amish producing communities in the area. To stabilize demand for the growers, the cooperative launched a "store CSA program" and is working to expand the food box program for produce prescriptions, a subsidized community box program, and a winter artisan box. The box program is an important stabilizing factor in this rural-based value chain. An example of the market coordination activities are the off-season meetings hosted by cooperative staff with producers to discuss the following season's crop planting plans and the crops the store intends to purchase. Prioritizing the CSA food box model is an important market channel strategy to grow emerging value chains, as it provides a higher degree of flexibility with products that can be sold, along with a guaranteed commitment to purchase whatever is produced, giving growers the flexibility to innovate with

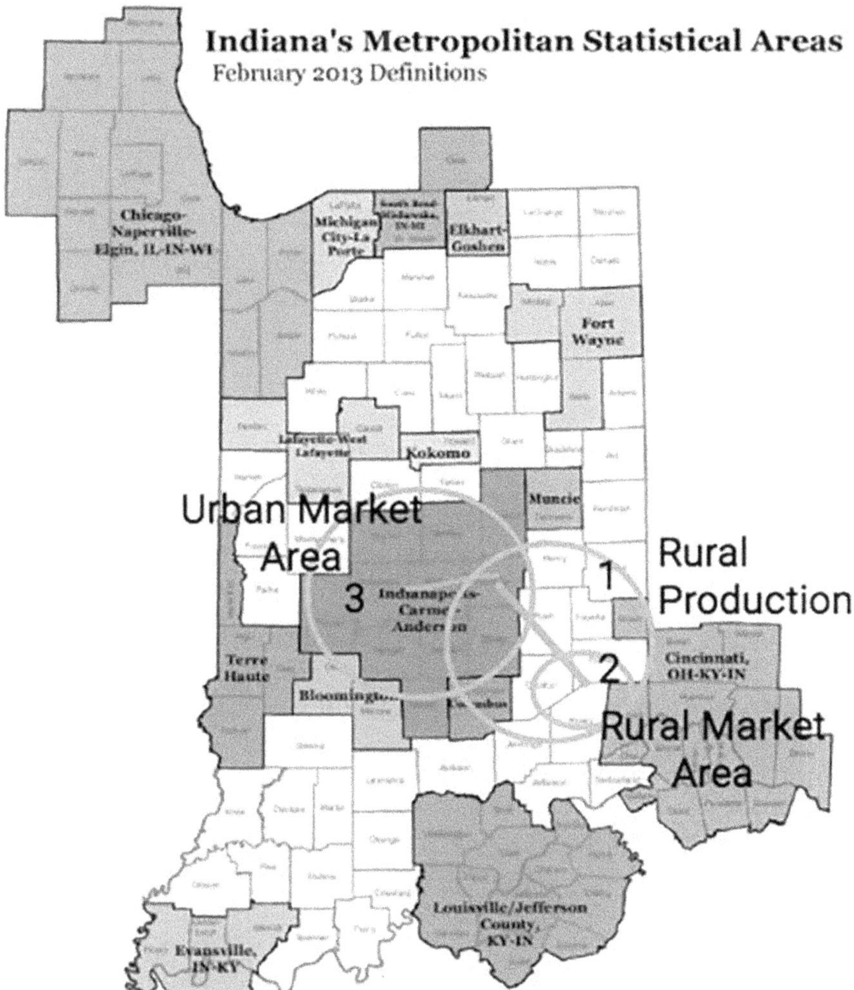

FIGURE 10.2 Coordinator A—rural production coordinated for rural and urban markets.

different crops and scale-up production while the logistics of the cooperative's future grocery retail operations are being developed.

As Tom Lyons describes in his chapter in this book, the challenges that small businesses and entrepreneurs face in rural areas include lower access to financial capital, physical infrastructure and training and development opportunities compared to urban areas (Lyons, 2021). He suggests that developing social capital through strong and weak ties in the community and out of the community is key to overcoming these challenges. The activities of Coordinator A to leverage the markets of nearby urban areas to build capacity for the rural producers and businesses is this strategy of building social capital in action.

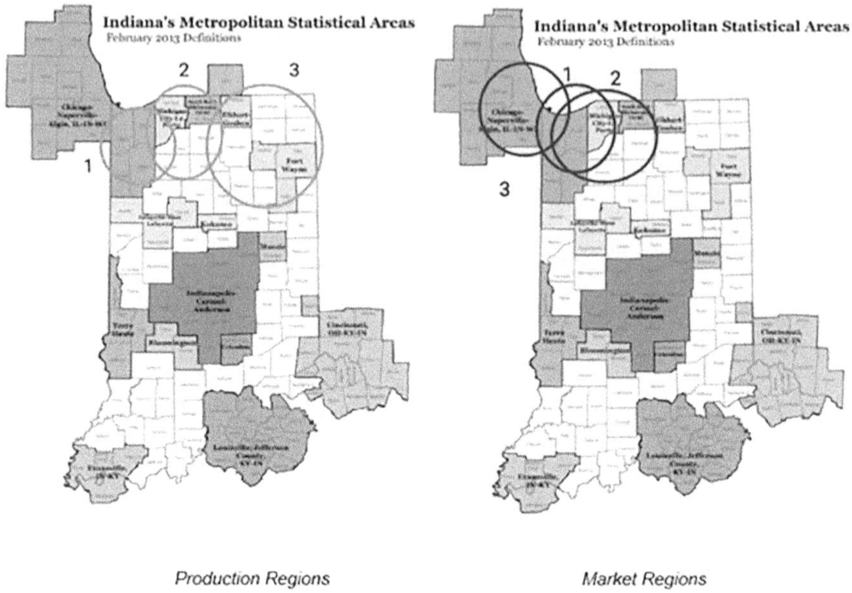

FIGURE 10.3 Coordinator B's production and market regions.

Another coordination professional working in northwest Indiana explains how the grant which funds her work influences the seven-county region, the small circle (1) where she focuses her coordination on supporting producers (Figure 10.3). She uses a series of concentric circles to show that her primary focus on producers starts with the smallest circle where her work is based out of, and the additional circles represent aspirational future development. The second circle on the production map is the area she believes directly influences the success of growers in her core area. The third and furthest away circle are other growers that she hopes to reach in the future once the establishment of an online market comes into existence, and aggregation and sales from growers further away could be possible.

In terms of market development, Coordinator B describes her work as primarily focused on that region as prescribed by the grant but says when she is able to assist with efforts that cross county or even state lines in adjacent states, such as Michigan, she sees the value in doing so. Like the previous example in which the coordinators working in the southern part of the state, Coordinator B working in the north defines her market areas by three circles. In circle one represents the current buyers that she works with, the 2nd circle is the rural oriented adjacent counties that the CP is aiming to grow, and the 3rd circle is the Chicago market area, which provides a source of stability for markets in the interim.

Coordinator B describes the systems nature of doing VCC work, which goes beyond geopolitical borders. This coordination professional has a particularly unique systems lens to the work. In addition to focusing on her seven-county region, she recognizes that the entire northwest area of Indiana is an important corridor for her colleagues in the south to access the large urban market of Chicago. Two of the colleagues in the network have expressed limitations from being able to work with certain partners in the state such as produce distributors who do not yet have customers and routes through their areas. As Coordinator B continues developing production capacity, aggregation, processing, distribution routes her work has the possibility to open pathways and potential for colleagues in the south to move products through this region. Not only can this northwestern-based coordinator provide access to physical kinds of resources like the possibility of new trade routes, pick up locations, processing centers, etc., but she also has access to the important soft infrastructure in this region through her networks of contacts. One example is that the northwestern coordinator invited Coordinator C to attend a conference that she was going to that she thought might be useful for them to make new business contacts. They attended and did in fact make a new retail account contact in the Chicago area as a result of the recommendation. Coordinator C says that this conference was never on their radar before, and they appreciate having the connections to the colleagues in their network to expand their thinking about the work, including to new regions and with new partners. Since that time Coordinator B has also provided market contacts to other Chicago-based buyers including several restaurants and a food processing manufacturer.

On one of the recent weekly calls, when the coordinators were asked about what benefits they receive from being in this statewide network together, they responded that their individual work has been enhanced by learning about new opportunities, resources, and business connections. They also spoke about the importance of having a community of professionals who they can discuss strategy with about the work and how it's going in their respective regions. Sharing and listening to what each other does provides a sense of validation and acknowledgement for this dynamic work, which is often described as having no roadmap whatsoever. Finally, one of the key benefits to a coordination network is the ability for coordinators to see beyond their immediate projects and regions and become more aware of the broader interconnectedness of the food chains and systems which they are helping to coordinate.

Discussion

These examples illustrate how soft infrastructure in the form of business relationships and opportunities can be created and extended through coordination professionals working together for a broader common goal. While each coordination professional represents their own unique geographic, market product, and stakeholder focus for prioritizing work, they can leverage these differences to refer and coordinate opportunities for who is best to serve the efforts as they arise. What is critical to recognize is that it is the network structure that makes possible this kind of sharing through regular communication flow, and the consistency of their communication over several years is what also fosters trust among these coordination professionals. This is akin to what entrepreneurship scholars suggest in developing coordinated systems of providing technical assistance. Lichtenstein and Lyons (2004) describe a "coherent and strategically deployed confederation" allowing each provider to do what it does best, and share opportunities with their colleagues to extend the best possible support to the clients who need their services. The Indiana value chain coordination network (VCCN) is the confederation in an early form. Though there are only five individual members from four organizations, comprised mainly of early adopters to the novel concept of value chain coordination, there is intention to grow the network to include many more actors across the state.

The Indiana VCPs benefit from the network in personal and professional ways that over time have had impact on their work. Each organization is building a new processing, aggregation, and market channel to serve farmers and buyers in their region, and the formalized support of the network was a key factor in their success. The network and the connection to one another fostered trusting communication lines with one another that created many critical benefits including: (1) support for each other to bring ideas to fruition as part of their VCP journey; (2) confidence in the outcomes of the work and strategies they employed to improve their regional value chain and food economy; and (3) personal support for carrying out challenging work in isolation. Each VCP is building their capacity as a leader for their value chain, and leadership needs support not just from the stakeholders and followers, but from other leaders who share the work.

While already having two years behind them, there are still many opportunities for this relatively young VCCN. For example, the federal grant which brought them all together ends in one more year. While the coordinators were initially brought together to fulfill the mission of the grant, building capacity for small and midscale producers in the state of Indiana, when that is over, they will have the opportunity to discuss the possibility to extend or create a new collective mission for their group. Several other questions remain for their future, including who is not currently a part of this network and who might be included in the future?

Some potential barriers to gaining additional members will likely include time, future funding, and securing lasting leadership for this statewide network. However, there may also be ideological challenges including the possibility that not everyone working discrete pieces of the Indiana food system will see the value of thinking or working in bigger systems. Some may prioritize certain market channels or certain producer or consumer groups. All the same complexities experienced in the day-to-day work of VCC will also be present in the mind of the coordinator of coordinators. The network should strive to maintain the ideological openness for a diversity of individual goals while also having a point of broader common ground mission to bring them together.

Additional questions also remain about the future of funding and leadership. In the absence this federal grant, what other funding resources will be needed to sustain the network convening? What resources will it take to incentivize participation and the critical role of coordinating the coordinators? And who will lead the efforts moving forward? Jodee who is the founder and current organizer of the network, who has been referred to as the "mother of local food in Indiana" provides the opportunity for them to exchange their knowledge, skills, and extend each other's professional networks and opportunities. Her role as the visionary and coordination of the network cannot be understated. The combination of specific knowledge, skills, and relationships to be a successful statewide network coordinator is a topic that deserves deeper investigation and attention. What we can see from this early pilot is that Jodee has a long history of working in food systems in the state and was able to draw upon those deep and trusted connections as well as her institutional positions within public universities. In addition, her connections to research and development projects more broadly in the United States helped inform and inspire her vision for Indiana. Other states looking to identify which individual or organization may be best suited to coordinate a network of coordinators can consider these dimensions of having trusted relationships, and ability to work in systems, and maintain relationships across a diverse array of stakeholders in the value chain as a few assets to consider.

Conclusion

This book is focused on the concept of rural innovations, and this chapter has set out to articulate an example of a development initiative with the goal of increasing the capacity and livelihood for predominantly rural producers in the state of Indiana. The innovation of a VCCN is not a high technology, but rather an organizing framework that helps to identify and deploy strategic agri-food development among coordination professionals in a shared geographic region. There are few examples more tangible that that of agri-food value chains to illustrate the point that production, processing, and markets need each other, and that the relative density of population, and natural and build resources logically correspond to rural areas being more typically well suited to the origins of the supply chain where the middle and end links of processing, aggregation, and markets fall in more dense areas. This chapter has drawn attention in the context of agri-food development, how rural and urban areas provide complementary benefits of food access and wealth exchange. Rural production to rural markets is also possible, but because developing markets takes time, diversified market channels and diversified market locations are key to growing at a pace that mitigates risk as rural producers and markets slowly and strategically grow capacity and scale. The statewide network of VCC is an additional layer towards supporting the development of regional agri-food value chains. This network organizes talents, skills, and scope of technical assistance efforts of the coordinators while also fostering trusted collegial support, leading to more efficient, resilient, and connected regional agri-food development across the state.

Notes

1 https://community-wealth.org/sites/clone.community-wealth.org/files/downloads/paper-yellow_wood.pdf.
2 https://www.ams.usda.gov/press-release/federal-philanthropic-partners-join-strengthen- local-food-supply-chains-food-linc.
3 Regional Food System Partnership Grant, https://www.ams.usda.gov/services/grants/rfsp.
4 https://www.ers.usda.gov/agriculture-improvement-act-of-2018-highlights-and-implications/local-and-regional-foods/.
5 https://acenetworks.org/central-appalachia-food-corridor/.
6 https://texaslocalfood.org/2018/02/09/kooking-local-foods-with-elgin-isd/.
7 https://batesvilleindiana.us/.

References

Block, D., Thompson, M., Euken, J., Liquori, T., Fear, F., & Baldwin, S. (2008). Engagement for transformation: Value webs for local food system development. *Agriculture and Human Values, 25*(3), 379–388. doi:10.1007/s10460-008-9113–5.

Clancy, K., & Ruhf, K. (2010). *Report on Some Regional Values Chains in the Northeast.* Northeast Regional Lead Team Project, National Good Food Network, Wallace Center, Arlington, VA.

Cohen, N., & Derryck, D. (2011). Corbin hill road farm share: A hybrid food value chain in practice. *Journal of Agriculture, Food Systems, and Community Development, 1*(4), 85.

Conner, D. S., Nowak, A., Berkenkamp, J., Feenstra, G. W., Kim, J. V. S., Liquori, T., & Hamm, M. W. (2011). Value chains for sustainable procurement in large school districts: Fostering partnerships. *Journal of Agriculture, Food Systems, and Community Development, 1*(4), 55–68.

Diamond, A., & Barham, J. (2011). Money and mission: Moving food with value and values. *Journal of Agriculture, Food Systems, and Community Development, 1*(4), 1–17.

Diamond, A., Tropp, D., Barham, J., Muldoon, M. F., Kiraly, S., & Cantrell, P. (2014). *Food Value Chains: Creating Shared Value to Enhance Marketing Success.* U.S. Department of Agriculture, Agricultural Marketing Service, Washington, D.C.

Donald, B., & Blay-Palmer, A. (2006). The urban creative-food economy: Producing food for the urban elite or social inclusion opportunity? *Environment and Planning A, 38*(10), 1901–1920.

Dunning, Rebecca. (2016). A Value Chain Coordination Framework. Kentucky Value Chain Coordination Practitioners Summit, May 26, 2016, Lexington, Kentucky.

Dunning. Rebecca. (2017). "National Value Chain Coordinators Network Year 1 Assessment Report" Report for Wallace Center at Winrock International. Retrieved through personal correspondence.

Federal Reserve, Molly Hubbert Dolye, Host, Access to Local Food Systems as a Rural Economic Driver, Interview with Sue Beckwith of Texas Local Food. (Podcast). September 2018. Retrieved from https://www.accesspodcast.org/

Jarosz, L. (2000). Understanding agri-food networks as social relations. *Agriculture and Human Values, 17*(3), 279–283.

Kloppenburg, J., Hendrickson, J., & Stevenson, G. W. (1996). Coming in to the foodshed. *Agriculture and Human Values, 13*(3), 33–42.

Lerman, T. (2012). A Review of Scholarly Literature on Values-based Supply Chains. University of California, Davis: Agricultural Sustainability Institute, Sustainable Agriculture Research and Education Program.

Lichtenstein, G. A., & Lyons, T. S. (2001). The entrepreneurial development system: Transforming business talent and community economies. *Economic Development Quarterly, 15*(1), 3–20.
Lyons, T. S. (2021). Social Capital Building for Rural Innovation. In French, C. (Ed.), *Building Rural Community Resilience through Innovation and Entrepreneurship.* New York: Routledge (this volume).
Lyons, T. S., & Lee, M. (2018). The Support Ecosystem for Regional Food Network Entrepreneurship. *Choices.* Quarter 2. Retrieved from https://www.choicesmagazine.org/choices-magazine/theme-articles/the-linkages-between-entrepreneurship-and-sustainable-regional-food-networks/the-support-ecosystem-for-regional-food-network-entrepreneurship
Lyons, T. S., & Wyckoff, B. (2014). Facilitating community wealth building: Understanding the roles played and capacities needed by coordinating institutions. *Community Development, 45*(5), 443–457.
Lyson, T. A. (2004). *Civic Agriculture: Reconnecting Farm, Food, and Community.* Lebanon, NH: University Press of New England.
Marsden, T. (2010). Mobilizing the regional eco-economy: Evolving webs of agri-food and rural development in the UK. *Cambridge Journal of Regions, Economy and Society, 3*(2), 225–244.
Meter, K. (2011). Breaking our chains. *Journal of Agriculture, Food Systems, and Community Development, 1*(4), 23–25.
Ratner, S., & Allen, K. (2013). Shared measures to achieve shared outcomes: Lessons from Central Appalachia. *Community Development,* 44(5), 567–581.
Ratner, S., & Markley, D. (2014). Linking rural assets to market demand: Wealth creation value chains in rural America. *Local Economy, 29*(4–5), 345–353.
Rocker, S. (2019). Value chain coordination: A new strategy for developing soft infrastructure in regional agri-food systems in the united states (Doctoral Dissertation). OCoLC 1107171233. Pennsylvania State University, University Park, PA.
Schmidt, M. C., Kolodinsky, J. M., DeSisto, T. P., & Conte, F. C. (2011). Increasing farm income and local food access: A case study of combined storage, marketing, and distribution strategies that link farmers to markets. *Journal of Agriculture, Food Systems, and Community Development, 1*(4), 157–175.
Stevenson, G. W., & Pirog, R. (2008). Values-based Supply Chains: Strategies for Agri-food Enterprises of the Middle. In Lyson, T.A., Stevenson, G.W., Welsh R. (Eds). *Food and the Mid-Level Farm: Renewing an Agriculture of the Middle.* Cambridge: MIT Press, 119–143.
United States Department of Agriculture. (2016, March 31). Federal, Philanthropic Partners Join to Strengthen Local Food Supply Chains, "Food LINC" to Boost Farm Sales, Grow Local Foods Sector in Ten Selected Regions [Press Release]. Retrieved from https://www.ams.usda.gov/press-release/federal-philanthropic-partners-join-strengthen- local-food-supply-chains-food-linc
Wallace Center. (2017). Food LINC Key Resource Report. Retrieved from personal correspondence.
Whatmore, S., & Thorne, L. (1997). Nourishing networks: Alternative geographies of food. *Reading Economic Geography,* 235–248.
Zajfen, V. (2008). *Fresh Food Distribution Models for the Greater Los Angeles Region.* Center for Food and Justice, Urban and Environmental Policy Institute, Los Angeles, CA, 1–23.

11

RURAL DESTINATION MANAGEMENT INNOVATION AND COLLABORATION IN APPALACHIA

Daniel Eades and Douglas Arbogast

Introduction

Issues such as overtourism and destination stewardship have emerged as central topics for the tourism industry (Destination Analysts, 2019; Destination International, 2019; Skift, 2020), and have gained new urgency in light of the recent COVID-19 pandemic. In places like US National Parks, "loved to death" headlines featuring litter, overcrowding, and mile-long traffic jams in peak seasons are featured in prominent media outlets (Brown, 2020; Stephan, 2020). The spread of the novel coronavirus beginning in early spring 2020 only increased these challenges. With mask and social distance requirements for indoor spaces, Americans have flocked to uncrowded outdoor areas where masks are not necessary, and the risk of virus transmission is low. Activities like walking the dog have become a "piece of paradise" (Coronavirus Impact, June 9, 2020), and consumers are increasingly looking for activities to help them stay occupied and healthy as COVID-19 necessitates social distancing. Several outdoor recreation activities have experienced growth including cycling, paddle sports, camping, bird watching, and nature sightings (America Outdoors, August 2020). This growth in domestic outdoor recreation activities, especially those close to urban centers, has quickly brought unforeseen management challenges for many destinations. Rural destinations in particular face considerable challenges as they work to promote economic prosperity through tourism, including limited funding for marketing and development, limited capacity, and perhaps most importantly balancing the competing objectives of increasing visitation while simultaneously managing growth and maintaining a sense of place (Lane & Kastenholz, 2015).

Many communities support tourism development through the activities of Convention and Visitors Bureaus (CVBs), not-for-profit organizations charged with representing a specific destination. Although they originated in urban areas

DOI: 10.4324/9781003178552-11

with higher visitor densities and an explicit focus on developing convention, meeting, and group business, they often serve as sole destination marketing and management organizations (DMOs) in rural areas also (Buehler, 2021; Midwest Meetings, 2012). The primary funding source for CVBs comes from accommodation taxes, thus most CVBs view their role as promoting those businesses that collect tax, e.g., putting "heads on beds." Rural destinations, with less tourism infrastructure than larger destinations are at a considerable disadvantage as they work to fill staffing needs, market the destination, and work to both grow visitation and manage the destination's asset base. Ultimately, the reliance on increased visitation and visitor spending creates little incentive to shift focus from marketing to management and destination sustainability. Unfortunately, CVBs across the country often find themselves ill-prepared to pivot from their traditional role of destination marketing to destination management.

In this chapter, we describe the innovative responses of three West Virginia destinations to the changing environment of destination management, and the successes and challenges rural DMOs face as they work to balance economic development, sustainable tourism, and residents' quality of life. Located entirely within the Appalachian Mountain region, with more than 78% of its land area covered in forest, West Virginia is recognized by U.S. Census Bureau definitions as the third most rural state in nation. As such, the state's tourism marketing efforts emphasize traditional rural tourism offerings like natural beauty, outdoor recreation, and authentic cultural experiences. Despite its rural nature, many parts of the state have seen rapid growth in visitation. This is especially true of the eastern mountain counties which have benefitted from major highway building projects and can now be accessed in less than four hours by visitors from eastern metropolitan areas in Washington, D.C., northern Virginia, and Maryland. As a result, many CVBs are reevaluating their role in the destination and exploring new ways to not simply market their local assets but develop and preserve them also.

The Challenge of Rural Destination Management

The challenge rural areas face in balancing tourism growth while maintaining authenticity and sense of place has been noted in the literature since the 1970s. Recently, these topics have been framed in the context of destination management versus destination marketing. Where once DMOs were tasked solely with a marketing approach to tourism, there is a recognized need to move towards a management role which includes adapting to technological changes, managing tourist expectations, mitigating impacts, confronting new avenues of competition, recognizing creative partnerships, and finding new measures of success (Gretzel et al., 2006). In fact, Ritchie and Crouch (2003) advocate the transition of the "M" in DMO to refer to "management" rather than "marketing" because the role of DMOs has strengthened and spread as truly innovative destinations have attempted to play a more proactive role in fostering and managing the benefits of tourism development.

Presenza, Sheehan, and Ritchie (2005) proposed a descriptive model to reflect an overall destination management effort in which the destination management organization's activities should include both an "external destination marketing" (EDM) function and an "internal destination development" (IDD) function including coordinating tourism stakeholders, visitor servicing, information/research, crisis management, human resources development, finance and venture capital, resource stewardship, and quality of the visitor experience. The importance of partnerships and collaboration between stakeholders as keys to success in destination management has been stressed by several authors (e.g., Holden, 2010; Pasape, Anderson, & Lindi, 2013).

Despite the important position of destination management and marketing organizations (DMMOs), there is a lack of DMMOs specifically established for rural tourism destinations (Adeyinka-Ojo, Khoo-Lattimore, & Nair, 2014), and no coordinated efforts between national, state, and regional level entities to manage and brand rural tourism destinations competitively (Adeyinka-Ojo, Khoo-Lattimore, & Nair, 2014; Cai, 2002; Pearce & Schanzel, 2013; Pike, 2008; Pike & Page, 2014). As a result, many rural destinations either fail to develop the complete tourism package necessary to attract and retain visitors, or experience growth that negatively impacts quality of life and destination sustainability.

National, Provincial/Regional, and Local Destination Management Roles

Given the breadth of tourism actors involved and their narrow roles in regulating, providing, and marketing tourism products, the responsibility for destination management is unclear and as a result often neglected. According to the UNWTO (2007) publication *A Practical Guide to Tourism Destination Management* responsibilities are traditionally split between national, provincial/regional, and local levels with the national level typically responsible for the more strategic roles while the local level will have responsibility for the more operational elements. In the United States, responses to destination management issues have varied in scale and scope. At the federal level, Congress responded by passing the Great American Outdoors Act which allocates funding for federal land management agencies' deferred maintenance on infrastructure at parks, campgrounds, forests, lakes, and rivers (Passing Great American Outdoors Act, n.d.).

Coordinated responses to management concerns at the state and local levels have been notably absent. At the state level, Oregon currently offers the Rural Tourism Studio which guides communities through the process of developing a shared vision and long-term strategy to enhance and manage tourism. Colorado offers the Destination Development Program which provides tourism-related education, funding, and support with the goals of increasing visitor spending, strengthening local economies, and bolstering community pride. However, preliminary research (Clasen, Vogt, & Andereck, 2019) suggests that most state-level organizations continue to emphasize marketing over management.

Conversations with industry experts (Bill Geist, DMOproZ, personal communication, April 3, 2020) suggest that local and regional efforts are also limited, with few DMOs possessing the financial capacity to move into the destination management field. In response, industry groups like Miles Partnership, which provides quarterly State of the American Traveler reports, published an Overtourism Toolkit to help local destinations address community level challenges linked to tourism growth including crowding and congestion, impacts on historical sites, and increased waste and environmental degradation. Similarly, the Global Sustainable Tourism Council (GSTC), a US-based nonprofit and tourism accrediting body that establishes and manages global sustainability standards for destinations and the industry (hotels and tour operators), is working with communities to address concerns about the impacts of overtourism on quality of life. Local leaders in Sedona, Arizona, looked for approaches to evaluate how tourism was impacting the community and more effectively manage tourism supply and demand. Following a community audit, the community engaged a team of social scientists to facilitate a participatory planning process that engaged a variety of stakeholders and produced a roadmap for future actions. The design and planning process implemented by the community in partnership with local DMO Visit Sedona, demonstrates best practices outlined in previous literature including participatory processes that engage concerned residents, business owners, tourists, public land management agencies, and local area nonprofit organizations; data collection that engages visitors and residents; and public meetings to engage residents at large. The resulting co-created plan provided concrete strategies to address resident quality of life, the local environment, the quality of the economy, and visitor experiences (Vogt, Andereck, & Pham, 2020).

While theoretical models, toolkits, and futures models exist as guides for destinations, there are few practical examples of how rural DMOs are innovating to successfully balance their dual mandates of preservation of place and visitation growth. According to Lane and Kastenholz (2015), rural tourism has failed to develop a destination management culture that can cope with the decentralized, multiplayer, multistakeholder nature of the rural tourism business and its essential links to the conservation and economic management of rural areas. Skift's (2020) Travel Megatrends report states that,

> Destinations that are to remain competitive and attractive to visitors for years to come will have to start protecting their communities and cultural capital now. This shift in approach requires reimagining the way that destination marketing and management intersect — as well as incorporating the concerns of local stakeholders into the tourism boards' strategic planning.

This reimagining requires that DMO leaders create, implement, and share best practices that allow destinations to innovate and remain competitive in the face of change.

Innovation in Tourism Systems

Kanter (1983) conceptualizes innovation as the capacity to change and adapt. It involves both the ability to generate new knowledge and the capacity to transform and implement that knowledge as new processes, products, services, or structures to solve problems. Compared to other industries, research on innovation in tourism is limited (Booyens & Rogerson, 2016); this is especially true of rural tourism innovations (Marasco, De Martino, Magnotti, & Morvillo, 2018). Those studies that do examine the phenomenon largely approach the issue from a firm level perspective with little attention to how entities like DMOs are contributing to more innovative destinations and tourism systems, either by adopting and facilitating the transfer of new knowledge or by innovating in their own right.

Tourism Regions as Systems of Knowledge

Tourism innovation literature identifies several types of knowledge. These include explicit knowledge, codified in documents, books, databases, and reports (Cooper, 2006; Hallin & Marnburg, 2008), or what Hjalager (2010) describes as research-based knowledge, and tacit knowledge, the intellectual capital and skills that individuals possess and employ but cannot fully articulate or codify. Cooper (2006) identified little evidence of knowledge transfer from academic research to practical applications in the tourism industry. Rather, Hjalager (2010) suggests that much of the knowledge used for innovation in tourism is derived from localized, tacit knowledge. According to Hoarau and Kline (2014), this is primarily the result of tourism's emphasis on shared experiences, thus the interactions of tourism stakeholders—visitors, firms, DMOs, government, residents—encourage both the sharing and co-creation of knowledge within the tourism system. In fact, Varra, Buzzigoli, and Loro (2012) characterize destinations as cognitive systems where knowledge, coupled with mutual learning, creates a culture of shared destination management, with successful destinations leveraging innovative techniques, tools, and leadership orientations for effective management.

Innovation through Knowledge Translation and Co-Creation

While shared experiences and co-created local knowledge are valuable, Hjalager (2010) argues that for innovation to occur within the industry, the knowledge must be transformed from tacit to explicit knowledge that can be disseminated using local structures and networks. Varra, Buzzigoli, and Loro (2012) advocate for destination management leaders to play a key role in the cognitive system by aggregating and disseminating this knowledge. Cooper (2006) also argues for a need to link tacit knowledge of local partners and organizations with explicit research-based knowledge to create a scientific community that facilitates knowledge transfer and innovation. Although existing tourism systems are largely informal networks, Hjalager (2008, 2010) identifies several examples of well-defined tourism clusters and demonstrates how partnerships, voluntary organizations, and the public sector have facilitated new innovations and increased competitiveness. Unfortunately, many rural areas are unlikely to have established networks in place to obtain and use explicit knowledge or codify tacit knowledge in ways that allow for easy dissemination and adoption between destination stakeholders.

Cooperative Extension's Role in Knowledge Transfer

Since its creation by the Smith Lever Act in 1914, the Cooperative Extension Service (CES) has served as the traditional vehicle for connecting rural communities and economies to research-based knowledge, especially research generated in the land-grant university system. University faculty members and disciplinary experts generate and translate research which is then disseminated to local networks of stakeholders and citizens via state and county-level educators (USDA, NIFA, n.d.). In addition to facilitating knowledge from the university to the community, these local networks allow for the evaluation of learning tools and program interventions, participatory research with community stakeholders, and input on future research needs (USDA, NIFA, n.d.).

While CES research and outreach originally emphasized the needs of agriculture producers and communities, the system has evolved to address a breadth of rural community and economic development needs. To place rural areas on more equitable footing with urban areas and established agglomeration economies, Lyons, Miller, and Mann (2017) propose a continued and active role for the CES as a network builder for rural innovation systems, and as a facilitator in the spread of both tacit knowledge and research generated within university settings.

Understanding Local Responses to Destination Management

We conducted interviews with three CVB directors to better understand how leaders conceptualize complex issues in tourist destinations, such as tourism resources and impacts, futures for tourism, and preferred tourism scenarios. We selected CVB leaders from targeted destinations that have achieved some success in navigating the dual mandates of effectively promoting and managing their unique cultural and outdoor recreation resources in ways that avoid negative impacts and preserve a unique sense of place. Our questions explored DMO roles that have been identified by tourism literature (Morrison, 2013) as important for achieving excellence in destination management. These include leadership and coordination, planning and research, product development, marketing and promotion, partnership and teambuilding, and community relations.

Although innovation is commonly framed in terms of business and entrepreneurship, we argue that tourism entities like CVBs should be, and are, playing a role in crafting creative and innovative solutions to rural tourism challenges, both as anchors of the local networks that link internal and external actors in the tourism system and as innovative leaders in their own right. We also demonstrate how university outreach initiatives can help DMOs develop innovative responses to present and future tourism development issues in their community, with particular attention paid to Cooperative Extension's role in co-creating knowledge with rural DMOs, sharing research and best practices, and translating tacit knowledge and learned experiences to explicit knowledge that can be shared within the state and across the nation.

Study Area

Tucker County, West Virginia, is a rural county located in the Potomac Highlands region of the state. With a population of 6,839 in 2019 it is West Virginia's second-least populous county. The county's economy boomed along with most of the state in the late 1800s and early 1900s fueled by the coal and timber industries attracting a population of close to 20,000 residents. These resources were largely exhausted by the mid-1950s forcing the industries to leave and population to drop precipitously. The median household income in Tucker County over the 2014–2018 time period was $45,655, while the median household income in the United States over the same period was $60,293 (United States Census Bureau, 2020). Today, due to more sustainable land management practices, Tucker County is a four-season tourism destination. Visitors contributed $46.4 million in direct spending to the county's economy in 2018, supporting 790 jobs (Dean Runyan Associates, 2019). Visitor attractions include the communities of Thomas, Davis, and Parsons; outdoor recreation on federal and state lands including the Monongahela National Forest, Canaan Valley and Blackwater Falls State Parks, Canaan Valley National Wildlife Refuge, and Dolly Sods Wilderness Area; downhill and cross-country skiing; a rich heritage of coal mining and timbering; and art galleries and live music. There is strong community-based support to develop and enhance these outdoor and cultural tourism components. Identifying and preserving these local assets has become of increased importance following the completion of Appalachian Development Highway System, Corridor H, a four-lane highway that puts the once isolated county within less than 2.5 hours of metropolitan centers in Washington D.C. and Northern Virginia.

Further south, in the Monongahela National Forest and the National Radio Quiet Zone, Pocahontas County (population 8,247 in 2019) provides a remote and rugged setting for a breadth of outdoor adventures. The county is home to five state parks and two state forests. Additionally, eight rivers which are protected by the MNF have their headwaters in the county. In sum, these state and federal lands provide more than 350,000 acres of protected spaces for recreation. Situated at a bowl-shaped convergence of two mountains, Snowshoe Mountain Resort offers 257 acres of skiable terrain for winter sports and was recently designated as the Mid-Atlantic's newest Bronze Level International Mountain Biking Association (IMBA) Ride Center. These and other attractions generated an estimated $112 million in direct spending in the county's economy in 2018 and supported 1,300 jobs (Dean Runyan Associates, 2019). The leisure and hospitality sector is the county's largest employer, representing nearly one-quarter of private employment. However, like many tourism-dependent economies, median household incomes are low, estimated at just $49,702 over the 2014–2018 period.

Located along the Ohio River, the City of Wheeling (population 26,430 in 2019) has long served as a transportation hub for north-south river traffic and for east-west road and rail transportation via the National Road and Baltimore and Ohio Railroad. The city's central location between raw inputs from the west and eastern population centers helped facilitate the city's rise as both an industrial center for iron and steel manufacturing, and a political center in the state where it served as West Virginia's first capital following secession from Virginia in 1863. Although industrial activity declined rapidly following the Great Depression and World War II, the city's downtown area still maintains its central market district and is home to three theaters: the Oglebay Institute's Towngate Theatre, the 700-seat Victoria Theater, the oldest theater in West Virginia, and the 2,500-seat Capitol Theater. The city's theaters play host to live acts throughout the year including the Wheeling Symphony Orchestra and the Wheeling Jamboree, the oldest county music radio broadcast in the United States after the Grand Ole Opry. While larger attractions like the Wheeling Island Hotel-Casino-Racetrack, and Oglebay Park, a self-supporting municipal park with five golf courses, including two championship courses, are the most actively marketed by the state tourism office, local destination leaders are working to develop and preserve the city's cultural assets. The diverse asset base attracted $334 million in visitor spending to the Ohio County economy in 2018, and supported 2,870 jobs (Dean Runyan Associates, 2019). However, as with other tourism-dependent economies in West Virginia, median household income in the city was just $42,489, approximately 70% of the national median household income.

Findings

Interview Findings

The challenges of destination management and proposed best practices have been identified in tourism literature for several decades. These include maintaining competitive advantage in light of technological change and competition (Gretzel et al., 2006; Pike & Page, 2014; Ritchie & Crouch, 2003), partnerships and the role of local communities and business in shaping rural tourism (Adeyinka-Ojo, Khoo-Lattimore, & Nair, 2014; Bramwell, 1994; Gretzel et al., 2006; Presenza, Sheehan, & Ritchie, 2005), the role and perceptions of visitors in destination management (Pearce & Schamzel, 2013), branding and maintaining destination image (Cai, 2002; Pike, 2008; Pike & Page, 2014), and planning for and measuring success (Gretzel et al., 2006; Morrison, 2013; Pike & Page, 2014; UNWTO,

2007) However, there are few examples of rural destinations balancing marketing and development activities in ways that achieve sustainable outcomes, engage the diversity of actors in the tourism system, and broadly address communities' tourism planning and community development needs. Our interviews with rural CVB leaders indicate that challenges and resource constraints exist. However, destination leaders are leveraging local assets and their relationships with local and external partners in the tourism system for organizational innovations (OECD, n.d.) that prepare the destination for success.

Moving Beyond Marketing

As with most DMOs, the primary activities of the CVBs we interviewed were focused on marketing activities. This is in large part a function of how CVBs in West Virginia are structured and accredited. To be accredited by the West Virginia Association of Convention and Visitor Bureaus (WVACVB), local and regional CVBs are required to allocate a minimum of 40% of their budget to advertising. According to Jessica Waldo, Tucker County's CVB director, only 20% of the organization's budget is allocated for improvements that enhance visitor's experiences once they are in the destination. However, there is a recognition among destination leaders that to remain relevant and competitive, the CVBs must also demonstrate tangible contributions to community development outcomes. As Frank O'Brien, the director of Wheeling's CVB, noted,

> Most of our strategic plan right now is still based on marketing, …but if that's all we're doing, then we can be replaced and we're not playing a significant enough role in the community's development to be viable. … Our revenue stream is very attractive to government people that want to put it for roads, or they want to fix a pothole. … If you can show them that you are involved in marketing *and* management *and* building a destination, they're not going to come after your revenue stream as much.

For Cara Rose, the Director of Pocahontas County's CVB, marketing and management activities like product development are intrinsically linked and equally important for success, "Its much bigger than marketing. Marketing is the number one thing, but in order to do marketing, you've got to have your product development."

According to Morrison (2013), product development activities are critical to destination sustainability. DMOs are recommended to maintain an active role in inventorying current destination offerings, identifying new tourism product development opportunities, and assisting in realizing projects and programs. The CVB directors we spoke to were aware of the need for continuous product improvement in order to remain competitive. In Wheeling, the community quickly realized negative impacts following the closing of one of their theaters. Realizing that these cultural facilities were essential to maintaining a unique identity and supporting small businesses in the city's downtown, the CVB took the lead role in acquiring and rehabilitating the 2,500-seat Capitol Theater. According to Frank O'Brien, Wheeling CVB Director,

> We had lost one more reason for people to come to Wheeling. And you can't afford to lose too many, because if you lose the things that make it a unique destination, [marketing the destination] is really tough. My board ultimately made the decision to allow us to buy the theater. We took revenue that was we received from hotels and motels, and we redirected that into a mortgage at the Capitol Theater and purchased that.

Even in the counties blessed with an abundance of outdoor recreation assets there was a recognition that investment was required to enhance and take full advantage of those resources. As Jessica Waldo, Director of the Tucker County CVB, noted, "we have to stop relying on our natural attractions to stay a competitive tourism destination...people like Ohio are dumping tons of money into trail development... [our destination] is going to fall behind if we don't reinvest." In Pocahontas County these investments first began by identifying assets that could be leveraged to take advantage of new recreation trends. For example, ski lifts and downhill ski trails, coupled with new trail building efforts, allowed Snowshoe Mountain to expand tourism offerings to include a mountain bike park which enhanced the county's tourism product, increased opportunities for year-round/multiseason tourism activities, and became a key element in the county's designation as an IMBA Ride Center.

The projects undertaken in the counties we investigated were substantial and destination leaders acknowledged that they could seem beyond reach for smaller CVBs with limited budgets. However, leaders in both the City of Wheeling and Pocahontas County were quick to point out that most of their efforts were dependent less on monetary resources and more on leveraging existing assets, partnerships, and relationships. As the Cara Rose, Director of Pocahontas County's CVB stated,

> If you don't have a whole lot of money, you might be really stressed to do a lot of product development. ... But I don't spend a lot of money. It's mostly time I probably spend on all these product development efforts. It's a very tiny percentage of our budget.

While monetary and personnel time commitments represent real costs to the CVB, the directors we spoke with recognize that the resources allocated to product development are investments that if spent wisely will produce dividends. For example, while Pocahontas County spent $30,000 for mountain bike development, "those investments paid off. We're going to get that money back in bed tax."

In addition to tax revenue there was a recognition that product development was not only a key tourism development strategy, but essential to economic development. Cara Rose, director of the Pocahontas County CVB stated, "Ultimately, it's not just tourism developments or community development…in the end, it's economic development. And for our county particularly, tourism is the economic driver. So, we're missing the boat if we're not doing development projects." Frank O'Brien expressed a similar perspective, noting that

> product development is small business development. … When there is an event, a Broadway show on a Tuesday night at the theater and there are 2,500 people going to that venue, filling up the Bridge Tavern, drinks before they go and drinks after dinner…this theater is driving that market… you can specifically say that it was the programming that brought the people to the community.

The influx of visitors has been recognized by the community and government officials, even those that were initially skeptical of the development efforts:

> One commissioner didn't understand why we were buying the theater and using money that should be used for advertising… But, after attending a few shows and seeing a couple of thousand people were coming to town… he actually came up to me, says 'Frank, I get it now. I mean, this is a different CVB with a different set of objectives and you are much more than a marketing organization'.

Community Partnerships

The destination leaders in the communities that we investigated took on leadership roles in setting the overall direction for local tourism initiatives. However, their accomplishments were the result of partnerships with local stakeholders, engagement with the community at large, and partnerships with external parties including faculty at West Virginia University. Cara Rose, Director of Pocahontas County's CVB summed up the destination and her role in it as "three primary things: the power of people, the power of product, and the power of partnerships. … that's my job: to make sure that those three things work together."

In line with Morrison (2013), destination leaders were team builders that leveraged their local network to achieve product development goals. In Pocahontas County, the establishment of the Snowshoe-Highlands Ride Center engaged a diversity of actors including Snowshoe Mountain Resort, the US Forest Service, Poca Trails, West Virginia University, IMBA, the Town of Marlinton, Pocahontas County Commission, Greenbank National Radio Astronomy Observatory, WV State Parks and Forests, and surrounding communities. And, while the community's built and natural assets were contributing factors, according to IMBA's Ride Center assessment report, the strong coalition of stakeholders, including commercial operations (Snowshoe Resort), local advocates (Pocahontas Trails), and land managers (United States Forest Service), were a key consideration in the designation of the community as a Bronze Level Ride Center. In 2020 the Snowshoe Highlands Area Recreation Coalition (SHARC) was formed to maintain these partnerships to achieve Silver level Ride Center designation in 2020, and develop a strategic plan for regional trail and service/amenity improvements in order to become the first Gold level Ride Center on the east coast.

In Wheeling, the size and scope of the Capitol Theater rehabilitation project necessitated buy-in from a diversity of local stakeholders. Fortunately, CVB staff had laid the groundwork for these relationships by contributing leadership support to other development initiatives including Main Street, Wheeling Heritage, and the Regional Economic Development Partnership, which engages municipal and county governments, labor organizations, local Chambers of Commerce, and business leaders. These relationships, the collision of ideas between stakeholders, and existing shared goals were seen as critical to building and maintaining the network that allowed the CVB to accomplish its objectives. In the words of Frank O'Brien,

> this sharing of ideas establishes the network...and can be effective for the community because everybody has similar goals and the mission is the same. We changed our focus to spend a lot of effort and substantial resources on destination management, i.e. buying a capital theater... but it was because we had really good stakeholders, ...we had a fantastic board of directors that represented a wide variety of economic, different types of government, and different types of tourism entities. And they're all sitting at the same table and trying to figure out how can we increase the number of people coming to the City of Wheeling.

To date, these partnerships have generated more than a million dollars in private sector support, in-kind contributions, and discounts; half-a-million dollars in federal grant funding secured by Wheeling Heritage for structural and façade improvements; and low-cost contracts for operation support by the Wheeling Sports and Entertainment Authority.

In addition to engaging leaders in the community, the DMO should also advocate for the destination by increasing local buy-in among residents. This includes educating the community on the benefits of tourism for the local economy, and consulting with residents on issues that impact local quality of life (Morrison, 2013). In Wheeling, according to Frank O'Brien, CVB Director,

> The first thing [the CVB] did was invite 2,500 local people for a free three-hour presentation on what this theater could do and what kind of programming it could have. And so we got a lot of community buy in that way.... we put out a call for some volunteers to come and kind of help us out...And we had 180 people show up on Saturday and Sunday of that designated clean up weekend. And they were just regular community people...The theater had some kind of meaning to them.

The role of community engagement was echoed by the Cara Rose who stated that,

> …to be successful in a rural area, you have to be engaged with your community. … People have to know you. They have to see our faces, and I preach that all the time. We have to pick up the telephone…We have to talk to them…We have to look them in the eye… that's really important.

According to Cara Rose, the CVB spends $10,000–$12,000 annually on "in-reach" efforts in the community including "tourism talks" that showcase a local public partner, and engagement with middle school and high school youth, including an 8th grade business lunch, hosting youth at local attractions, and sponsoring the high school's tourism club—the largest club in the school with membership numbers greater than the high school's band.

In addition to internal partners, external partners can serve as a key source of explicit knowledge that can be injected into the tourism system to facilitate innovation and move projects forward. In Pocahontas County, funding from the Claude Worthington Benedum Foundation is allowing the SHARC to work with IMBA Trail Solutions to develop a detailed plan for purpose-built mountain bike trails on a section of the Monongahela National Forest near the town of Marlinton. IMBA Trail Solutions has extensive experience working on large-scale projects with multiple stakeholders including the USDA Forest Service; this knowledge and technical assistance will allow the destination to wisely invest resources for continued product development.

In Tucker County, West Virginia University played a critical role in facilitating structural and organization innovations in the destination's management framework that brought together separate entities with distinct tourism management and marketing functions. The potential of the county's unique cultural and natural resource asset base had been acknowledged by both internal and external development entities, and in 2013, the West Virginia State Legislature created the Tucker County Cultural District Authority (CDA) to preserve and enhance the county's unique artistic, cultural, historical, and recreational assets for culture, education, and tourism development. In 2016, the Claude Worthington Benedum Foundation funded work to develop a common vision for cultural tourism in the county, link assets, develop a leadership network, and create a performance agenda for the county and organization. To fully address the complexities of the project the CDA engaged the WVU Rural Tourism Design Team (RTDT), a transdisciplinary group led by Extension Service specialists with support from faculty and students from the Recreation, Parks, and Tourism Resources; Landscape Architecture; and Graphic Design programs. The project engaged a breadth of local tourism and economic development stakeholders including the local Chamber of Commerce, Economic Development Authority, County Commission, and CVB representatives; county and municipal government leaders; and businesses and nonprofit organizations.

The RTDT employed a mixed-methods and multiperspective approach to tourism development planning (Arbogast, Butler, Faulkes, Eades, Deng, Maumbe, & Smaldone, 2020) that collected primary and secondary data via key informant interviews, resident attitudes surveys, visitor preference surveys, economic impact analysis benchmarking, participatory asset identification and mapping. The data gathered from these exercises were paired with local knowledge and community dialogue to map opportunities and priorities for tourism development. Landscape design helped stakeholders visualize sites targeted for development, and social design projects helped residents to express a shared cultural identity.

Research outputs and recommendations were translated into community impacts including establishing a destination management framework (Figure 11.1), hiring a full-time county planner, and signage improvements that incorporate a unified branding strategy. Although community capacity and resource development remain a challenge, new partners have been engaged to maintain momentum (Arbogast, Deng, & Maumbe, 2017).

Cooperative Extension's Role in Promoting Innovation in Destination Management

The previous examples demonstrate the innovative practices destination leaders are employing and how CVB directors' tacit knowledge and social capital are used to leverage their natural, built, human, and cultural assets for sustainable

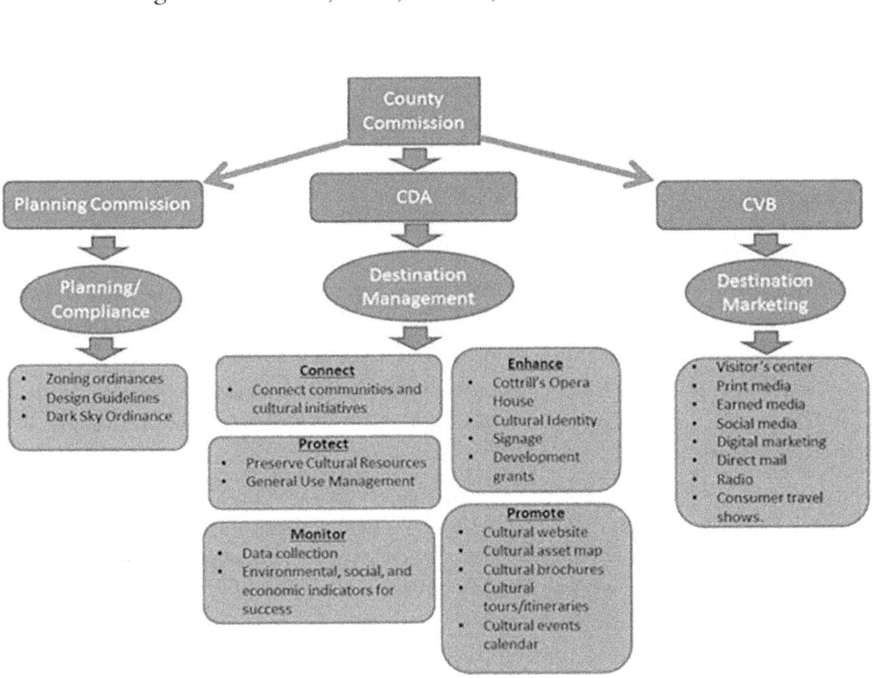

FIGURE 11.1 Tucker County, WV destination management framework.

tourism development. The structural innovations in Tucker County demonstrate the success rural destinations can achieve when they combine local knowledge with explicit knowledge and technical services from experts outside the community. By linking the tacit knowledge of local partners and organizations with explicit research-based knowledge, destination stakeholders can create a scientific community that facilitates knowledge transfer and innovation (Cooper, 2006).

Lyons, Miller, and Mann (2017) discuss how Cooperative Extension can take a lead role in creating these rural "scientific communities" and spurring rural innovation. Recommendations include encouraging economic specialization beyond agriculture; promoting systems thinking; importing knowledge created by the university into rural areas and utilizing experts and industry to spread that knowledge; co-creating knowledge with industry; building rural regional networks of industry, educational institutions, entrepreneurship support organizations, economic development organizations, and others to recreate the agglomeration effects; and networking with other land grant universities across state boundaries to foster innovation on a broader scale. As partners in the rural tourism system, Cooperative Extension in West Virginia, and in states across the country, are fulfilling these key roles in network creation, knowledge dissemination, and the co-creation and sharing of innovative best practices that facilitate the sustainability of rural tourism destinations.

Research-Driven Approaches

Extension's community and economic development efforts across the country emphasize putting knowledge to work to help rural communities identify research and data-driven solutions to their economic challenges. In rural destinations, the capacity to generate and use data is often limited. As Cara Rose stated,

> We need to do a better job at collecting on the ground, Pocahontas County data. It could probably help to have some of that data on a regular basis. But, you've got to look the visitor in the eye and then you have to have partners willing to help do surveys…all of our partners are small businesspeople and ask them to hand out a survey to everyone that walks in the door, it's a stretch. …So I've got to figure out how I do it for them … I would say to being able to do that research and that data collection is a weakness.

In West Virginia, and in other states that emphasize tourism development initiatives, Extension works with destination leaders to share best practice case studies to improve product development and co-create new data and research useful for preparing tourism policies, plans, and strategies. For example, Michigan State University Extension's "Understanding Tourism for Michigan Communities" uses tourism industry statistics to expose communities to new trends and travelers' interests, as well as opportunities for niche tourism markets and products.

Likewise, their Tourism First Impression's program uses an established Extension program for assessing communities' assets from the eye of a first-time visitor. The University of Minnesota Tourism Center also engages communities around current issues and emerging trends that affect the tourism industry. Data programs include visitor profiles for communities and businesses, and research addressing mobility and workforce issues. In West Virginia, West Virginia University Extension Service's (WVUES) rural development process for rural economies uses a mixed-methods, participatory research approach to collect data from visitors and residents, benchmark current tourism economy activities, and identify community assets.

The data collected from these research processes and the existing tourism networks can be brought together for strategic planning initiatives that address community challenges by blending local assets and relationships with explicit knowledge and best practices from tourism literature. Michigan State University Extension offers planning workshops that not only walk communities through the process of establishing readiness and engaging stakeholders but also expose destination leaders to theoretical concepts like Butler's (1980) tourism life-cycle model. WVUES's rural tourism specialist has guided rural destinations through several strategic plans including in Tucker and Pocahontas Counties. Plan goals emphasize both marketing and management elements including increased shoulder season visitation, hospitality training for frontline workers, signage improvements, and internal stakeholder relationships. The strategic plan for West Virginia's Mountain Music Trail, a multicounty initiative that promotes music and cultural activities along the US 219 corridor, emphasized elements of product development not by creating new places and spaces, but by marketing and branding existing and cooperatively sponsored events.

Creating the Backbone Organization to Share Knowledge

The innovations and activities occurring in towns and counties are important for local destinations. However, Lyons, Miller, and Mann (2017) emphasize the need to broaden the reach of innovative activities and create regional innovation systems. WVUES's Mon Forest Towns (MFT) initiative is taking the lessons learned from activities in Tucker and Pocahontas Counties and creating a tourism knowledge system across eight counties and ten gateway communities in the Monongahela National Forest. The initiative demonstrates how university tourism research, education, and planning are being combined in regional tourism knowledge systems to link internal and external partners and funders, bring explicit knowledge from the university system to communities, provide a platform for networking and an opportunity for local destination leaders to share their knowledge with peers, and generate new, co-created knowledge.

The MFT initiative began with an acknowledgment that the environmental, social, and economic challenges impacting forest communities were complex, interrelated, and beyond the scope of any single program or organization. Rather than impose a vision of success or solutions, destination leaders, government entities, and other stakeholders recognized that addressing regional challenges would require sustainable partnerships built on successful community approaches already occurring across forest communities. The Monongahela National Forest (MNF) in partnership with West Virginia University, and USDA Rural Development began bringing diverse stakeholders together in 2017 to create a shared recreation vision for each county and the greater region surrounding the MNF. The MNF Recreation Economies Partnership cultivates relations across forest lands and gateway communities that enhance the economy and quality of life for residents and visitors while simultaneously sustaining the quality of the environment and local communities.

Later, in 2018, USDA's Forest Service, Rural Development, and the National Institute for Food and Agriculture collectively published a toolkit to empower Rural Development field staff and Forest Service district rangers in identifying funding, best practices, and technical assistance resources to better support small business development in the communities they serve, thereby enhancing the local recreation economy, and improving quality of life and recreation experiences. To achieve these goals, the USDA encouraged field staff to collaborate with the Cooperative Extension and Land Grant University Systems to access the broad educational, research, and technical assistance resources available for recreational economy planning initiatives.

The partnership between local communities, destination leaders, the USFS, and WVUES was solidified in 2019, when the MNF's ten forest towns entered into a formal agreement to work collectively on the development and delivery of an integrated regional recreation partnership. The partnership agreement includes operational guidelines that cover how the partnership conducts business and interacts with the steering committee, town representatives, and partnership organizations, and how the partnership can grow to include new members.

The processes and activities of creating a common agenda, establishing a shared measurement framework, engaging in mutually reinforcing activities, communication, and backbone support are in line with existing collective impact frameworks (Hanleybrown, Kania, & Kramer, 2012) and are encouraging knowledge sharing and forest-wide impacts. The MFT have adopted regional branding; local CVB directors are finding a platform to share their experiences and knowledge and are recognized as leaders in the regional tourism system; local partners have obtained funding that allows them to expand the reach of their work. For example, two local CDFIs were able to extend their lending territory and offer business assistance and funding to tourism-based businesses across the ten-county area.

Similar initiatives have also been established in the Ohio Valley and Northern Panhandle. Building on the results of a university-led regional competitiveness study, Extension campus and field faculty established the Visit Upper Ohio Valley Regional Partnership in 2013. The team has active participation from each of the state's five northern panhandle counties, and representatives from seven counties in neighboring Ohio and Pennsylvania. The organization has successfully engaged local governments, libraries, CVBs, local businesses, museums, parks, and other tourist destinations in the Upper Ohio Valley Region; maintains an evolving list of regional assets; and engages in collective marketing efforts. The group has received the attention of the WV Division of Tourism Secretary and Assistant Director who regularly promote the effort as a model for regional tourism development across the state.

Sharing Best Practices and Creating Explicit Knowledge

In addition to disseminating knowledge to communities, and co-creating knowledge with communities, Cooperative Extension collects and shares this research through its peer networks, ensuring that innovative solutions at the local level are codified, and best practices can be adopted across the country. Many of the activities outlined above are currently being advanced by the National Extension Tourism Design Team (NET). Drawing representatives from the USDA Regional Rural Development Centers (RRDC), USDA NIFA, and two representatives from Canada, the Design Team is a loosely structured group with two tourism-focused land grant and sea grant representatives from each region. Key external stakeholders for NET are federal agency partners such as USDA, US Forest Service, Environmental Protection Agency, Economic Development Administration, National Park Service, NOAA/National Sea Grant Program, National Travel & Tourism Office, and US Department of Commerce/ International Trade Association, as they most align with Extension and tourism (either via direct reports, funding, research, and/or programs). Additional stakeholders include collaborating academic institutions and faculty, nonprofit agencies such as The Conservation Fund, and tourism industry organizations such as US Travel and state tourism offices. Other external stakeholders include the communities, organizations (e.g., Destination Marketing Organizations, Chambers of Commerce, and Economic Development Authorities), and tourism-related businesses served by Extension programing.

In addition to providing Extension tourism with an overarching structure that emphasizes partnerships, NET provides a forum for sharing research and best practices in sustainable community tourism. For example, the Design Team has hosted biennial conferences attracting between 50 and 200 attendees since 1995; recently NET leadership collaborated with the World Leisure Centre of Excellence in Sustainability and Innovation to produce the peer-reviewed publication, "Innovative and Promising Practices in Sustainable Tourism" to provide an opportunity for academics, extension professionals, industry stakeholders, and community practitioners to reflect, discuss, and share the innovative approaches that they have taken to develop sustainable tourism in a variety of different contexts (Vaugeois, Phillips, Arbogast, & Brouder, 2019). Extension tourism research is further enhanced by cooperative research efforts between Extension field professionals and colleagues at the RRDCs.

Finally, the organization continues to engage in strategic activities to elevate the role of Extension tourism. In February 2020, land grant and sea grant representatives met to determine how the Design Team could expand its support to grow and enhance the provision of tourism programming within both land grant and sea grant Extension. One outcome of the retreat was the National Extension Tourism Strategic Plan 2020–2025 which serves as a roadmap for sustainable tourism research, education, and outreach within Cooperative Extension and sea grant in collaboration with land grant universities, federal agencies, and other partners. The document reaffirms the core values of Extension tourism first laid out in 1993, and considers a pathway for elevating Extension tourism activities and broadening their reach including further engagement of faculty and students at land grant universities to deliver applied scholarship to community stakeholders; inventorying and assessing existing Extension and sea grant tourism programs; providing professional development opportunities for Extension and sea grant staff, and other key stakeholders; and sharing applied research, special programs, or other tourism development and outdoor recreation technical expertise with key stakeholders and audiences (Mission, Vision and Strategic Plan, n.d.).

Implications

Innovation in tourism, especially in the destinations we examined, is a continuous and incremental process. Our research demonstrates how rural destination leaders are navigating the process and provides lessons for other destinations working to embrace their dual mandates of destination marketing and sustainable destination management.

First, reorienting the DMOs' role to management activities requires a deliberate shift in mindset and intention to engage in activities beyond marketing. The destination leaders we interviewed recognized that marketing and management activities like product development are intrinsically linked and equally important for the destination's success. As a result, destinations require continuous product improvement in order to remain competitive. This, in turn, requires continuous investments in the relationships and knowledge search processes that drive innovation.

Second, monetary resources are always limited; this is especially true for small, rural DMOs. As a result, the destination leaders we engaged recognized a need to leverage their relationships and creatively engage human resources through active partnerships. This requires destination leaders to actively engage in-reach efforts that involve local stakeholders and communicate to residents the importance of resource development for economic growth and local quality of life, and outreach efforts that engage funding and technical assistance partners. Partnerships with businesses, government leaders, and other stakeholders allowed the CVBs to undertake work that would otherwise be beyond their capacity and created synergies that resulted in greater impacts than would have been realized acting alone.

Third, CES can serve as a critical partner in supporting and enhancing rural tourism development initiatives. WVUES, Michigan State Extension Service, the University of Minnesota Tourism Center, and others across the nation offer educational programs to build, lead, and facilitate community-based tourism development and should be engaged as a primary resource partner. This is especially true in rural communities where Extension may already be viewed as a trusted resource. These partnerships encourage shared learning, networking, and knowledge sharing that benefit local stakeholders, local tourism economies, and the field of rural tourism development.

Finally, while our research emphasized the work of local DMOs, it also points to a clear need for active state level initiatives to share and promote best practices and provide resources that support product development. In West Virginia, each of the CVB directors interviewed expressed a need for peer sharing supported by the WVACVB, the association that leads the accreditation process. According to Cara Rose,

> We talk a lot about, educational sessions. We're supposed to be doing those. And, you know, something like [the importance of destination management] could be one of those educational sessions where we talk about different ways that CVBs can impact their overall marketing and strategic plan by doing these sorts of things. … I really do believe people should do more of this.

Frank O'Brien discussed his experiences with the Certified Destination Management Executive program and how participation "gave me the confidence to go out and buy the Capitol Theater, to become involved in management, because not only is this a trend, but it's going to make us viable in the future." Like Cara Rose, he also saw value in sharing his experiences with other\destinations across the state, how can we help and possible play more of a role with these smaller organizations and help them understand these trends and help them understand what they could be doing? Because, you know, we've helped you with [this] research to have better sense of what we could be doing to support them. But the industry is really recording this need for this management role. And so, I'm thinking, if the CVB Association [shared] case studies of organizations, CVB's going beyond marketing and how they've been able to do that, whether they're large or small and identify resources, identify an appropriate role and the impact that that's had, that could be a valuable thing and potential partnership we could play with the association.

As a result of this research, WVUES has established dialogue with the WVACVB about offering educational sessions on how CVBs could better implement best practices in destination management. Linking this education with other on-the-ground programing either through Extension or through programs offered by state entities could allow rural destinations to implement lessons learned and engage the community in the destination development process. Programs like those in Oregon, Colorado, and southwest Virginia show how state tourism offices can help to facilitate these processes in communities and could serve as a model for other states.

Establishing funding streams to assist rural destinations in product development, after participatory planning, could also provide seed funding for further development. According to Cara Rose,

> there are opportunities for the state to step in and help with those kinds of good products. It's authentic. We have the assets. It is not like we have to create them. We just need that financial boost. We're all kind of throwing up our hands and when they give us a carrot, we grab it. But we don't feel like we have any avenue to make proposals. Virginia, Oregon must be getting it right.

Conclusions

CVBs serve as the key, and often sole, destination marketing and management organization. While marketing remains their primary role, literature and best practices advocate for their increased attention to coordinating the development of the destination's tourism product base and managing the tourism system in a way that is sustainable and equitable for the diversity of stakeholders. Despite their limited resources, our research shows how rural tourism destinations in West Virginia are combining CVB directors' tacit knowledge and social networks to creatively enhance their destination. When local knowledge is combined with the explicit knowledge of university and Cooperative Extension partners new and innovative structures and knowledge sharing networks are formed that enhance both local and regional destinations. For rural destinations especially, Cooperative Extension should disseminate research and best practices, co-create knowledge with local stakeholders to solve problems, provide a platform to share the tacit knowledge of destination leaders within larger tourism networks, and translate this local knowledge to explicit knowledge that can be shared with peers and widely disseminated across the country. Through knowledge sharing and the adoption of innovative practices at the state and local levels, rural destinations will be better equipped to creatively address the destination management challenges of the 21st century.

References

Adeyinka-Ojo, S. F., Khoo-Lattimore, C., & Nair, V. (2014). A framework for rural tourism destination management and marketing organizations. *Procedia-Social and Behavioral Sciences*, 144(144), 151–163.

America Outdoors: Consumers Are Flocking to These 5 Activities. (2020, August). *npd*. Retrieved from https://www.npd.com/wps/portal/npd/us/news/thought-leadership/2020/consumers-are-flocking-to-these-5-activities/#.XzrOJ41OU3o.linkedin

Arbogast, D., Butler, P., Faulkes, E., Eades, D., Deng, J., Maumbe, K., & Smaldone, D. (2020). Using social design to visualize outcomes of sustainable tourism planning: A multiphase, transdisciplinary approach. *International Journal of Contemporary Hospitality Management*, 34(4), 1413–1448.

Arbogast, D., Deng, J., & Maumbe, K. (2017). DMOs and rural tourism: A stakeholder analysis the case of Tucker County, West Virginia. *Sustainability*, 9(10), 1813.

Booyens, I., & Rogerson, C. M. (2016). Tourism innovation in the global South: Evidence from the Western Cape, South Africa. *International Journal of Tourism Research*, 18(5), 515–524.

Bramwell, B. (1994). Rural tourism and sustainable rural tourism. *Journal of Sustainable Tourism*, 2(1–2), 1–6.

Brown, J. (2020, August). Lake Tahoe Tourists Who 'Aren't Showing the Same Respect' Creating Prolific Trash Issues. *SFGATE*. Retrieved from https://www.sfgate.com/renotahoe/article/Lake-Tahoe-grapples-trash-issue-15493664.php

Buehler, B. (2021). *The difference between a CVB, DMO, and DMC*. Destination Colorado.

Butler, R. W. (1980). The concept of a tourist area cycle of evolution: Implications for management of resources. *Canadian Geographer/Le Géographe canadien*, 24(1), 5–12.

Cai, L. (2002). Cooperative branding for rural destinations. *Annals of Tourism Research*, 29(3), 720–742.

Clasen, D., Vogt, C., & Andereck, K. (2019, October 8–12). U.S. states and local destination support [Conference presentation]. NET STORC 2019 Conference, Astoria, OR, United States.

Cooper, C. (2006). Knowledge management and tourism. *Annals of Tourism Research*, 33(1), 47–64.

Coronavirus Impact: How a Crisis Is Changing the U.S. (2020, June 9). *New York Times*. Retrieved from https://www.nytimes.com/live/2020/coronavirus-usa-03-27

Dean Runyan Associates. (2019). West Virginia Travel Impacts, 2000–2018. Portland, OR.

Destination Analysts. (2019). *State of the American Traveler Destination Management Edition*. Retrieved from https://mk0destinationajcrrq.kinstacdn.com/wp-content/uploads/2019/12/The-State-of-the-American-Traveler-Fall-2019-002.pdf

Destinations International. (2019). *DestinationNEXT Futures Study*. Retrieved from https://destinationsinternational.org/reports/destinationnext-futures-study

Gretzel, U., Fesenmaier, D. R., Formica, S., & O'Leary, J. T. (2006), Searching for the future: Challenges faced by destination marketing organizations. *Journal of Travel Research*, 45(2), 116–126.

Hallin, C. A., & Marnburg, E. (2008). Knowledge management in the hospitality industry: A review of empirical research. *Tourism Management*, 29(2), 366–381.

Hanleybrown, F., Kania, J., & Kramer, M. (January 26, 2012). *Channeling Change: Making Collective Impact Work*. Stanford Social Innovation Review. Retrieved from https://ssir.org/articles/entry/channeling_change_making_collective_impact_work

Hjalager, A. M. (2010). A review of innovation research in tourism. *Tourism Management*, 31(1), 1–12.

Hjalager, A. M., Huijbens, E. H., Björk, P., Nordin, S., Flagestad, A., & Knútsson, Ö. (2008). Innovation systems in Nordic Tourism. *Technology Analysis and Strategic Management*, 11, 527–539.

Hoarau, H., & Kline, C. (2014). Science and industry: Sharing knowledge for innovation. *Annals of Tourism Research*, 46, 44–61.

Holden, A. (2010). Exploring stakeholders' perceptions of sustainable tourism development in the Annapurna conservation area: Issues and challenge. *Tourism and Hospitality Planning & Development*, 7(4), 337–351.

Kanter, R. M. (1983). *The change masters: Innovation for productivity in the American corporation*. Simon and Schuster.

Lane, B., & Kastenholz, E. (2015). Rural tourism: The evolution of practice and research approaches–towards a new generation concept? *Journal of Sustainable Tourism*, 23(8–9), 1133–1156.

Lyons, T. S., Miller, S. R., & Mann, J. T. (2017). A new role for land grant universities in the rural innovation ecosystem? *Journal of Regional Analysis & Policy*, 48(2), 3775.

Marasco, A., De Martino, M., Magnotti, F., & Morvillo, A. (2018). Collaborative innovation in tourism and hospitality: A systematic review of the literature. *International Journal of Contemporary Hospitality Management*, 30(6), 2364–2395.

Midwest Meetings. (2012). History and Purpose of CVBs. Retrieved from https://www.midwestmeetings.com/blogs/history-and-purpose-of-cvbs#:~:text=The%20first%20CVB%20was%20actually, hotels%20to%20bid%20for%20business

Morrison, A. (2013). Destination management and destination marketing: The platform for excellence in tourism destinations. *Tourism Tribune*, 28(1), 6–9.

Organisation for Economic Co-operation and Development. OECD Innovation Strategy, Defining Innovation. Retrieved from https://www.oecd.org/site/innovationstrategy/defininginnovation.htm

Pasape, L., Anderson, W., & Lindi, G. (2013). Towards sustainable ecotourism through stakeholder collaborations in Tanzania. *Journal of Tourism Research & Hospitality*, 2(1), 2–14.

Passing Great American Outdoors Act Is Just Beginning for the Outdoor Recreation Industry. (n.d.). Outdoor Recreation Roundtable. Retrieved from https://recreationroundtable.org/passing-great-american-outdoors-act-is-just-beginning-for-the-outdoor-recreation-industry/

Pearce, D. G., & Schanzel, H. A. (2013). Destination management: The tourists' perspective. *Journal of Destination Marketing and Management*, 2, 137–145.

Pike, S. (2008). Five limitations of destination brand image questionnaires. *Tourism Recreation Research*, 33(3), 361–363.

Pike, S., & Page, S. J. (2014). Destination marketing organisations and destination marketing: A narrative analysis of the literature. *Tourism Management*, 41, 201–227.

Presenza, A., Sheehan, L., & Ritchie, J. B. (2005). Towards a model of the roles and activities of destination management organizations. *Journal of Hospitality, Tourism and Leisure Science*, 3(1), 1–16.

Ritchie, J. B., & Crouch, G. I. (2003). *The competitive destination: A sustainable tourism perspective*. Wallingford, Oxon, GBR: CABI.

Skift. (2020). *Travel Megatrends 2020*. Retrieved from https://skift.com/megatrends-2020/

Stephan, T. (2020, August 5). Crowds, Trash, Overrun the Eastern Sierra, CA. *Snowbrains*. Retrieved from https://snowbrains.com/crowds-trash-overrun-the-eastern-sierra-ca/?fbclid=IwAR2waOxHUJ-Mnv5vqB4tRDu4T53d-ICXwkS9A7ZAddbI9_nrQ-JWrV18kAEg

United Nations World Tourism Organization. (2007). *A Practical Guide to Tourism Destination Management*. Retrieved from https://www.e-unwto.org/doi/abs/10.18111/9789284412433_

U.S. Census Bureau. (2020). Quick Facts. Retrieved at https://www.census.gov/quickfacts/tuckercountywestvirginia

USDA, National Institute for Food and Agriculture. (n.d.). Cooperative Extension System. Retrieved from https://nifa.usda.gov/cooperative-extension-system

Varra, L., Buzzigoli, C., & Loro, R. (2012). Innovation in destination management: Social dialogue, knowledge management processes and servant leadership in the tourism destination observatories. *Procedia-Social and Behavioral Sciences*, 41, 375–385.

Vaugeois, N., Phillips, M., Arbogast, D., & Brouder, P. (2019) *Innovative and Promising Practices in Sustainable Tourism*. World Leisure Centre of Excellence. Vol. 1. Retrieved from https://viurrspace.ca/handle/10613/16372

Vogt, C. A., Andereck, K. L., & Pham, K. (2020). Designing for quality of life and sustainability. *Annals of Tourism Research*, 83, 102963.

12

NATURE-BASED ECONOMIC DEVELOPMENT

Innovating at the Intersection of Nature & Main Street

Shannon Rogers, Molly Donovan, Cathryn Porter and Geoffrey Sewake

Introduction

Bristol, New Hampshire is like many rural towns in the United States. A beautiful river flows through the town and once served as an economic driver. There are trails in the nearby community forest and a mountain in the background and just a few miles down the road sits a pristine lake. Its small, walkable main street comprises the town's center. The town's citizens and leaders are looking for a solution to the downtown vacancies and the economic downturn the town has faced. They seek to bring vibrancy and economic activity back to their community and enhance civic pride in their main street. Bristol has begun to see its natural features as an asset to be leveraged for economic development.

Over the past decade we have witnessed several communities in New Hampshire that are rich in natural resources and have experienced economic decline. As small towns experience decline, they seek new economic opportunities to create jobs, enhance the tax base, and create community vibrancy. Communities often ask, "how can we get people who use our trails to spend time and money in the downtown?" They perceive a potential market in the trail visitors, and we have found that trails can also be an important location factor for new residents or those seeking to start or retain a business. A new and innovative approach to capitalize on this market is to look to the natural assets within a community as economic assets that can support the quality of life of new residents, draw new residents and entrepreneurs, enhance tourism, and catalyze long-term investment. Innovation lies in the leveraging of underutilized resources such as trails and other natural assets. The program we will discuss is also innovative in the sense that it brings together volunteers, staff, and researchers in a community capacity building manner to learn together and catalyze action that improves the

DOI: 10.4324/9781003178552-12

economy. This synergy produces results that would be much less likely through traditional economic development approaches and conservation initiatives working separately.

We developed the Downtowns and Trails program in response to these needs to link users of trails to the businesses on main street. This is an innovative approach to connect natural features with economic centers in rural communities. This new program is rooted in community development practice and requires four major conditions: natural, built, economic, and social/leadership that need to be in place for nature-based economic development. UNH Extension plays a key role in the innovation ecosystem as we have access to a national network of practitioners and researchers to consult with when we identify a community need and are considering new programming. We also have access to funding through our regional research center for peer exchanges as was done for Downtowns and Trails. As this chapter unfolds, we share the background on our Nature Economy approach as context and then discuss the story of how UNH Extension researched, developed, and piloted the Downtowns and Trails program to assist New Hampshire communities in connecting their downtowns and trails to achieve economic vibrancy. While specific recommendations for implementing nature-based economic development vary from town to town, the following lessons may be applicable to communities interested in pursuing strengthening these connections.

Nature Economy Principles

Nature is a key component of outdoor recreation but also contributes to a community's economy in other ways. When introducing this topic, we often ask communities, "what has nature done for you lately?" Many are surprised by the myriad answers that come to mind when one stops to think about it. The benefits can include provision of shade and water filtration, aesthetic benefits, access to spaces for exercise and meditation, outdoor seating and dining, and space to hold cultural and artistic events. We call our work in this space "Nature Economy" because of the many connections between various aspects of nature and the way that local economies function. The actual tools and community education we have developed are termed "nature-based economic development" and include innovative programs and education related to quality of life, outdoor recreation, community services, and visitor attraction. Nature-based economic development is a new framework for communities to explore the potential economic benefits of natural assets and the deliberate efforts to sustainably leverage natural resources for positive economic impact.

There are three main beneficiaries of the nature economy: (1) Residents of a community; (2) Potential new residents/ entrepreneurs to said community; and (3) Visitors to the community. The mechanisms through which economic benefits flow from nature to these beneficiaries are as follows.

Natural Assets Support Quality of Life for Residents

Nature can provide many aesthetic benefits, including the values people derive from the visual appearance of a place or feature. Many properties have natural views of mountains, water, and pastureland. These views translate into real revenue and other economic benefits to communities through increases in property values and subsequent property taxes. The benefit is dependent upon the quality and health of nature, and many of us have benefited from years of environmental quality improvements. However, one does not have to have a million-dollar view to enjoy benefits of nature. Data from numerous studies show us that there are benefits to health and well-being from being in nature briefly or simply looking at pictures of nature. *The Nature Fix* documents a number of these, including a reduction in blood pressure levels when walking through forests and improvements in one's concentration and mood from that come from looking at pictures of nature (Williams, 2017).

The outdoor recreation economy is becoming recognized as a truly important industry to the U.S. economy, representing over $800 billion dollars in direct and indirect expenditures in 2017 (Outdoor Industry Association) and growing at a faster pace than other industries, outdoor recreation has become an asset and opportunity for rural economies. Outdoor recreation is a rapidly growing component of our national economy. Moreover, residents who live near nature—often in rural parts of the country—can take part in recreational activities for little or no additional cost. This can impact real estate values and other attributes of local economies. For instance, homes near trails can also garner higher prices because of the benefits that proximity provides to homeowners who value outdoor recreation. The following are findings from studies that show the economic impacts of cycling and cycling infrastructure on communities, such as bike paths and rail trails (All findings are from the League of American Bicyclists).

- People who ride bikes buy other things and are more likely to make multiple or repeat trips to local stores
- Bicycling tourism brings millions of dollars to cities and towns across the country
- Bike accessible business districts benefit from catering to cyclists as customers

Natural Assets Can Be a Strong Attraction for New Residents Looking to Move to Your Community or Start a Business in Your Community

Businesses large and small must consider several factors when determining where to locate a business. The overall quality of life of a place has long been a factor for business owners themselves and for the recruitment and retention of employees. Quality of life includes access to good schools, cultural amenities, and recreation. Residents who live near nature often use natural assets as a "location factor" in choosing where they live and even start businesses (i.e., Halstead & Deller, 1997).

Natural Assets Can Attract Both Day and Overnight Visitors to Your Community

Potential visitors to a community can be enticed to stay for the day or longer if there are natural assets to explore and enjoy along with the supporting infrastructure to accommodate visitor needs. Sustainable and nature-based tourism rely upon clean and functioning ecosystems.

Innovation in Program Development: Matrix for Nature-Based Economic Development

For the development of the Downtowns and Trails Program, we used our Nature-Based Economic Development matrix as a foundation. We developed this by identifying the conditions needed to achieve economic vibrancy with our program model. This matrix is based on a foundation of community development practice, community capitals framework (Emery & Flora, 2006), economic development, and nature economy practice in New Hampshire.

Based on our research and experience, we developed a matrix to describe four major conditions that need to be in place for nature-based economic development (See Figure 12.1). In this specific case, these conditions need to be met to make a successful connection between downtowns and trails. What makes this unique is incorporating the economic component as a condition not as an outcome. This allows us to connect the trail user with the downtown. Natural, economic, built, and social/leadership conditions need to be assessed when considering how to better leverage natural assets for economic vibrancy.

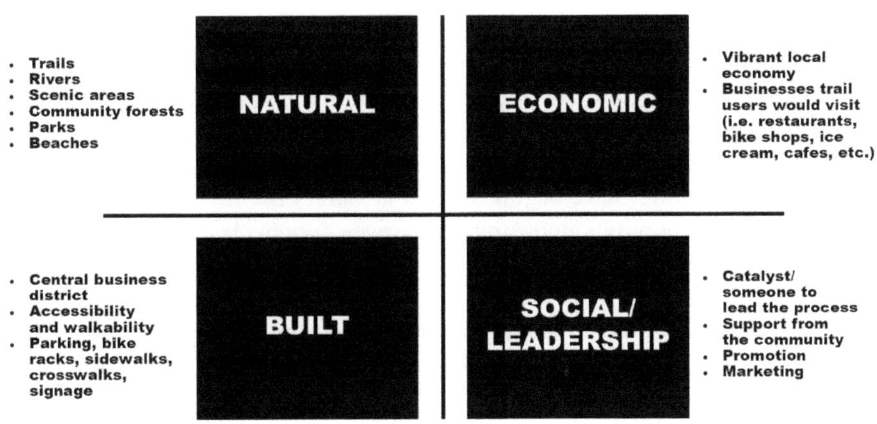

FIGURE 12.1 Nature-based economic development matrix.

Conditions for Connecting Downtowns and Trails for Economic Vibrancy

Trails and natural features like rivers, lakes, beaches, and community forests serve to enhance connectivity because they provide opportunities for residents and visitors to recreate and enjoy enhanced quality of life that these natural assets provide. Additionally, certain economic conditions need to be in place to draw trail users to the downtown, such as businesses that a trail user might frequent, including bike shops and sporting goods stores, restaurants, breweries, cafes, and overnight accommodations. There are also features of the built environment that are important for safety, connectivity, and the overall vibrancy of the downtown, such as a thoughtful layout of the central business district, the presence of bike racks and bike parking, restrooms, sidewalks, benches, community art, and landscaping. Finally, the most successful programs tend to have strong community leadership and participation that can be sustained over a long period (The Progress Fund, 2015).

In many communities, residents enjoy natural assets. But some may be unaware of the assets, and many potential visitors and new residents alike are not sure where the trails begin and end, or how they can safely use them. There may not also be stores and restaurants that visitors and others might expect to see in a place where they would want to live or just visit for the day or weekend. The Downtowns and Trails program creates the linkages between trails and an enhanced main street, thus encouraging trail users and visitors to spend money and take in activities on main street.

Case Study Background-New Hampshire's Natural Assets and Rural Downtowns

New Hampshire's natural resources are some of the state's greatest assets. Our local economies grow when our forests, trails, and waters are well taken care of, used by residents and visitors, and linked to our downtowns. Communities have begun to understand and actively work on forging the link between the local economy and natural assets. Over the past two decades, communities have suffered from job losses and population declines and have adopted economic development strategies to address these challenges. Drawing upon an asset-based community development approach, communities have begun to see and value their natural amenities as a major source of economic opportunity. However, insights learned from over 80 community visioning processes conducted by UNH Extension in New Hampshire over the past 20 years suggest that over half of all towns believe they are not effectively leveraging their trails and natural amenities to foster vibrant communities. In response, many communities formed volunteer trail committees and are making efforts to map and publicize their trails. Similar themes and patterns have been noted in other New England states and across the country.

Trails in New Hampshire

Trails are a key component of the economy in NH as well as something that contributes to high quality of life for residents. Trails are used for walking, hiking, horse-back riding, snowmobiling, and skiing. The NH Bureau of Trails includes more than 1,200 miles of wheeled OHRV trails, over 500 miles of state-owned rail trails, and over 7,000 miles of snowmobile trails (NH Trails Bureau, 2018). Further, volunteer organizations manage more than 4,000 miles of hiking trails in the state (NH State Parks, 2018). Special interest organizations also have their own estimates of the number of certain types of trails. For example, the Rails to Trails Conservancy reports that New Hampshire currently has 75 rail trails which extend a total length of 558 miles (Rails to Trails Conservancy, 2018). New Hampshire has a cherished and unique tradition of allowing public access to private land which has made a significant amount of land available to people for various recreational uses.

Downtowns

Cities and towns in New England tend to have a similar development pattern, which often includes a town center that was historically the center of commerce for the community. This might be a town square, a village center, a downtown, or a main street. These areas of commerce may include local businesses, government buildings, churches, libraries, housing, and outdoor places for people to gather. So, it is no surprise that downtowns are valued for being the historic center of commerce and a symbol of the community's vitality.

Some downtown areas have experienced a loss of commerce and seen disinvestment due to development extending out beyond the historic commercial base, in addition to job and population losses. This translates to empty storefronts, lack of facade and building maintenance, and lack of community activities. Communities typically see their downtown as an economic center and the heart of the community and often recognize that there is a lot of work to be done to maintain, enhance, and revitalize the center. Such efforts include improving the physical characteristics of the downtown through renovation and streetscape improvements, creating vibrancy through community events to attract residents and visitors, and retaining and recruiting businesses to the downtown.

In addition to valuing their historic town center, New Hampshire communities value their natural assets and features. This has led to efforts to preserve expand access to scenic lands and waterways. Communities often develop trails in these areas to give residents and visitors an opportunity to enjoy the natural assets. In recent years, community leaders focused on enhancing their downtowns have noted that the trails and natural areas are increasingly being used by residents and visitors. Thus, they see the potential links between trails and their downtowns. As part of their revitalization efforts, leaders are looking to capture trail users as a new market for their downtowns.

Developing the Downtowns and Trails Program for New Hampshire

Following years of working in community economic development, the UNH Extension team identified the need to actively and systematically link trails with downtowns for economic development. To address this need, we began the process of program development and planning. This entailed researching programs and initiatives in small, rural communities that were actively leveraging trails for economic benefit, such as the Trail Town program in PA. Through the Cooperative Extension national network, we identified the *Trail Towns* program in Kentucky. Inspired by the PA program but modified for a more rural communities, this program seemed especially relevant because New Hampshire and Kentucky have similarly sized rural communities and both states are home to large national forests that lie in mountainous regions. An Extension colleague in Kentucky who had been studying the Kentucky program expressed interest in collaborating with us, so UNH Extension pursued and received a grant from the Northeast Regional Center for Rural Development (NERCRD), along with Vermont and Connecticut Extension colleagues, to study the Kentucky Trail Towns model to determine its relevance to New Hampshire and New England states.

In late 2017 and early 2018, the research team began extensively reviewing other programs and literature on the topic of "Trail Towns." We traveled to Kentucky to assess the Kentucky Trail Towns program, with the overarching goal of identifying the conditions necessary to connect trails with downtowns for economic development. We were especially interested to apply our matrix of nature based economic development to the Kentucky program, using the four components we had identified as crucial to success: natural, built, economic, and social/leadership. We visited four Kentucky Trail Towns based on their unique characteristics, the types of trails they featured, and for their varying demographics and leadership structures. Using the aforementioned matrix as a framework, the team assessed the four downtowns for trail user amenities, the connection between the downtown and the trail, and the trailhead. Team members also met with volunteers and leaders from each community to learn more about the Kentucky Trail Town program, including how it started in each community, the challenges and successes in implementing the program, and how the program has impacted the community.

Based on what we learned from our visit, the Trail Town model resonated with our team. Much like Kentucky, New Hampshire's communities vary with respect to the various types of trails and natural assets, differing levels of economic vibrancy, and the fact that many communities are not located along the same trail. Our findings, summarized below, helped to inform the development of the UNH Cooperative Extension Downtowns and Trails program (Rogers et al., 2019).

- Each Trail Town has unique characteristics and uniformity is not necessary.
- Trails and trail users vary by town. Trails may be for walkers, hikers, riders, kayakers, or multiuse. The connection between the downtown and trail does not need to be walkable but can be reached by car or bike.
- Visitors are exploring trail towns due to their designation as trail towns even without using the trails. Deliberate efforts need to be made to understand where trail users would spend money and provide for the visitor market.
- Committed leaders, broad community support and volunteers are necessary to initiate and sustain the Kentucky Trail Town program.
- Collaboration and partnerships are essential. Local, regional, state, and federal government are key partners. These partnerships may bring funding, connections, technical assistance, and credibility to the effort.
- Colleges and Universities in Kentucky Trail Towns play an important role in leadership and visitor attraction due to their developed downtowns.

The network of Kentucky Trail Town is valuable in bringing knowledge and shared experiences to each town in the program.

Downtowns and Trails Program Development and Implementation

The research team came away understanding that we could develop a program that linked trails and downtowns without the need for a state-wide effort or *Trail Town*-like designation. We felt we had learned enough to begin working with New Hampshire communities, helping them to link their trails with their downtowns.

Based on what we learned from our visit to Kentucky, as well as our experience with other community economic development programs, we developed and piloted the Downtowns and Trails program in the small, rural town of Bristol, New Hampshire (2020). Aware that Bristol municipal staff had an interest in nature-based economic development from past interactions, we felt the town met the criteria for a pilot effort. The town had a municipal staff person to work with, engaged volunteers, a deep value for both their natural resources and the downtown, and a willingness to try something new. The community and civic leaders of Bristol recognized their natural assets and were interested in leveraging these assets to support their economic vibrancy goals. Thus, beginning in the spring of 2018, Bristol entered a formal partnership with UNH Extension to conduct the program.

Bristol lies 25 miles northwest of Concord, the state capitol, and is an economic center. It has a traditional town center filled with small businesses and office spaces—some located in historic buildings—situated around a town square. The town has a strong social infrastructure, including a library, community center, and a robust school system. Community members also have a strong sense of connection and a culture of volunteerism. With respect to natural amenities, Bristol has a total of 42 trails extending 330 miles through the surrounding hills and along the lake. There are state parks and a ski resort in the region. The town is located in the NH Lakes region at the southern tip of Newfound Lake, a well-known tourist resort area (Table 12.1).

Bristol demonstrated some early capacity and leadership by enlisting their volunteer economic development committee to work on the Downtowns and Trails Program. The pilot program involved the following:

- Reviewing the importance of, and opportunities for, linking downtowns and trails
- Assessing the downtown area, linkage area, and appropriate trails using Esri ArcGIS Collector mobile application
- Developing and training volunteers to conduct interviews with businesses, residents, and community leaders on their interest in this initiative.
- Developing and training volunteers to administer an intercept survey for those using the trails to determine their interest and use of downtown.
- Sharing the findings of the assessment and prioritizing actions to work on nature-based economic development projects.

Development of Downtowns and Trails Assessment Characteristics

A key piece of the Downtowns and Trails program is assessing the natural and built environment to determine whether the conditions exist for successfully connecting the two. The assessment is completed through a set of characteristics that determine the connectivity between a downtown and nearby trails and assess amenities in the downtown for trail users. These characteristics are research based and adapted by UNH Extension from multiple sources, including the First

TABLE 12.1 Characteristics of Bristol, New Hampshire (RHIhub)

Population	*3,050 (2016)*
Municipal budget	$7 million
Government	Elected select board
Median household income	$53,280 lower than the county (63,100) and state average of $74,991
NH region	Lakes Region and as part of the gateway to the White Mountains.
Poverty rate	9% of which is higher than the state average of 7.4%
Commuting	66% commute to another town for work

Impressions program and the National Civic League's Civic Index. The downtown characteristics that are used in the First Impressions program are based on what makes a downtown vibrant for a resident, visitor, or business owner, and are based on the built environment.

The downtowns and trails assessment characteristics build upon the First Impressions downtown characteristics and include new characteristics specific to assessing the connectivity of downtowns and trails and trail user amenities. The characteristics specific to downtowns and trails (described below) are adapted from multiple trail town guides, including the Trail Town Program in Pennsylvania and Michigan's Trail Town Program. Key characteristics for assessing downtowns and trails include the following:

- The *trailhead* is where a trail begins and should be well marked. Ideally, there is a kiosk with trail maps and information about nearby amenities, adequate parking, and restrooms.
- The *pathway* leads people from the trail to the downtown area and vice versa. There should be adequate wayfinding signage.
- The *downtown entrance* is the first impression of the downtown and should be well marked, attractive and welcoming.
- *Overnight accommodations* are important for capturing multiday visitors. This includes hotels, motels, campgrounds, or home rentals.
- The availability of *public restrooms* near the trail and around the downtown are important to encourage trail users to spend time in the area.
- A variety of *businesses* contributes to the economic vibrancy of the downtown. Businesses can support trail users' needs, for example, casual restaurants, breweries, coffee shops, drugstores, bike shop/gear rental, grocery store, and local shops.

Other characteristics in the built environment that contribute to the vibrancy of a downtown include community art, signage, landscaping, lighting, parks, points of interest, public restrooms, seating, sidewalks and crosswalks, streets and transportation, and receptacles for waste and recycling. It is important to have a diverse mix of these characteristics. For example, while businesses are key to attracting people to the downtown, it is also important to have good access to seating in the downtown to encourage people to stay awhile. The presence of another natural feature in addition to a trail—such as a river, mountain, or forest—can also support longer stays in the community and thus further spending potential. Similarly, infrastructure like sidewalks and crosswalks are important for safety and connectivity, but without landscaping or community art, the downtown may lack interest.

Implementation of Innovative Technology for Assessment

The downtowns and trails assessment is conducted using the ArcGIS Collector mobile application, a free app that serves as a tool for collecting data in the field.

The Collector app allows the assessor to quickly and easily identify characteristics while also collecting the geospatial location for each item. For each item collected, the assessor selects the appropriate characteristic from a list, writes a brief description, rates the item as an asset or opportunity for improvement, and takes a photo. Assessors are encouraged to take note of items that are missing in the downtown that could promote vibrancy or connectivity, such as a blank wall that could serve as a backdrop for a mural, or a restroom at a trailhead. The assessment is conducted over the course of half a day, whereby assessors visit the community and walk and/or drive around the downtown, the trailhead, and the pathway. The purpose of the assessment is to identify the assets and opportunities for improvement that stand out and not to conduct an inventory of all characteristics that exist. Following data collection, all of the items collected are viewed on a map. Community members can click on a point to see an item and the description, rating, and photo.

While this assessment could be completed using pen and paper, the innovative use of GIS technology allows for all of the data points to be viewed by multiple users at once on a digital map. The visual of the data points on the map helps to identify areas where there are assets that can be built upon or areas where there is opportunity to make improvements. Importantly, the assessment visually depicts the pathway between the downtown and the trailhead. The photos and geospatial data are critical to helping communities determine where to take action.

Innovative Local Leadership Collaborations

The Bristol staff and leadership signed on to the program via a memorandum of understanding with UNH Extension and embraced this pilot program which demonstrates their leadership, creativity, and spirit of innovation. They took a risk and were willing to try new ideas to add economic and social value to their town. Our many years of working in NH tells us that communities often find the process of change tackling community challenges to be difficult, as there is a tendency to manage the status quo. Yet, Bristol recruited volunteers and adopted new tools that were developed for the program. The UNH Extension staff introduced them to an engagement process that entailed use of key informant interview protocols, intercept surveys, and an assessment of downtown characteristics for spatial analysis. These customized tools were developed for the Downtowns and Trails program and embraced by Bristol residents, thus demonstrating community capacity to continue the trail connection effort and future nature-based economic development efforts in the community.

Leadership emerged from the economic development committee along with staff at the local library and greatly contributed to the success of the pilot. The town librarian played a significant role in the Downtowns and Trails program, given their understanding of the economic potential of the program for the community. The local library is viewed as a community center, ready to provide many services to residents and visitors that go beyond book circulation. The library serves as information center and welcome center for the community, complete with rest rooms, and even hosts events on relevant topics. It is an important institution for both the residents and visitors of Bristol. In fact, the community forum for the pilot program was held in Bristol's library because of its welcoming nature.

Ultimately, the forum led to the formation of two action committees focused on both short- and long-term goals. One of the short-term goals was better signage and wayfinding, particularly in the downtown and at the trailhead. Bristol has already significantly updated its trailhead with a new kiosk created in partnership with the Newfound Lakes Region Association. The community also implemented a new wayfinding plan in the village center. It has longer-term plans to partner with the State Department of Transportation to upgrade the road on which the bike path is located. While the process was smooth for many, the challenge of some solutions being very long term was a challenge for some.

Robust and Innovative Community Engagement

Bristol leaders and community residents participated beyond traditional vehicles for community engagement such as providing comments at public meeting and engaging in project work through a municipal committee. They adopted a broad and deep community engagement strategy instead of the conventional public meeting format with limited time and interaction. This strategy included both thick and thin engagement techniques which provided a variety of ways for community members to participate (Nabatchi & Leighninger, 2015). This included spatial analysis, key informant interviews, intercept surveys, and a community forum. Thin engagement focuses on shorter interactions for individual responses such as the intercept surveys used in Bristol while a more intensive, or thick engagement took place through dialogue and deliberation at the community forum. The initial organizing committee consisted of eight active volunteers and over 20 volunteers participated in our training on how to conduct surveys and interviews. They then went out into broader community over the course of the summer and gathered over 100 survey responses from residents and visitors, exceeding our expectations.

Ultimately, Bristol has adopted an economic development strategy to "promote a positive business climate that positions Bristol as a business-friendly community with a superior quality of life" (Bristol Economic Development Committee, 2020). The strategy focuses heavily on supporting existing business to help sustain and grow them, as well as attracting new businesses. Downtowns and Trails is one of several local and regional initiatives and efforts aimed at supporting high quality of life and therefore supporting the business environment. This past year, a new trail opened on the far side of the village center. In recent press coverage about the trail, the town attributed this opening of the trail and the momentum the town has had in connecting natural assets to the downtown to their participation in our Downtowns and Trails program (Caldwell, 2020).

Because of the program, participants learned about the economic benefits of trails and gained a deeper understanding of how both residents and visitors to their community perceived the town. According to the Town Administrator and to volunteer leadership, this information was previously unknown and key to the successes attained by the community.

Conclusion

Rural communities that leverage their natural assets, particularly trails, to further economic development goals demonstrate innovation and resilience. Doing so demonstrates a certain level of adaptation and willingness to work with existing assets, drawing upon asset-based approach to build economic vibrancy in rural communities. Municipal leaders and community volunteers see their natural resources as an asset and came together in Bristol to implement an economic development strategy including the nature economy. They adopted the Downtown and Trails Program to expand their local economy and strengthen their downtown. This program identified the trails users and put amenities in place to draw them to the local businesses. Bristol is an example of a community that addresses the challenge of economic decline by bringing together the library, municipal staff, citizen volunteers, and elected officials to understand and embrace the nature economy and linking their trails with the economic center, their downtown.

To help communities tap into their natural assets and unleash innovation, our Downtowns and Trails program seeks to assess each of the four conditions discussed above through different tools. The natural, built, and economic conditions are assessed via the downtown assessment using spatial analysis and crowdsource mapping. Social and leadership conditions are assessed through the key informant interviews with community leaders and businesses. The program was successful because it entailed innovative program design elements. Although the innovation has been incremental and at a small geographic scale, it was nonetheless important to the program's success.

The result is that community leaders and volunteers are trying new initiatives, implementing a broad engagement strategy, and developing an economic development strategy embracing quality of life based on findings from the downtowns and trails assessment, intercept surveys and key informant interviews.

Bristol has developed an innovation ecosystem that supports their ability and interest to improve their downtown by linking with their trails. They recognize their natural features and trails as an asset and were willing to explore the new idea of understanding the trail users and drawing them into town to spend money and create vibrancy. They have a strong network of local players such as municipal staff, committees, elected officials, business leaders, and institutional leaders such as the librarian. Bristol is resilient because they cultivated an innovative ecosystem to strengthen their downtown and local economy by linking with the local trail system. They have not limited their economic development strategy to the nature economy but are also working on expanding broadband as a critical tool in business attraction, retention, and expansion.

Our Downtowns and Trails program is replicable in other communities as a first step to assessing the opportunity to connect downtown with a nearby trail for economic benefit. The program is disclosed through UNH Innovation indicating that it is unique and has value to other communities. The disclosure process represents another innovative aspect of the program and was done to ensure that we had a high quality and replicable program that could be adapted to a variety of community types and levels of readiness. Interested communities should consider their readiness for the program regarding the four conditions we have described: natural, economic, built, social/leadership. To participate, communities need to have at least one trail or natural asset and a downtown, though this could be a village center or four corners. In addition, volunteer and leadership capacity is important as a diverse steering committee will lead the implementation of the program. While these pieces are important to get started, the Downtowns and Trails program also provides an opportunity for a community to assess these four conditions and continue to strengthen and build capacity for future nature-based economic development.

Although we launched the Downtown and Trails program prior to the pandemic, we find that this work gained importance during the pandemic and will continue to be relevant post pandemic. In fact, anecdotal evidence suggests that the use of trails has increased during the COVID-19 pandemic as New Hampshire residents and visitors seek out and use trails as a safe form of recreation. There is an increased awareness of what the state's natural resources can offer to individuals and families. While the state is seeing increased trail use, towns and some main streets are suffering a significant loss of small businesses due to COVID-19 restrictions that impact their ability to serve their customers. Local leaders and residents are experiencing an increase in trail use and restrictions on the local economy. There are multiple local and statewide efforts to support struggling small businesses and local leaders see an opportunity to enhance the downtown economy by drawing trail users to spend money at local businesses. As such, now is a good time for communities to begin downtown assessments, to engage with businesses and community members, and to determine the retail, service, and hospitality needs of trail users as they prepare for economic recovery.

As a response to the pandemic, NH communities are being encouraged and supported by UNH Extension and the University of New Hampshire Small Business Development Center to begin economic recovery with a focus on community economic resilience planning. This planning will entail stabilizing and strengthening the local economic base while building on the abundant natural resources such as our rich forests, mountains, and lakes. Based on what we learned from the 2008 Great Recession, there is also an expectation that we are likely entering a period of entrepreneurial growth. New businesses will develop out of necessity and fill vacant commercial spaces in town centers and along main street. There is an incredible opportunity for these businesses to cater to the needs of trail visitors. Bristol is showing characteristics of resilience because they have mobilized their leaders and volunteers together and recognized their trails as an economic asset to enhance their downtown and local economy.

References

Caldwell, T. (2020, August 6). Trails Blend Health & History. *The Laker*. Found on the web at: https://thelaker.com/2020/trails-blend-health-and-history

Emery, M., & Flora, C. (2006). Spiraling-up: Mapping Community Transformation with Community Capitals Framework. *Community Development*, *37*(1), 19–35.

Halstead, J.M., & Deller, S.C. (1997). Public Infrastructure in Economic Development and Growth: Evidence from Rural Manufacturers. *Journal of the Community Development Society*, *28*(2), 149–169.

Nabatchi, T., & Leighninger, M. (2015). *Public Participation for 21st Century Democracy*. Hoboken, NJ: John Wiley & Sons, Inc.

New Hampshire State Parks. (2018). Recreational Use Statues. Found on the web at: https://www.nhstateparks.org/about-us/trails-bureau/laws/recreational-use-statutes

Rails to Trails Conservancy. (2018). New Hampshire Rail Trail Stats. Found on the web at: https://www.railstotrails.org/our-work/united-states/new-hampshire/

New Hampshire Trails Bureau. (2018). Snowmobiling in New Hampshire. Found on the web at: https://www.nhstateparks.org/activities/snowmobiling

RHIhub. Rural Health for New Hampshire. Found on the web at: https://www.ruralhealthinfo.org/states/new-hampshire#:~:text=New%20Hampshire%20covers%208%2C968%20square, areas%20(USDA%2DERS)

Rogers, S., Donovan, M., Porter, C., Chase, L., Brown, L., Koo, J., & R. Sero. (2019). *Connecting Downtowns and Trails*. NH Cooperative Extension. Durham, New Hampshire. Found on the web at: https://extension.unh.edu/resource/downtowns-and-trails-information-brief

The Progress Fund. (2015). *Trail Town Program*. Found on the web at: https://www.trailtowns.org/

Town of Bristol NH. (2020). Economic Development Committee Report. Found on the web at: https://www.townofbristolnh.org/economic-development-committee

Williams, F. (2017). *The Nature Fix: Why Nature Makes Us Happier, Healthier, and More Creative*. New York: W.W. Norton & Company.

13

GIVING RISE TO INNOVATION ECOSYSTEMS IN RURAL HONDURAS

A Case Study of Sustainable Harvest International

Egbert Ospina, Alexandra Croteau, Elliott Powell and Ricardo Romero-Perezgrovas

Introduction

Building rural community resiliency demands tackling some of the world's most pressing challenges, such as environmental destruction and ever-increasing levels of hunger and food insecurity, not to mention the current COVID-19 pandemic. Unfortunately, failed international development projects in impoverished rural communities outnumber success stories. Building human capacity from the ground up is key to ensuring more positive outcomes and reimagining the approaches to failed interventions. Of the myriad of stakeholders whose work intersects with rural community development, civil society organizations (CSOs)—organizations that are not associated with the government, as defined by van Laerhoven and Barnes (2019)—play a particularly important role in tackling environmental, social, and economic challenges in remote areas of the Global South where government agencies fail to cover. Rather than relying on quick-fix or "handout" approaches that can create dependency and limit idea adoption, communities can set themselves up for greater success in achieving resiliency by directing outside CSO intervention efforts to foster an innovation ecosystem within the community (Waters-Bayer & Bayer, 2005). CSOs that rely on close relationships with local people and that have an intimate understanding of community issues can act as a catalyst for a community-built innovation ecosystem.

According to Grandstrand and Holdersson (2020, p. 1), an innovation ecosystem is, "the evolving set of actors, activities, and artifacts, and the institutions and relations, including complementary and substitute relations, that are important for the innovative performance of an actor or a population of actors." Through this framework, this chapter explores the work of a CSO supporting community efforts to establish local innovation ecosystems in rural regions of the Global

DOI: 10.4324/9781003178552-13

South with low coverage from government institutions. Establishing an innovation ecosystem requires building local leadership, knowledge-share practices, and relationship networks that promote local and culturally appropriate solutions that are easy to adopt and adapt.

Sustainable Harvest International (SHI), a U.S.-based environmental CSO, recognizes that environmental degradation and rural poverty are inextricably linked and that the solutions to these challenges must therefore be integrated in innovative ways. In addition, the organization's proven and time-tested agriculture extension model promotes the creation of local innovation ecosystems by building long-term relationships with local farming families in partnering communities. Key components of SHI's approach that support innovation ecosystems include: (a) locally hired field trainers assigned to work directly with farmers, (b) promotion of knowledge sharing and environmental stewardship within farmer groups, (c) establishment of local financial structures where farmers have access to microloans to start individual or collective entrepreneurial activities, and (d) a structured methodology based on a multiphase five-year approach to transitioning from conventional agricultural practices to organic and regenerative agriculture.

After successfully completing the program and SHI's formal presence has left the community, participant families are expected to further develop the skills and knowledge necessary to implement regenerative agriculture techniques and reforestation projects, and to maintain food sovereignty. These activities result in improved health, livelihood, and greater resiliency in the face of environmental and economic shocks. Moreover, after participating in SHI's five-phase program, participants find in themselves the confidence and capacity to continue innovating, organizing themselves to access micro or community credit sources, and continue to develop their new knowledge and skillsets with community members (French & Romero-Perezgrovas, 2020). Examining SHI's work in Honduras as a case study, this research explored how an international CSO fostered an innovation ecosystem by using a long-term local intervention.

One key goal of this chapter is to illustrate and understand the successes and limitations of SHI's people-centered, participatory approach to advancing the community's efforts in cultivating an innovation ecosystem. The authors employed a case study methodology. The primary purpose of using this approach is, "to do an in-depth study of a phenomenon in its real-world context" (Yin, 2018, p. 127). The following research question guided this study:

How Has SHI's Innovation Ecosystem Model Promoted Sustainable Development in Rural Honduras?

To answer this question, the researchers collected quantitative and qualitative data from interviews, baseline-intro, and baseline-exit surveys. With these methods, the study was able to adequately capture data and analyze how the CSO facilitated the development of an innovation ecosystem in four rural communities of the Yoro Department, Honduras (Figure 13.1).

FIGURE 13.1 Location of the four study communities in Yoro Department.

Local Leadership

Participant families gained confidence in their abilities through SHI's learn-by-doing approach and by completing work on their own land. This confidence enabled them to take on leadership roles particularly related to spreading and enhancing local knowledge. Participatory approaches forge farmer leaders, including women, who typically perform extension work in the most effective manner given limited resources (Feder et al., 1999; Sachs et al., 2020). This case study explored instances of participants taking on the role as a promoter of regenerative agriculture techniques: first with the SHI field trainer in Yoro, followed by other program participants.

Jaime Soto, SHI's field trainer in Yoro, was a former SHI participant. Jaime showed strong enthusiasm for regenerative agriculture, the program's methodology, and sustainable development in his community. Upon graduation, SHI continued the already established partnership and benefited from his expertise and years of experience as a participant. Furthermore, Jaime is of the same Tolupan indigenous group as the participants whom he trained, suggesting that he afforded culturally attuned guidance. Jaime served as an example of how SHI builds robust local relationships that promote the benefits of the CSO's intervention and stand to improve outcomes. Reiber et al. (2010) state, "continuous promotion can lead to significant and sustained adoption [of extension intervention] with subsequent potential benefits to smallholders via increased locally-available know-how." Not only were participants more prone to embrace SHI's intervention when exposed to community-level promotion but also those who saw the improved outcomes of their neighbors sought to replicate it in themselves and pick up the mantle of role model for others.

This study found that participants adapted and spread the ideas they learned around sustainability and regenerative agriculture techniques to surrounding communities. One program participant in Yoro, Carlos Sandoval, provided advice to around 50 families in neighboring communities in the region (J. Soto, Interview, May 11, 2020). This example revealed that SHI participants became local leaders either by taking roles with the CSO as a field trainer or by promoting valuable knowledge and information through their own networks and communities.

Develop a Culture of Continuous Learning

The analysis found that through participating in SHI's program, small-holder farmers embraced a culture of continuous learning that engendered a custom of knowledge sharing. This, in turn, sparked innovative practice across the community. With the field trainer's mentorship, participants established improvement plans that delineated their learning objectives around regenerative farming, nutrition, enhanced agribusiness management, and entrepreneurial skills. Within five years, families experimented with techniques and explored themes to successfully execute their improvement plans. By carrying out the work on their own land, participants gained hands-on experience, strong technical understanding, and a deeper appreciation for innovation. Through their experience of enhancing their own conditions, and learning from others who have done the same, participants in the program developed a growth-oriented mindset and welcomed further learning and innovative experimentation with new techniques.

Prior studies have shown that participants of SHI's intervention learned by executing their own projects and gained confidence that enables them to improve their livelihoods (Romero-Perezgrovas et al., 2017). This study found that participants, in addition to developing new technical skills, adopted a culture of learning exemplified by the following characteristics:

- A change in mindset to one that is growth-oriented
- A greater value placed on sustainability and continuous learning
- An eagerness to seek and share knowledge and try new techniques

As SHI participants developed a deeper appreciation for learning, they sought and shared knowledge which gave rise to new relations and institutions that generate local innovations and adaptation strategies.

Changing to a Growth-Oriented Mindset

Participants developed a growth mindset which is essential to experiment with and implement new technologies and practices. The local field trainer in Yoro recognized that when participants harnessed new skills, their attitude changed.

> It's not just a project with the family that you are working with; the work can change their self-esteem… it is not at all easy to change the family's

> attitude just through building a garden. Our work also builds self-esteem so that the family knows that they are building a project that will have lasting impact.
>
> (*J. Soto, Interview, May 11, 2020*)

This study found that participants showed a change in their outlook towards a greater value for learning and knowledge acquisition. Evidence of a change towards a growth-oriented mindset among older participants was particularly strong. Elderly individuals are often more reluctant to deviate from time-tested techniques (Noack & Federwisch, 2020), yet older Yoro participants demonstrated a growth mindset and formed an important part of the innovation ecosystem.

For example, Alberto Romero—a 60-year-old participant in the community of Agua Fria—learned regenerative techniques to expand his agricultural operation. The following is a testimonial from Romero's assigned field trainer, sharing his experience on the partnership:

> Romero was a hardworking farmer who worked long hours. Prior to his participation in SHI's program, Romero was earning around 100 Honduran lempiras a day [the equivalent to 4 US dollars]. Romero's aspiration was to not work past the age of 65, so he decided to partner with SHI to achieve this goal. I worked with Romero to diversify his banana cultivation with pineapple and several other fruits. We worked to empower Romero to diversify his crops on his own. Now Romero does not work daily and has been able to double or triple his daily income to 200–300 Honduran lempiras [equivalent to 8 to 12 US dollars].
>
> (*J. Soto, Interview, May 11, 2020*)

Additionally, Miguel Garay Snr. from the community of San Francisco, in his 70s, exemplified how older Yoro participants adopted a growth mindset through gradual experimentation, "he had a small plot where he planted corn and beans because he didn't take advantage of the slope on his terrain. We started to change that little by little." (J. Soro, Interview May 11, 2020). Miguel eventually cultivated and integrated a variety of crops including pineapples and plantains on his sloped terrain. Optimizing new techniques, Miguel's agricultural production expanded and began generating additional income based on improved productivity.

Placing a Greater Value on Sustainability and Learning

Participants demonstrated that they cultivated a new set of values that enabled a culture of learning to flourish. These values also guided sustainable practices that contributed to improved resiliency. By striving for sustainability, participants recognized their own capacity to innovate with the resources at their disposal. Additionally, this study found evidence that these new skills, values, and attitudes support the case that SHI participants engaged in a culture of learning. Adan Jose Rivera stated,

> I must admit that before Sustainable Harvest International, I was a destroyer of the forest. I am very regretful of [practicing slash-and-burn]. My field trainer has taken my blindfold off and made me conscious of the importance of protecting the forest.
>
> *(A. J. Rivera, Interview, May 6, 2014)*

Adan's personal account illustrates that SHI participants adopted the practices of sustainability and changed their attitudes towards the environment.

Nelson Aníbal, an SHI participant from a different region of Honduras (Santa Barbara Department), worked hard to regenerate his land even prior to participating in SHI's program. He embodied a strong value for the environment and dedicated his time and energy to planting trees, "I invested a lot of effort in reforesting my land... To date, I have planted over 1,000 trees of various species for shade and timber, over 8,000 coffee trees, and 500 plantains" (N. Aníbal, Interview, July 14, 2014). The interview with Nelson illustrates how participants enhanced their value of sustainability and innovation by expanding reforestation efforts and increasing crop diversity in an agroforestry system.

Adan, Nelson, and other program participants learned to incorporate new agricultural techniques that rely on minimal external inputs with which they could experiment, adapt, and improve on their own or as a community. SHI participants routinely test and adopt new practices, revealing a sustained culture of learning. One example of this comes from SHI participant, Rufina Perez, from the community of Santa Cruz del Dulce in the Department of Comayagua. She made it a practice to prepare organic fungicide with the materials in and around her home. Rufina would prepare a recipe for lime sulfur, or *caldo sulfocalcico*. This local alternative to expensive and dangerous toxic chemicals is a low-cost, natural, and safe way to control fungus and bacteria on certain crops (R. Perez, Interview, March 25, 2020). Nelson speaks of this transition,

> before working with Sustainable Harvest International-Honduras, we used to burn our fields and depend on chemicals to make our soil productive. Now we know how to take advantage of all the resources around, such as coffee pulp and papaya leaves, to make natural fertilizers.
>
> *(N. Aníbal, Interview, July 14, 2014)*

Nelson and Rufina displayed how participants adapt to their circumstances by innovating with local resources.

An eagerness to Seek and Share Knowledge and Try New Techniques

Participants in SHI showed eagerness to adopt innovative projects to improve their agricultural production and livelihood. Patricia Hernandez discussed how she came to rely on her own entrepreneurial activities by employing innovative strategies in the form of making barbecue and chili-flavored plantain chips with the plantains she grew using agroforestry techniques. She recalled,

> I have had a change in my life, the life of my kids, and my family because what we have learned helps us improve our health and income generation. Now I don't have to go into town to look for work because I have a micro-business.
>
> *(P.M. Hernandez, Interview, March 19, 2015)*

Other interviews revealed similar accounts. SHI-Honduras Country Director, Zoila Reyes, shares her experience with a participant in Yoro.

> Eliodoro Romero told me that he would leave his home early in the morning in search of work and sometimes return home by lunch without a dollar in his pocket because he couldn't find any work. He then came up with the idea of taking some plantains or malanga with him when he goes out to find work, and that way he at least has something to sell and doesn't return penniless. He then learned that if he sold just plantains, he could only earn about 60 lempiras, but if he fried them up into plantain chips, he could sell them for 300 lempiras [equivalent to 12 US dollars], so he started preparing fried plantain chips for each of his outings to find work. Now when he leaves, he always takes something to sell.
>
> *(Z. Reyes, Interview, May 8, 2020)*

The Eliodoro Romero case illustrates how SHI participants learned to appreciate experimentation. Innovative approaches are observed in more than just plantain production. For example, using old tires that are normally a source of pollution in rural communities, participants recycled them for innovative horticultural use. Additionally, they utilized these same old tires to build slow filtration systems to recapture greywater for irrigation. According to Zoila,

> some of our program participants have found a way to effectively grow their crops in containers formed with recycled car tires. They have filled their [tires] with tomatoes, cabbage, and paprika. This is a great way to repurpose old materials and keep that waste out of landfills.
>
> *(Z. Reyes, Interview, March 5, 2019)*

SHI participants are also eager to create partnerships in support of innovative projects, revealing a custom of knowledge sharing and a thirst for experimentation. As is shown in Figure 13.2, one program participant worked with an EARTH University intern to come up with an innovative way to provide food to chickens.

Creating an Innovation Ecosystem for Resiliency

Using surveys from the graduated cohort of participant families in the four Yoro communities, this study corroborated the findings that participants developed and innovatively applied new knowledge to a variety of circumstances. As each

FIGURE 13.2 Cirilo Alvarado from El Caliche, Honduras, and Dasha Montcalm, an EARTH University intern from Costa Rica, collaborated on the innovative project of using a plastic tank to trap black soldier flies as a sustainable food source for chickens.

family explored practical solutions, they actively participated in key components of an innovation ecosystem such as knowledge creation and sharing. The specific techniques SHI graduates executed were intended to restore and protect their environment and sustain their families. Participants integrated a minimum of four regenerative agriculture techniques, demonstrating their capacity to design innovative adaptations suited to their unique circumstances. This led to building resilience in the face of common local environmental hazards such as soil erosion—which in extreme cases results in dangerous landslides—and contamination from agrochemicals or synthetic fertilizers. The variety of integrated agriculture techniques also serves as a testament to a model design which allows for individual families to explore and innovate at their own speed.

SHI's methodology provides for a certain amount of flexibility contained within the program structure, allowing for families to move through the training curriculum at a pace more comfortable to their needs while still achieving preestablished objectives. This ability to meet farmers where they are is critical to ensuring that, within the SHI methodology, families can pursue innovation according to their specific circumstances. As opposed to SHI's highly personalized, participant-centered agricultural training model, the principal critique of other extension training programs like Farmer Field Schools (FFS) is that they function under strict timetables of sessions focused on a prespecified curriculum (Anderson & Feder, 2003). As a result of SHI's inclusive approach, the program incorporates participants' contexts, interests, assets, and capacity to innovate and formulate their own improvement strategy.

Yoro participants were able to identify their problems and execute solutions, as the following interview excerpt notes,

> The participant needs to be involved in every step of the process because they are learning... All the work that goes into creating the compost, maintaining their parcels for cultivation, building and maintaining the infrastructure - its 80% the work of the participants so that if there is ever anything that breaks or needs maintenance, the participant will be able to do it themselves.
>
> *(Z. Reyes, Interview, May 8, 2020)*

Although not a single Yoro family reported practicing regenerative agriculture techniques before the program, by the time of graduation they had adopted, on average, seven out of the ten regenerative techniques the field trainer introduced. Additionally, eight of the 29 households adopted nine techniques and only one household adopted a minimum of four techniques (Table 13.1).

In addition to new regenerative agriculture techniques, families also adopted nutrition and livelihood related household infrastructure projects (chicken coops, water harvesting modules, wood conserving stoves, water filters, pigsties, fishponds, etc.) and agroforestry practices that cultivated new species and associations of trees and annual crops.

The number and type of infrastructure projects depended primarily on the resources available to the families (J. Soto, Interview, May 11, 2020). In the Yoro Department, every family reported building a vegetable garden and a chicken coop. In addition to vegetable gardens, 27 families cultivated fruit orchards, 17 built metal storage silos, and 12 families-built pigsties. These infrastructure projects provided households with greater storage and handling capabilities. With these new assets, families increased the productivity and quality of their

TABLE 13.1 Percentage of Participants that Adopted Regenerative Techniques

Participants (%)	*Regenerative Techniques Adopted*
100	Organic Fertilizers
93	Soil Conservation Practices
89	Organic Repellents
86	Seed Storage Conservation Techniques
79	Crop Rotations
76	Crop Diversification
69	Agroforestry Plots

food for both their own consumption and market use. This study found that households each executed different projects and thus developed diverse expertise across the community. Each household innovated based on their own context to find the strategies that best suited their needs. This allowed community members to rely on each other to learn diverse innovative practices.

In addition to changing cultivation practices, Yoro families began to reforest degraded areas by cultivating indigenous species in agroforestry plots. Prior to participating in SHI's program, only eight families grew coffee (*Coffea arabica*) and one family grew other tree species: mahogany (*Swietenia macrophylla*), cedar (*Cedrela odorata*), and sweet orange (*Citrus sinensis*). After graduating from SHI, families adopted the following tree species (Table 13.2).

Altogether, SHI families planted a total of 19 new tree species. With new varieties, the four Yoro communities now have access to 11 new and useful plant species, marking a 171% increase. The diversity of crops grown in the Yoro communities illustrated how each family innovatively designed their own cultivation strategies rather than follow a standardized and stagnant approach. Therefore, each household became a source of knowledge on the cultivation of the unique varieties of fruits, flowers, nuts, and hardwood trees that they cultivated. The diversity of crops illustrated the existing knowledge maintained by the community and the increased resilience of its members through improved nutritional and livelihood outcomes.

Participants also took action aimed at meeting household nutritional needs and achieving food sovereignty. Families diversified their diets by growing a greater variety of nutrient-rich vegetables, fruits, and grains. Home gardens have been found to contribute significant positive impacts on ecosystem health, family nutrition, and household income (Leakey, 2017). Before partnering with SHI, 21 families reported growing two crops and only three families grew three types. The crops were cultivated in a conventional manner relying on slash-and-burn and synthetic chemical inputs. The variety of crops only included corn, beans, and some soy. After participating in SHI's program, 22 families grew between 5 and 11 crops, the average family grew 10 types, and the family with the largest variety grew 15 different crops. The varieties now included bananas, plantains, coffee, sweet potato, squash, onions, yuca, pineapple, carrots, and chilies to name a few.

TABLE 13.2 Number of Families Introducing New Tree Species

Number of Families	*Tree Species*
26	Sweet Orange (*Citrus sinensis*)
24	Mango (*Mangifera indica*)
22	Coffee (*Coffea arabica*)
19	Lemon (*Citrus citrus*)
15	Avocado (*Persea americana*)

The literature supports the notion that a diversity of crops is beneficial to helping people meet their nutritional needs while also improving their attitudes (Cherrett, 2001; Leakey, 2017). As the Yoro Department field trainer and former SHI participant stated, "You cannot discount how big the impact on your confidence is when you go from just beans and corn to having options" (J. Soto, Interview, May 11, 2020). Once farmers have attained food security, they can focus their energies on improving their living conditions, attaining better education, expanding agriculture businesses, enhancing access to capital through the community bank, managing natural resources such as water, and participating in community social structures (Cherrett, 2001).

As participants decreased their reliance on agrochemical and other external inputs, they increased their ability to sustain their farms with local resources. In fact, participants reduced their use of synthetic fertilizers by 93% and herbicides by 35% by adopting compost, mulching, and other techniques. SHI families discovered that they could maintain their plots of land using their knowledge of regenerative agriculture and local resources. By eliminating use of synthetic inputs which need to be bought regularly, they also saved money.

Participants changed their value towards the environment and altered their farming practices to address degraded soils resulting in reduced environmental damage and increased resilience to external shocks. For example, 100% of Yoro participants ceased the practice of slash-and-burn farming, a major contributor to soil degradation and poverty (Harwood, 1996). In fact, after completing the program there were no reports of soil erosion nor contamination from agrochemicals and synthetic fertilizer residues. Furthermore, the number of families that dedicated their time to reforestation and watershed protection doubled. Before the program, 87% of Yoro participants reported soil degradation and/or erosion problems.

In addition to the environmental benefits, families that developed regenerative agriculture techniques reallocated precious time and energy to other worthwhile endeavors. For example, interviews revealed that, before the program, participants were often forced to leave their community to find day-work—or *jornaleo*. Adopting regenerative agriculture techniques lessened this pressure. These families could continue to meet their household food needs without relying on off-farm income. SHI participants built a safety net by cultivating diverse food staples in and around the home in case of unforeseen and catastrophic events, such as the COVID-19 pandemic. Avoiding the constant need to seek scarce off-farm work, families sustained the means to produce food. In this sense, participants invested in economic prosperity by reducing dependence on using income to purchase food.

It is important to note that new techniques promoted by extension services, particularly those focused on conservation, are only adopted if they appeal to and fit with the families' income-earning strategies (Jansen et al., 2006). This study found that SHI participants recognized the potential for increased savings as well as income generation opportunities by selling their surplus. SHI's solutions deliberately focused on viable markets and effective business strategies to increase income from agricultural activities. The program assisted participants in developing and implementing their business models and encouraged them to innovate upon strategies that address market needs and allow for future expansion. As participants' business models became more robust, they increased the income generated from their agricultural activities.

Participants in the Yoro Department have shifted their reliance on income earned from low-paid and scarce off-farm work to more sustainable options. Before starting the program, participants earned between 80% and 100% of their income from unreliable and low-paid off-farm employment. However, after completing the program, this reduced by an average of 20% (Figure 13.3), thus allowing them to dedicate resources to generate income by developing and selling value-added products in local and regional markets.

SHI assists families in building their financial capital through helping to organize collective rural banks referred to a *caja rural*. After completing the program, 62% of the Yoro participants gained access to credit through a *caja rural,* which they shared with other SHI participants. Another positive effect associated with organizing a *caja rural* as a community is building social capital by uniting the members around a shared objective (Axin, 1988; Bunch, 1982; Claridge, 2018). By working, learning, and practicing together, community members built mutual trust that created new knowledge sharing channels and fostered an innovation ecosystem.

Recommendations and Lessons Learned

By focusing on the family to create lasting impacts, SHI promotes a culture of learning and knowledge sharing mindset. However, this study found scant evidence that SHI explicitly considers family dynamics and gender roles. The interviews revealed that SHI staff and trainers appear to assume that families and

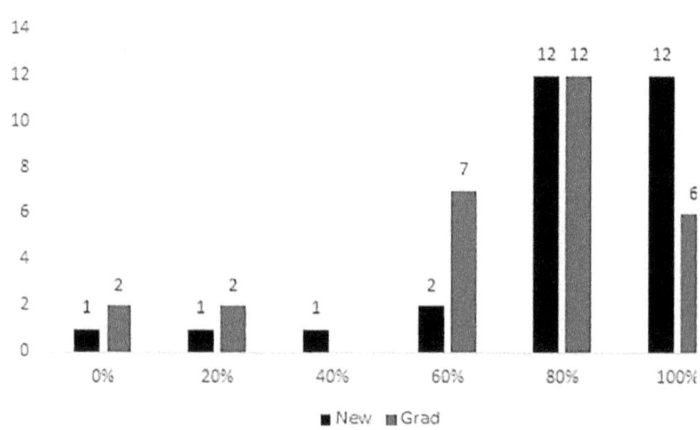

FIGURE 13.3 Percentage of family income from paid employment.

their communities are cohesive units and that they can work through projects together without explicit consideration of family dynamics, power relationships, and gender roles. However, there was no clear indication that staff were equipped with proper tools to analyze these dynamics; ensuring that they avoid inadvertently reinforcing imbalances of power. Interviews with field trainers showed, for example, that SHI staff typically invite the male of the household to join the program after the family has expressed interest. However, by the end of the five-phase program, the entire family is expected to engage in the work and exchange of ideas to substitute a static relationship with knowledge. It was unclear though how field trainers managed to engage the entire family and whether there were protocols for negotiating power dynamics particularly around gender roles. Although the program showed evidence of successfully ingraining values of learning and environmental sustainability, there was no indication that the program supported establishing value of gender integration for natural resource management and economic development.

Additionally, this study found no evidence that SHI promotes political engagement among its participants or the communities it serves. While SHI can remain nonpartisan, there is a need for advocacy to further sustainable development efforts in rural areas to decrease environmental degradation and improve rural infrastructure. Prior studies of SHI Panama found that external factors, such as lack of access to roads or transportation, contribute significantly to program outcomes (Dupre et al., 2016). Therefore, it is in the participants' best interest to advocate for improved infrastructure in rural areas to advance their potential. Although SHI avoids engaging in public policy discussions with the Honduran government, it might do well to mobilize participants for active political engagement at the local level through their new relationship networks central to their innovation ecosystems.

Finally, this study found a need for participatory monitoring and evaluation approaches that improve the understanding of the formation innovation ecosystems. CSOs, like SHI, typically employ surveys to collect this information, which is not the best method of gathering information about knowledge-sharing relationships. SHI has, however, employed a variety of evaluation methodologies in Panama, such as ripple effect mapping, which offered insight into a wider range of changes in relationships and impacts. The organization should consider systematically incorporating participatory evaluation methods across their programs to reveal the change in the communities' capacity to create innovation ecosystems and the ensuing results.

Conclusion

This case study shed light on the practices and organizational features that enable a small sustainable development CSO to have a lasting impact on the communities where it works. This study showed that SHI participants assumed leadership roles promoting regenerative agriculture and sustainability, sought out and shared knowledge and innovations, and built both infrastructure and institutions that enable them to sustain local knowledge and further economic development. Together, these characteristics lead to the continuous modification and adoption of behaviors that lead to personal and household well-being, catalyze innovation, preserve the environment, and ultimately elevate their role as knowledge nodes in the community. SHI's success in promoting agroforestry and other regenerative agriculture techniques is largely a result of its participant-centered approach, whereby each participant develops new skill sets based on their individual circumstances and context. With the knowledge gained and confidence built as a result of having completed their own improvement plans, participants embraced their roles as purveyors of sustainable development and innovative practices in their community. This change led to increased resiliency in the face of environmental and economic shocks, such as the dire challenges communities faced during the COVID-19 pandemic.

To better understand the unique intricacies and dynamics of a CSO's role in fostering the development of an innovation ecosystem, further research is needed to better understand the dynamics of how innovation is both infused into families' practices and into the broader community. Considering that SHI focuses on families, studies that critically examine the cohesion of the family unit could shed light on how a household operates given gender roles and power imbalance. Furthermore, this study did not examine the interplay of the Yoro community's indigenous Tolupan identity and program outcomes. Research specifically focused on the results of this or other minority group, and how the CSO's initiative affects their outcomes, could elucidate what aspects of the innovation ecosystem worked well and what needs improvement. Finally, capturing the experience of participants through their personal stories and other qualitative data, such as images, would generate a deeper contextual understanding of the unique ways that innovation ecosystems are leveraged by individual families.

References

Anderson, J. R., & Feder, G. (2003). *Rural extension services*. Washington, DC: The World Bank.

Axinn, G. (1988). *Guide on alternative extension approaches*. Rome: FAO.

Bunch, R. (1982). *Two ears of corn*. Oklahoma City, OK: World Neighbors.

Cherrett, I. (2001). Decentralization, rural poverty, and degradation of uplands in Central America. *Mountain Research and Development*, 21(3), 221–225. doi:10.1659/0276-4741(2001)021[0221:drpado]2.0.co;2

Claridge, T. (2018). Functions of social capital–bonding, bridging, linking. *Social Capital Research*, 20, 1–7.

Dupre, S., Holland, M., Jones, K., Romero, R., & Fisher, S. (2016). Comparative Impact Study – Panama. Unpublished.

Feder, G., Willett, A., & Zijp, W. (1999). *Agricultural extension: Generic challenges and some ingredients for solutions*. Washington, DC: The World Bank.

French, C., & Romero-Perezgrovas, R. (2020). Evaluation on a shoestring: One international development organization's experience measuring impact in Central America.

In P. R. Lachapelle, I. Gutierrez-Montes, & C. B. Flora (Eds.), *Community capacity and resilience in Latin America* (pp. 94–109). Abingdon: Routledge.

Granstrand, O., & Holgersson, M. (2020). Innovation ecosystems: A conceptual review and a new definition. *Technovation*, 90, 102098.

Harwood, R. R. (1996). Development pathways toward sustainable systems following slash-and-burn. *Agriculture, Ecosystems & Environment*, 58(1), 75–86. doi:10.1016/0167–8809(95)00655-9.

Jansen, H. G., Rodriguez, A., Damon, A., Pender, J., Chenier, J., & Schipper, R. (2006). Determinants of income-earning strategies and adoption of conservation practices in hillside communities in rural Honduras. *Agricultural Systems*, 88(1), 92–110.

Leakey, R. B. (2017). *Multifunctional agriculture: Achieving sustainable development in Africa*. Oxford, England: Academic Press.

Noack, A., & Federwisch, T. (2020). Social innovation in rural regions: Older adults and creative community development. *Rural Sociology*, 85(4), 1021–1044.

Reiber, C., Schultze-Kraft, R., Peters, M., Lentes, P., & Hoffmann, V. (2010). Promotion and adoption of silage technologies in drought-constrained areas of Honduras. *Tropical Grasslands*, 44, 231–245.

Romero-Perezgrovas, R., French, C., Chazdon, S., & Mendoza, A. (2017). Sustainable harvest international's work in two rural communities: Program participants perceptions. In R. Sero (Ed.), *A field guide to ripple effect mapping* (pp. 125–132). Minneapolis: Minnesota University Libraries Publishing

Sachs, C. E., Jensen, L., Castellanos, P., & Sexsmith, K. (Eds.). (2020). *Routledge handbook of gender and agriculture*. London, England: Routledge.

van Laerhoven, F., & Barnes, C. (Eds.). (2019). On the roles of civil society organizations in the governance of shared resource systems. In *Routledge handbook of the study of the commons* (pp. 360–375). London: Routledge.

Waters-Bayer, A., & Bayer, W. (2005). The social dimensions in agricultural R&D: How civil society fosters partnerships to promote local innovation by rural communities. In EFARD 2005 Conference on Agricultural Research for Development: European Responses to Changing Global Needs, Zurich (pp. 27–29).

Yin, R. K. (2018). *Case study research and applications: Design and methods*. Los Angeles, CA: SAGE.

INDEX

Note: **Bold** page numbers refer to tables, *italic* page numbers refer to figures and page number followed by "n" refer to end notes.

For Product Safety Concerns and Information please contact our EU representative GPSR@taylorandfrancis.com
Taylor & Francis Verlag GmbH, Kaufingerstraße 24, 80331 München, Germany

www.ingramcontent.com/pod-product-compliance
Ingram Content Group UK Ltd.
Pitfield, Milton Keynes, MK11 3LW, UK
UKHW020147200926
475702UK00016B/2593
* 9 7 8 1 0 3 2 0 1 4 2 0 3 *